CORPORATE
irresponsibility

CORPORATE
irresponsibility

AMERICA'S NEWEST EXPORT

LAWRENCE E. MITCHELL

Yale University Press   New Haven & London

Set in New Baskerville type by Keystone Typesetting, Inc.
Printed in the United States of America by R. R. Donnelley & Sons.

Library of Congress Cataloging-in-Publication Data
Mitchell, Lawrence E.
Corporate irresponsibility : America's newest export / Lawrence E. Mitchell.
    p. cm.
Includes bibliographical references and index.
ISBN 0-300-09023-4 (acid-free)
1. Social responsibility of business — United States. 2. Corporations — Corrupt practices — United States. 3. Corporations — Moral and ethical aspects — United States. I. Title.
HD60.5.U5 M585 2001
658.4'08'0973 — dc21   2001001529

A catalogue record for this book is available from the British Library.

The paper in this book meets the guidelines for permanence and durability of the Committee on Production Guidelines for Book Longevity of the Council on Library Resources.

10   9   8   7   6   5   4   3   2   1

For my parents, who taught me

CONTENTS

ACKNOWLEDGMENTS

A book of this type can never succeed without the help of others. A number of friends and colleagues have helped me along the way. I particularly want to thank Bill Bratton, Theresa Gabaldon, Kent Greenfield, Andrew Mitchell, Marleen O'Connor, Harold Porosoff, Lauren Porosoff Mitchell, Peter Raven-Hansen, and Tamar Frankel for their insightful comments, and Joe Singer for his early encouragement. At Yale University Press, Henning Gutmann saw the potential in my proposal, and Lara Heimert helpfully saw it through to completion, while Lawrence Kenney did an artful job of editing my sometimes prolix prose. Lesliediana Jones of the Jacob Burns Law Library at The George Washington University Law School was of immeasurable help in identifying and assembling sources. LaTonya Brooks-James helped me with the manuscript and endless computer headaches and was always there to provide encouragement. Mariya Talib, Jennifer Hu, Josh Levy, and Elizabeth Leise provided research help. I would also like to thank the Alfred P. Sloan Foundation and the Ford Foundation (and especially Gail Pesyna and Lance Lindblom, respectively, of those organizations), whose funding of related projects reinforced my ability to complete and refine this one.

INTRODUCTION

The modern American business corporation has been a subject of wonder and horror for much of the past century. Wonder for the limited liability and liquid shares that have given entrepreneurs and professional managers the power to concentrate and use capital for innovative and risky projects that create technological miracles and human comforts. Wonder for the corporation's specialized structure, which encourages millions of people to invest their money and go about their daily lives, leaving to skilled managers and workers the responsibility for the businesses they have financed. Wonder for the fabulous wealth that this protected capital has produced, freeing so many people to pursue other dreams and lead lives of greater meaning than merely making a living. Wonder, because in these ways modern American business corporations have created material well-being that allows so many people to live the eighteenth-century liberal ideal on which America was founded, an ideal of individual freedom, autonomy, and choice.

But the business corporation has also been a subject of horror. Horror for the way its limited liability permits it to dump the costs of production onto those who are powerless to affect the corporation's conduct: victims of environmental pollution, consumers of dangerous and poorly made products, and workers whose wages have stagnated and, in real terms, dropped. Horror as continuing massive layoffs treat workers at all levels as little more than disposable chattel, destroying their economic futures and personal satisfaction simply to increase stock price by a few points. Horror as plant closings devastate entire communities that have grown up around them. Horror as corporate political pressure distorts democratic processes, as corporate welfare in the form of tax breaks and subsidies deforms the course of the economy. Horror as the fabulous wealth produced by business corporations ever more exaggerates the difference between the haves and the have nots, not only in America but in the world beyond our shores. And all of this is justified by one very simple goal: to get stock prices to rise ever higher.[1]

American corporations and American capital have extraordinary power. The *New York Times* recently identified twenty-two American corporations which had market capitalizations[a] greater than the gross domestic products of twenty-two individual countries, including Spain, Kuwait, Argentina, Poland, and Thailand.[2] Public perception and reported facts tell us that American capital is overwhelming traditional and culturally diverse ways of thinking about, organizing, and conducting business throughout the world.[3]

Surprising as it might be to Americans, not every culture — not even every Western culture — puts the acquisition of wealth at the top of its list of values. It may even be true, as analyses from Max Weber's study of Protestantism to more recent research suggest, that cultural differences can account for disparities in a society's wealth, that there are cultures whose traditions of family, community, and hierarchy deter their people from making individual wealth their priority — and that they're happy with this ordering of values. Before we export our own methods and our own values, we need to consider whether it is our right to do so, for through the power of our corporate form and capital markets we are in fact doing so. And we are doing so for the glorious goal of making American stockholders richer.

Trickle-down answers don't work. American dominance doesn't benefit these nations; in fact, our increased wealth is often at their expense. A study by the United Nations Development Program in 1999 reports that American economic and cultural world dominance has accelerated the widening wealth divide between rich and

---

[a]The market capitalization of a given corporation is its stock price times the number of its outstanding shares.

poor nations.[4] I will help explain at least part of the reason for American hegemony, the reasons it is causing this problem, and the reasons why, if we continue on our current course, we are likely to self-destruct—but not before we cause a lot more pain. And I will explain why the pain is felt at home as well as abroad, for the same factors that allow American corporations to dominate the globe have helped to make America itself, at least in economic terms, the most unequal country in the world.[5]

The argument is fairly straightforward; the explanations are far more complex. Simply put, I will argue that the main problem with American corporations — the main cause of their irresponsibility — is their drive to maximize short-term stock prices, a result that no thoughtful person really wants. The root of the problem is the corporate structure itself: the corporation's legal structure encourages managers to aim for exactly this short-term result, and it does so by constraining their freedom to act responsibly and morally: the result is immoral behavior. Such behavior is in nobody's best interest and has especially pernicious effects on groups outside the traditional legal corporate structure, that is, everyone but the stockholders and managers. Compounding the problems caused by the short-termism built into the corporate structure is the fact that for almost all legal purposes we treat the corporation as if it were a natural person, granting it the freedoms of a natural person to increase stock price however it likes, but without the moral and social conscience that leads real people to care about how they do business. A long-term focus, which includes not only investing for the future but caring that profits are made responsibly and morally, is good not only for society, but also for business. The way to achieve this result is, paradoxically, to free managers from the structural pressures of stockholders and capital markets, to loosen the legal and cultural constraints upon them so that they can act as we expect them to — as natural human beings who work to increase corporate profit the way people with human moral and social values act — not in the artificial and dangerous way we have constructed them to act. The best way to achieve this result is through changes in cultural and business norms. I will make the argument for the necessary changes but will also suggest a number of other more intrusive possibilities within our existing legal framework that could be used if persuasion fails to work. These range from creating self-perpetuating boards to changing financial reporting practices to creating tax incentives through capital gains reform.

THE NEED FOR REFLECTION—
THE PURPOSE OF THIS BOOK

The extraordinary contemporary success of the American corporation, the corporation that appears to bring great prosperity at home and has come to dominate economies abroad, is based on a false premise. That premise is that it is the purpose of the corporation to maximize shareholder value or, in more common parlance, stock price. This is not a legal requirement. It is not even a norm that has governed corporate practice for most of our history. It is, however, the watchword by which we live today. And it is an ethic that will destroy us in the long term.

The observation that the ethic of stock price maximization is both new and destructive isn't novel. My explanation for it is. The explanation lies in the structure and legal rules with which we have created the corporation, and the markets in which it operates. I will show why, under current law, we should expect the corporation and its managers to care only about stock price maximization. And I will show that even in its pursuit of this goal we should not expect the American corporation to behave responsibly. Indeed we have every reason to expect it to behave irresponsibly. You need not believe in a broad notion of responsibility to accept my argument; you only need believe that corporations, like other people, should be accountable for their actions. We have designed corporations so that they are unaccountable for their actions, irresponsible in their behavior.

MAXIMIZE STOCKHOLDER PROFIT

Maximize stockholder profit. This is the watchword of our corporate faith. It is a dictate that arises from the legal structure of the American corporation and the rules of corporate law. But it is an imperative that is as destructive as it is simple. It is a message that keeps managers' and stockholders' focus on the short term.[b] And short-term management is irresponsible management: it leads to layoffs, plant closings, alienated workers, unsafe products, and a polluted environment, all in the name of today's profit; it leads to underinvestment in worker training and research and development; it has dangerously increased stock market volatility and turned our capital markets into unstable casinos of unimaginable proportions which threaten the long-term economic well-being of our society. As players in these casinos, short-term stockholders have abandoned the idea of individual corporations in favor of an invisible and faceless market.[6] We no longer invest in corporations, but in analysts' projections of future stock prices. And we shift those investments the moment the reality doesn't appear to meet projections or as soon as projections change, just as bettors at the racetrack adjust their bets as the odds at the track are continually shifted until post time.

This state of affairs is not the fault of corporate managers, at least not of managers alone. While equity markets have always had a quality of gambling about them, the degree to which long-term investing has given way to pure speculation has reached alarming proportions not seen since the 1920s. On average, stockholding periods have gone from two years in 1990 to eight months in 1999, and the period in NASDAQ stocks is five months. Even mutual fund holding periods have gone from eleven years in 1990 to four years or less.[7] It may be that markets have gotten more efficient so that stock prices reflect fair value more quickly than they used to. If this is true, then what appears simply to be speculation reflected in the eightfold increase of the NASDAQ turnover rate really is investing. But the increased instability of stock prices makes this explanation

---

[b]The largest and, in governance terms, the most active, public pension fund in the United States, the California Public Employees Retirement System, discovered this truth after embarking on a study of corporate governance. As set forth in their U.S. Corporate Governance Principles: "Company managers want to adopt long-term strategies and visions, but often do not feel that their shareowners are patient enough." http://www.calpers-governance.org/principles/domestic/us/page02.asp.

seem incredible, as does the fact that investors who trade more heavily tend to show lower-than-average profits.[8]

The long-term consequence of this collective pursuit of short-term stock price maximization is to risk America's prosperity and that of the rest of the world as well by making corporate directors and managers more than ever slaves to the stock market instead of professionals in search of better products and better ways of serving their constituencies. Followed to its logical conclusion, it may well lead to the ruin of our economy. Maximize stockholder profit is a message that is believed to embody the purpose of American corporations. But it is as incompatible historically, socially, economically, and politically with a sustainable and responsible economy as we once claimed socialism and communism to be. Looked at in the long run, it is even inconsistent with the goal of maximizing stockholder profit itself.[9]

My thesis is, on one level, unremarkable: responsible corporate management and sustained prosperity require long-term management and long-term investment. We must allow corporate managers to turn their attention to running businesses rather than manipulating stock prices. What is remarkable is to note how the legal and financial structures of the traditional American corporation create significant disadvantages for long-term management and strong competitive advantages for short-term management. These structures converge on the command to maximize stockholder profit. If we expect responsible corporate behavior and sustainable prosperity, we must rethink these legal and financial structures and their emphasis on stockholder profit. In order to do that, we must understand how deeply they are embedded in American law and American economic policy.

Maximize stockholder profit. To make this our corporate goal ignores the undeniable fact that the modern corporation is a social and political institution as well as an economic institution — an institution in which people go to work not only to make a living but to help find meaning and friendship in the process; an institution that by the products it produces, the services it offers, and the methods by which it markets them has an enormous effect on the way we think about our lives and the goals we pursue; an institution that involves itself in the mechanisms of government to help determine the ways our laws are made and the way our wealth is distributed. To make this our corporate goal ignores the power and the corresponding responsibility of the corporation.

It's also bad for business. As research increasingly shows, healthy business and a healthy economy depend upon a rich understanding of the corporation's role in modern society and its responsibilities as well as its rights. A truly sustainable prosperity depends upon a long-term view because a constant short-run focus skimps on research and development in favor of advertising and marketing, worker training, intelligent use of resources, and important considerations of social health. As *Fortune* magazine's list of the 100 Best Places to Work shows, companies that realize the importance of the long term perform better than those that don't.[10] In the meantime, corporate managers plunge thoughtlessly ahead, leaving a trail and creating a future of economic and social dislocation.

Maximize stockholder profit. It's a self-defeating maxim. But that hasn't stopped us from exporting it abroad. American ideas about business and American styles of management appear to be taking over the world.[11] American (now global) consulting, accounting, law, and financial firms are selling their stockholder-value services to companies in the European social democracies, including countries like Germany, where the concept is so foreign that the language has no word for "stockholder value', in emerging capitalist markets, and throughout Asia and the rest of the developed world. American business and legal consultants have written entire corporate codes for emerging capitalist economies with little appreciation of the distinct legal, cultural, and social environments in which they operate — sometimes, as in the case of Russia, with disastrous results.[12] American corporations are merging with or otherwise joining forces with businesses throughout the globe. And they are doing so on the basis of a single message: maximize stockholder profit.

European and Japanese managers appear to be buying this message, largely because of pressure from American capital. Institutional investors in Germany and Japan, most of whom are American,[13] want these and other nations to abandon their systems of corporate governance.[14] These investors believe that "companies everywhere should follow the British-American model of placing shareholder value above the interests of other 'stakeholders' like employees and suppliers, or considerations like the health of the environment." If European and Japanese corporations abandon their systems of corporate governance and adopt the American system, they too will be caught up in the whirlwind of short-term management and for the same reasons we are. They will also become enmeshed in a particularly American view of law and responsibility, a view which I argue is one that even Americans find unsatisfying. It is a consequence they will ultimately regret.

Despite its relative novelty as an operating ethic and its grip on contemporary American culture, the idea that the corporation exists solely or even primarily to maximize its stock price does arise from some fundamental truths about American social thought and policy. As I shall explain, it is part and parcel of the extreme and distorted version of Enlightenment liberalism that currently dominates our culture, the radical individualism and rampant selfishness that have been gaining steam since at least the late 1970s, an individualism and selfishness that can be seen everywhere from the elimination of affirmative action in Texas and California state universities to welfare "reform" in the 1990s to attempts to eliminate the estate tax and institute other tax cuts to benefit the wealthy. It can be seen in the grabbing behavior of society's winners, who want even more for themselves in a U.S. society described by the economist Robert Frank as "winner take all." It is part of the same phenomenon that produced the young investment banker we'll meet in chapter 9, who demanded that his firm provide free meals, free clothes, and a nurse's room for resting — and got them. It is part of the same phenomenon that has created the CEO we'll meet in the same chapter, whose concern for the value of his stock options not only leads him to check his company's stock price ten times daily but also to post it three times a day in the lobby of corporate headquarters. It is part of the same phenomenon that has led average CEO salaries to boom to 475 times that of the average worker, with average raises well into double digits, while workers' wages, for the lucky few, barely keep pace with inflation. It is part of the same phenomenon that has left most American workers with stagnant or declining wages so that executives can keep stock prices up by exporting jobs abroad. It is part of the same phenomenon that has led even the labor union pension funds we'll see in chapter 7 to demand that corporations produce higher stock prices in the short term even at the cost of jeopardizing their members' jobs. It is part of the drive of American investment bankers and institutional investors we'll also see in chapter 7, ever on the lookout for greener pastures, to demand so-called reforms in other countries that threaten traditional cultures of community and stability, cultures of high employment and deep social welfare — all to provide even more investment vehicles with which to increase their already substantial wealth.

It is from this ethic of stock price maximization specifically and excessive individualism generally that many of our major corporate problems derive. I do not mean to claim that stockholder wealth maximization is the only cause of our corporate problems. But I argue that this singular focus explains a great deal and fits neatly with other aspects of American society that combine to suggest that this narrow corporate purpose may be the taproot of the problem. My purpose in this book is to explain why this is so and to offer some ways of rethinking the corporation so that we can retain its obvious benefits and at the same time ameliorate its problems.

I want to be very clear, before beginning, that while I don't find greed especially attractive, this book is not an extended attack on greed. Neither is it an attack on capitalism as a broadly conceived economic system or on the simple fact of globalization, which itself attracts much fire, as the violent World Trade Organization demonstrations in Seattle in 1999 and the recent spate of books on the subject show.

The book is, instead, a warning. It is a warning that if we don't restrain ourselves, if we don't restrain our drive to accumulate even more wealth, if we don't rethink the way we do corporate business, we may find that in the long run we have much less prosperity than we do now, and, in the process of losing for ourselves, we will harm much of the world as well. It comes from a lesson we are all taught as children and all teach our children, much as I tell my fourteen-year-old son to practice the violin, from which the short-term rewards are negligible, before he plays video games, much as I tell him to lay off the delight of McDonald's in favor of the asceticism of fruit. It's a simple lesson about deferring gratification, about foregoing short-term pleasures for long-term benefits. But although it's a lesson we all know, we easily forget it. And we most easily forget it when we are acting alone but together, in the faceless, soulless, thoughtless markets of American corporate capitalist society. It's a lesson that we remember only when we stop to ask a simple but elusive question, the question that the reluctant revolutionary played by Woody Allen in the movie *Antz* dared to ask about a similar situation in which everyone acted alone but together: alone in the sense of acting without collective reflection, together in the sense that only in unreflective concert could they accomplish their own self-destruction. The purpose of this book is to ask that question — Why? — and to explore some of the answers.

I'll do more than analyze the problem. After all, it's easier just to criticize, and I don't want to stand accused of taking the easy way out. I will also make several concrete policy recommendations which flow directly from the problems I identify. While I have described the central problems as structural, many of my suggestions will not address corporate structure at all. There is much that works well in the American corporation, and much of it lies in the very same structure that causes us problems. Most of my suggested reforms, therefore, are aimed at allowing us to retain what is, unarguably, an efficient structure, but to correct for the distortions that structure produces.

Some of these suggestions will look familiar: they have been floating around in the miasma of academic literature or are variations on proposals by politicians like Senator Ted Kennedy, former labor secretary Robert Reich, and public intellectuals like the Nobel laureate James Tobin. Some are entirely original. Some are unlikely to be adopted anytime soon, but I nevertheless suggest them because of the way they refocus our thinking, starting with the long term rather than the short term. Others are practical suggestions, and I will spend more time discussing these. Taken together, they represent a logical and coherent response to the problems I identify—they provide managerial freedom to manage without the need to be obsessed with stock price. They give stockholders incentives to invest for the long term. They give us time and space to think about what individual corporations are doing and decide whether we are happy with their actions. They give corporations incentives to care about the rest of us. Ultimately, they help to resolve the collective action problem faced by any single stockholder or manager whose desire is to achieve long-term investment goals by tying us all to the mast of the long term to prevent us from being destroyed on the rocky shoals toward which the sirens' song of the short term is leading us. They will not solve all of our problems. But they will, I hope, help to reorient the way we think about the goals of our corporations and corporate law and lead us in the right direction.

CLEARING THE GROUND— SOME STARTING ASSUMPTIONS

Before I begin my argument, let me make several important points on which I want to be clearly understood for, despite my protest to the contrary, it may be easy for the reader to see this book as another in the series of recent attacks on greed and globalism. To see it that way is to miss the point.

First, my argument has nothing directly to do with the virtues or vices of capitalism, although I will have occasion to discuss the nature of capitalism itself, the multiplicity of forms it takes, and its relation to the corporate form and to democracy generally. For the most part, I view capitalism as a good thing, although I think its modern American form is a perversion, much as Aristotle saw democracy as a perversion of a polity, or government by the many.

Second, although I will be very critical of the modern corporate ethic of stock price maximization, I want to be clear about two things: first, *profit* is essential to corporate survival, and I begin with the assumption that continued corporate profitability is important for any number of reasons; profit *maximization*, however, even in the accounting sense of maximizing earnings per share, may not be an ideal target. In fact, one point of this book is to argue that even if we want corporations to maximize profits, aiming directly at that goal is a less effective way to accomplish it than focusing on other things, like the production of goods and services.[15] In a Tao-like way, naming profit maximization as the goal will, in the long term, defeat it. *Corporate* profit maximization may, depending upon the way profits are sliced up and distributed, be a good thing. I am focusing on what has come to be accepted, in scholarly and popular circles alike, as the purpose of the corporation: *stock price maximization*.

Maximizing *corporate* profits may increase real wealth. It may make a bigger pie for everybody, leaving only the serious question of how to distribute it. Maximizing stock price may be only the illusion of creating real wealth.[16] Nevertheless, as far as terminology goes, I will use the phrase "stockholder profit maximization" interchangeably with "stock price maximization" because it is the phrase used throughout the literature. Simple financial theory, which I will discuss later, makes it clear that profit maximization in the accounting sense and stock price maximization are not necessarily the same thing and in fact may rarely correspond except in the very long term. It is the latter which is my focus.

Third, while I will have something to say about globalization of the world's capital markets and, in particular, the dominance both of American capital markets and the increasing influence of the American corporate form in the world, this book is not another attack on globalism. In fact, although the limits of globalization are not yet known, it does seem rather obvious that some forms of globalization are here to stay, in product markets (facilitated by the media and by electronic commerce) as well as labor and capital markets. I am not arguing that we should turn back the clock, even if we could. Rather, what I shall be examining is what globalization means in terms of the relations among markets, states, and cultures. I will be at pains to point out the negative effects of globalization. But what I will be criticizing is a particular form of globalization, a relatively unregulated free-market form of globalization in which the power of capital overtakes the power of states and in which the power of the product overtakes the will of culture and tradition. And I will be critical of the way in which states and cultures have started to cave in to the exportation of American-style corporate capitalism. Just as the corporation is not inherently evil, neither is globalization. It's the way we deal with it and regulate it that matter.

Controlling globalization is a far greater problem than simply reining in the all-embracing exuberance of any particular markets in a given country. For each country has its own sovereign authority, its own national government and political and economic structures, through which it can choose to limit the penetration of its borders by other systems and other cultures. But when we seek to restrain — or to control or reform or direct or whatever you like — globalism as a world effort, we lack that sovereign. There is no one world authority that can serve as a focal point for our choices about globalization, that can act as a mediator among competing interests and allow for compromise solutions. In the absence of such a world authority, we have let the markets rule. That is the aspect of globalization I will criticize.

Fourth, I begin with the assumption that most corporate directors, officers, and employees are, for the most part, decent people, at least no less decent than the rest of us. Generally they want to do the right thing as they perceive it through their own moral and ethical constructs, at least as much as the rest of us. To my way of thinking, this is an assumption that they do not always seek to maximize their self-interest, although self-interest is something they pursue part of the time. I recognize that in the preceding two sentences I have of course made a value statement: Free moral actors do not pursue their self-interest all of the time. This point may be controversial in academic circles, but I suspect that the reader who lives in the world of people rather than the world of books will find it obvious.[17]

The last assumption is highly important. Without it I am left with two alternatives: either to assume people generally are selfish and uncaring or to assume nothing about peoples' motivations. If I assume self-centeredness (which I genuinely believe not to be true, although presenting the assumption as a belief rather than as an empirically established fact may not satisfy some readers), there would be no purpose in writing this book, since my argument boils down to the simple point that we ought to free corporate actors to follow their best instincts. If I assume nothing about human motivations and behavior at all, then I would have precious little to say about anything, for how can one make any predictions without some assumptions? My assumption that people—and in the particular context of this book, corporate actors—have good motives is decidedly *not* an assumption that they will act well all of the time or even most of the time, I suppose. It is only an assumption that most of them *want* to act well most of the time, and this is all I need to support my argument.

Finally, a word about the numbers. There are a myriad of financial statistics, and new ones seem to appear every day. Often they are based on different methodologies and time periods, and sometimes time periods for similar types of statistics don't match up perfectly. Using and comparing these statistics is a tricky process and must be done carefully. I have tried, as much as possible, to use the same sources for given categories of data, and where this has not been possible have so indicated. Nonetheless, while the precision of the numbers and their comparisons may be open to debate, they all point in the same direction, and the conclusions I have drawn from them are not in doubt.

CULTURE MATTERS

One last point. Contrary to most economists, who mistakenly believe that the same economic policies, applied everywhere, will produce the same results, I hold that culture matters. It has been demonstrated, for example, that there is a definite relation between the level of corruption and economic productivity in a society and its roots in Protestant-based individualistic cultures in contrast to Catholic and other cultures, in which community, loyalty, and family ties are more highly prized. At the same time that democracy reduces corruption, there is an interesting case for the proposition that loyalty and markets are "antithetical" to one another, the first privileging obligation and community and the second, individualism and merit.[18] Who is to say which is better?

Culture is critical to politics and to economics as well. As the political scientist Ronald Inglehart points out, it is culture that shapes democracy, not the other way around. And as another commentator notes, economic values are always instrumental, designed to achieve a particular purpose. They are not intrinsic to a society or to the way a culture defines itself. As such, economic development can be shaped only by the cultural values that exist in a society.[19] Alan Greenspan, perhaps the developed world's most famous economic guru, abandoned the economists' gospel that economic policies are not culturally dependent for the conclusion that capitalism is a matter of culture, not of human nature.

Culture matters. As the historian David Landes puts it, "Culture Makes Almost All the Difference."[20] This view may be unpopular in politically correct circles when it leads to the observation that some cultures are economically more "backward" than others. But as a simple observation about wealth creation, it is unmistakably right. There is nothing intrinsically wrong with noting the importance of cultural differences in a variety of areas, from politics to social organization to economics. And it seems undeniable that economic growth and productivity are greater in some cultures than in others. The important question is what you do with the conclusion. Do you (futilely, I suspect) try to make other cultures like yours, in the hope that they will develop economically like yours? Do you view them as inferior in some way and therefore not to be bothered with or, to the contrary, to be colonized, figuratively or literally? Or do you understand that cultural variations might well reflect different values, that culture matters a lot, and that the kinds of economic institutions a culture develops reflect more than simply its economic needs? I start from the last point, and it is that point that forms an important part of my final critique of the exportation of American corporate capitalism.

In the meantime, the thing to note is that America is very much a society grounded in Protestant values and that the individualism born of Calvinism is very much intertwined with, and to some extent is part of, the individualism born of liberalism. Culture and politics reinforce one another. But when these particular aspects of our culture and politics are cut loose from their ethical moorings, they can be a shipwreck waiting to happen. We have done precisely that, as our individualism and spirit of acquisitiveness have drowned out an important underpinning to our individualism, a caring and communal impulse that we've all but destroyed but that, carefully considered, shows itself as the very legitimation of our individualistic spirit.

This book is organized in three parts. Part 1 explores the philosophical and social environment in which the modern American corporation is grounded and explains why, from a cultural perspective, we ought not to expect our corporations to behave responsibly and accountably. Part 2 examines the legal structure of the corporation in finer detail, demonstrating how each aspect of that structure contributes to the problems I identify and suggesting ways in which we might create an environment in which managers, stockholders, and workers can use the best aspects of the structure to more likely assure responsible, long-term management. Part 3 is a brief examination of the nature of capitalism and its various forms and an explanation of the way American corporate and cultural mores are taking over the globe.

I

GROUNDWORK

THE PHILOSOPHY

OF THE AMERICAN

CORPORATION

AMERICAN LIBERALISM AND THE FUNDAMENTAL FLAW— THE FOUNDATION OF THE CORPORATE PROBLEM

How widespread are our corporate problems? How severe is corporate irresponsibility? Sometimes we know it when we see it: Firestone makes exploding tires and Ford knowingly allows them to remain on SUVs; Hooker Chemical pollutes Love Canal; Union Carbide builds a substandard factory in Bhopal. Sometimes it's less easy to see: General Electric lays off tens of thousands of workers and in the process destroys entire communities; Mattel's board of directors grants itself obscenely valuable stock options so complex that their value is hidden from the stockholders, who vote to approve them; some of America's largest corporations abuse federal tax laws in order to pay almost nothing in taxes even as their profits soar.

Pinning down the problem is difficult; good statistical data are almost impossible to come by if for no other reason than that the notion of corporate irresponsibility is notoriously hard to define. Moreover, much of what I will discuss as corporate irresponsibility is behavior that does not rise to a highly visible level but results from a day-to-day way of thinking about and running large corporations.

So you could, if you chose, decide that the problem is not terribly important and close this book right now. But that would be a serious mistake. For whether or not I can provide information that might pass as scientifically acceptable, it is clear that the vast majority of Americans believe that corporate misbehavior is a serious problem

—and this despite our widely celebrated unprecedented prosperity. In September 2000, *Business Week* published the results of a poll which found that fully three-quarters of Americans believed that their lives were too dominated by business (and that same number agreed with Al Gore's aggressive stance against big business). Among the findings were that 66 percent of Americans believed that "large profits are more important to big companies than developing safe, reliable, quality products for consumers. Adding to the disenchantment is the perception that companies often buy their way into government." The poll found a general perception that business had grown beyond the capacity of government to control it, creating a dangerous power imbalance in American society as well as in the rest of the world, an imbalance in which American business is perceived to overwhelm local sovereignty and culture for the sake of increasing profits. The poll's findings were consistent across age and income groups and are particularly notable for their discovery that the sentiments expressed were not so much antibusiness as anticorporate.[1] So perhaps I can't prove that corporate irresponsibility is a widespread problem, although I'll try. But the fact that the overwhelming majority of Americans believe that it is provides a powerful incentive to try to find out why.

Our corporate problems, including the ethic of stock price maximization, largely lie rooted in the structure of the American corporation. But the corporation also functions in a more fundamental social, political, and ethical ideology of radical individualism that dominates American culture and reinforces and exacerbates the problems arising from structure. This chapter will establish the groundwork for analyzing corporate responsibility by situating the issue in our cultural context.[2] In order to have a concrete basis for understanding the link between corporate behavior and culture, let's first look at several examples of what I consider to be corporate misbehavior, and then see how they fit in.

THINGS GO BETTER WITH COKE

In fiscal 1999, the Coca-Cola Company, an icon of American business success, suffered an $813 million charge to earnings—that is, a loss — as a result of poor overseas operations, primarily in Russia and Eastern Europe. Coke suffered a significant decline in stock price during the course of 1999, with several peaks (including rebounds in early 2000) but lapsing to lower levels. The solution for this corporation (with its new chief executive) described by the *New York Times* as one "known for generous benefits, job security and unflagging optimism about its future" was to lay off 20 percent of its workforce (six thousand of its thirty thousand employees worldwide) at a cost of $800 million.[3] While the company defended the move as a way of focusing on its core business, it appears that dropping stock price was the driving motivation. Coupled with the layoff announcement was the disclosure that some of Coke's foreign bottlers would reduce their levels of inventory, with one expert quoted as saying that this implied Coke had overstated its earnings growth for the preceding two years and expressing concern that it might continue to do so in the future. Of course overstating earnings growth is a way of increasing stock price in the short term. Although there is no suggestion that Coke was behaving fraudulently, the overstatement, coupled with the layoffs, suggests (especially after a year in which the stock price was beaten down) that current stock price was at the forefront of management's concern. That's no surprise given the state of American corporate law and financial markets. Does it justify terminating the employment of six thousand people? Might Coke have found a different way to get through a difficult time? Even if the corporate decision makers decided that Coke employed too many people, does the fact that they hired them in the first place give Coke's executives a moral obligation to make layoffs the last possible option? to make them as painless as possible?

If you were the owner of a small business that was having a hard time and you worked every day with loyal, longtime employees, how hard would you try to find other alternatives before walking into their offices, looking into their eyes, and telling them they were fired? Of course the Coke board and CEO Douglas Daft didn't have to work with most (if any) of the fired employees every day. They didn't personally have to go and look them in the eye and tell them they were being fired. They had underlings to follow orders, to do their dirty work for them. They had protection against the experience of actually having to fire people. And they had the protection of corporate law and the demands and expectations of capital markets to prevent them from having to own up to the consequences of their decision; after all, business is business, and business is about maximizing profits. Sorry.

UNOCAL AND CORPORATE SLAVERY

Sometime around 1991, Unocal established the Yadana gas pipeline project as a joint venture with the ruling Burmese junta (through a corporation controlled by the junta) to engage in off-shore drilling for natural gas and to transport that gas to Thailand through pipelines running through the Tenasserim region of Burma. It was well known at the time of this agreement that the junta, which went by the ironic name of the State Law and Order Restoration Council (SLORC), had engaged in extensive human rights abuses and violations of international law. Nonetheless, SLORC allegedly acted as agent for the project, with financial support from Unocal, "to clear forest, level ground, and provide labor, materials and security for the Yadana pipeline project."[4] In an opinion denying Unocal's motion to dismiss the complaint of farmers from the region, the federal district court described allegations not only of rape, intimidation, and forced relocation, but SLORC's use of slave labor for the project. As the case approached its resolution in federal district court in California, where Unocal is headquartered, National Public Radio's program *All Things Considered* did a story on it.[a]

I will deliberately leave out the potentially inflammatory details and horrifying stories of the way the slave labor allegedly came about and was conducted. I don't need those details for my purposes, because NPR reporter Daniel Zwerdling's interview with Unocal's vice chairman, Jon Imle, is enough to make the point:

[a]The case was dismissed on jurisdictional grounds in August 2000 and is now on appeal.

Mr. John Imle (Vice Chairman, Unocal): I don't believe those charges. I wouldn't call them lies. I—maybe confusion about what has been going on where. I mean, I've heard stories that—I just don't believe those stories.

Zwerdling: Imle says when he and his fellow executives decided to get into the pipeline project with Myanmar's government, their first goal was to make a profit. After all, he says, they're a business.

Mr. Imle: But right behind that and as a condition—always a condition of that investment, we will only invest in places where we can improve the lives of people.

Zwerdling: And Imle says the gas pipeline will improve lives across the region. The project is pumping gas across Myanmar to a power plant inside Thailand, and that'll help bring electricity to people who still cook with firewood and light up their homes with kerosene lanterns. Still, Imle says, he and his colleagues realized that they caused controversy when they formed a partnership with the military rulers in Myanmar. They know that everybody from U.S. presidents to human rights groups to United Nations officials, all these people have repeatedly denounced Myanmar's dictators as some of the most brutal on the planet. And Imle says he realized that Myanmar's government is infamous for using what some people call forced labor or conscripted labor . . . .

Mr. Imle: I accept that conscripted labor is used broadly in civil projects in that country in Myanmar.

Zwerdling: But Imle says he was determined to make their pipeline project a model of the ethical way to do business. Maybe they'd even nudge the dictators toward democracy. [Zwerdling then describes the structure of the project, including the Myanmar army's intended role of providing security.] He [Imle] says company executives wouldn't tolerate it if the military forced villagers to work on the project against their will.

Mr. Imle: We worked very hard . . . to determine that we would be able to conduct our business in an absolutely ethical, honest, and moral manner.

Zwerdling: And do you feel, deep down inside, convinced that the military did not abuse workers in any way connected to the pipeline?

Mr. Imle: I'm not in a position to know that much about the internal conduct of the military on the ground. But I guess what I'm trying to say is there was no contractual relationship with the military. We were not in any way in control. . . . But the use of conscripted labor in connection with this project was a non-starter from the beginning, and everyone knew that. Now what the military may or may not have done that nobody knows about, I can't address. But whatever happened in the area of this pipeline, I don't think those things happened in the area of this pipeline, I don't think these things happened, in my heart of hearts, I really don't.[5]

Now I didn't highlight anything in the conversation, just to avoid any advance signaling of my own view. But I don't think you can help notice Imle's logic: First, Unocal's goal was profit; second, despite Unocal's insistence on ethics, Unocal executives knew that the Myanmar regime was brutally repressive and used slave labor, and they frankly had no idea what was going on in Myanmar; third, Unocal had "no contractual relationship" with the junta, apparently implying that the absence of a direct contract to provide slave labor relieved Unocal of the responsibility for investigating and asserting control.

Leave aside the scary resonances of early American political reactions to reports of the atrocities Germans were committing against Jews during World War II, as well as the echoes of President Bill Clinton's extraordinary technical responses in the far more trivial Lewinsky affair. Just look at the bare outline of Imle's defense, taking what he said as entirely accurate: Unocal wanted to make a profit, its executives knew all about the Myanmar government, they evidently didn't ask or investigate at high corporate levels what the military was doing, they had no contract with the military to provide slave labor, they therefore had no legal control over the military's behavior in Unocal's name and for its benefit, and Imle's deepest intuitions told him the story couldn't be true. Would we accept this from a politician? from our friends or neighbors? Would we accept it as an excuse from our children?

Why should we accept it from Unocal? Was Unocal's decision a legitimate corporate decision? It sure is cheaper to force people to relocate than to pay for their land or to redirect the pipeline in order to permit them to continue their lives. It's obviously cheaper to use slave labor than to pay someone to work for you. And if Unocal's executives were acting through these agents in whose country such activities were legal (or at least let's assume that they were, to make Unocal's case easier), why shouldn't they do what is necessary to maximize stock prices? Posing the question this way and on these facts pretty much answers it.[6] And yet the answer is not so clear as a matter of American corporate law.

EXPLOSIONS AT GENERAL MOTORS

On July 9, 1999, a California jury awarded the highest liability award in American history, $4.8 billion, including $107 million of compensatory damages and the remaining $4.7 billion in punitive damages, to Patricia Anderson, who, along with her children and a family friend, were seriously burned when the fuel tank of their 1979 Chevrolet Malibu exploded in a rear-end collision. The plaintiffs offered to reduce the punitive damages by $4 billion if GM recalled the cars and all those built on the same frame, but the company refused. Although the punitive damages award was later reduced to $1.09 billion, significant evidence was admitted regarding a memorandum discovered by lawyers in the early 1980s (but for various reasons never produced at trial). Written by GM engineer Edward Ivey, the memo analyzed the cost of making safer fuel tanks ($2.40 per car) against the possible losses from damages GM would have to pay in the event of accidents and resulting fires. Obviously, GM declined to recall the cars or redesign the fuel tanks. In reducing the punitive damages award, Judge Ernest Williams observed that the placement of the fuel tank was intended "to maximize profits, to the disregard of public safety."[7]

Was General Motors' decision a reasonable corporate decision? If the purpose of the corporation is to maximize stock price, then a cost-benefit analysis is perfectly appropriate, and the answer is yes. Was the decision a *human* decision? No. One way of getting at the answer is to ask what Ivey would have done with his report had he known his wife, children, or other loved ones would be driving Chevy Malibus.

It's not that we don't make cost-benefit decisions all the time. We do. Our resources are scarce. We have little choice but to make cost-benefit decisions. But there's a difference between a human making those decisions and the same decisions made by a corporation.

The difference between a natural person and a corporation is that we natural persons experience the costs of our decisions as well as pay them. If we behave in a way that harms other people, we typically not only are aware of it but feel the pain of it as well. If, for example, a colleague from another law school sends me her paper and asks me to comment on it, and I decide that it's more beneficial for me to get my own writing done, I may well decline to read it — but I'll feel bad about it and will almost certainly feel the need to apologize.

Corporations may sometimes pay the costs, but they don't experience them in the same way. GM and its executives had no experience of explaining to its customers that their cars might explode and, short of being hauled into court, no experience of the need to apologize. In other words, they didn't feel responsible because they didn't experience the consequences of their decision to keep profits up at the expense of human life.[8] How would GM's executives react if they had to confront the Andersons or any of their other customers face to face? We don't know; they might make the same decision. But they would make it with a more human understanding of its consequences, with a full appreciation of its costs. How does their ability to avoid this confrontation, to externalize costs and not feel responsible, affect our evaluation of the nature and purpose of the American corporation?

MISAPPROPRIATION—THAT IS, THEFT—AT MARRIOTT

In December 1991 Marriott Corporation issued convertible preferred stock. The company also issued $400 million of debt in early

1992. On October 5, 1992, Marriott announced a restructuring of its business in which its highly profitable and fast-growing management and services businesses (producing more than half of Marriott's operating profit) were to be placed in a new subsidiary and spun off to Marriott's common stockholders. Its far less profitable real estate and concession businesses were to be left in Marriott, along with all of the debt and the preferred stock. The new business was expected to be highly profitable; the remaining business (with which the debtholders and preferred stockholders were stuck) would be heavily leveraged and was expected to produce rather minimal cash flow after debt service. Why did Marriott do this? Well, the new company, with all the good assets and no debt, would be significantly more valuable to stockholders than a Marriott burdened by debt. In other words, stock price would be maximized. Not so for the debtholders. The market value of this relatively newly issued debt plummeted, and, although the preferred stock price increased, the corporation into which the preferred stockholders could convert their stock was one that was largely denuded of the assets the preferred stockholders thought they were getting.[9] Marriott put the costs of maximizing its stock price onto the debtholders and preferred stockholders. At the stockholders' meeting called to approve the deal, one sensitive shareholder said to Chairman J. Willard Marriott, "Your father would be ashamed of you."

Why wasn't J. Willard Marriott ashamed? Well, for one thing, he didn't (or so he might have thought) have to confront the people who were suffering from his decision. For another, he undoubtedly saw his job as being to maximize common stock prices — after all, that's the job we told him to do.[b] While taking money from bondholders hardly rises to the level of tolerating slave labor or knowingly installing faulty fuel tanks, it is in line with this behavior in that the two things that permit it to occur are the same: the mandate to maximize stock price, and the separation of the decision maker from the consequences of the decision.

[b]It also didn't hurt that his family owned a large block of common stock.

Death and taxes, as the old saying goes, are the only things about which one can be certain. But death is not inevitable for the artificial corporate person. Sure, it can die after a fashion — in bankruptcy court or after being swallowed up in a merger — but these are hardly certain, and even when corporations experience their own form of death there is always some sort of afterlife for the assets and often for the business as a going concern. But what about taxes? Corporations surely are subject to taxes just like the rest of us, in their case at a flat rate of 35 percent on all of their reported profits. But there's the rub: reported profits. Recent evidence suggests that the pressures of making profits for stockholders have made even good corporations turn bad as they find ways to avoid reporting profits to the Internal Revenue Service, in the process diminishing their tax burdens and increasing profits to stockholders.

On February 20, 2000, the *New York Times* reported how widely corporations have begun to engage in these schemes. For example, AlliedSignal got slammed by the tax court after it sold an investment for $400 million and, in a scheme cooked up by its investment banker, Merrill Lynch, moved the profits to a Dutch partnership. It thus neatly avoided a $140 million tax liability. When it reclaimed the profits from the partnership, the tax liability had disappeared, and AlliedSignal reported a $4 million gain on the partnership investment itself!

This is not an isolated case. According to the *Times* the situation has become so bad that corporate tax lawyers (discharging their ethical obligations) have been ratting to the IRS on their own clients. But IRS resources are limited so that fewer than 10 percent of corporate dodges are being picked up. The result is that while individual income tax revenue increased 6.2 percent in 1999, corporate tax revenue fell by 2.5 percent.[10]

AlliedSignal is only one example. As the *Times* reports (and the numbers suggest), more than a few highly respected corporations are engaging in these and other tax evasion practices. Some of these may be legal, but many others push the envelope of legality and frequently come out on the other side. Why would they do this?

The *Times* gave an answer: pressure to increase stockholder profits. One of the major corporate expenses, taxes, is being pushed onto the rest of us through corporate bilking of the federal treasury. It leaves less money than we are entitled to for our social infrastructures. And it limits our ability to redistribute wealth the way our tax system was designed to do.

Why behave in these ways? Why should corporations be particularly susceptible to the kinds of behavior that most individuals — even if the thought crossed their minds — would reject as unethical to say the least? What is it about the way we structure the corporation and the nature and purpose we envision for it that gives the corporation a different moral construct, or at least makes a different moral outlook easier for them to adopt and easier for us to swallow?

THE FOUNDATIONS OF CORPORATE MISBEHAVIOR

In order to understand the problems underlying the structure of American corporate law it is essential to understand the foundations of American law upon which it is built. This in turn requires us to look at the political, social, and ethical theories underlying our laws, the concepts of enlightenment liberalism that are implicit in our Constitution, and the social and political philosophy that frames our public and private relationships with one another. It is these concepts that form what we might see as the tectonic plates undergirding our entire social structure. Like the tectonic plates upon which Earth's surface sits, these theoretical plates sometimes shift imperceptibly to shade our prevailing moods, giving us only the faintest shudder as they settle into our collective consciousness. Sometimes, though, they clash violently, as they do in earthquakes, changing for a time or forever our social outlook. When we have looked at these deepest levels of our common understanding, we will begin to see that the fundamental flaw of our corporate structure is the fundamental flaw of liberalism itself, a flaw which is hard to see in the purest theoretical forms of liberal philosophy but which becomes pronounced and even pathological when the shifting plates create distortions in those forms.

The metaphor is useful. But it's not perfect. The problem is that the Earth's shifting surface is a natural phenomenon. We can no more control it than we can control the rotation of the planets around the sun. Our philosophical plates are different—they are entirely of our own making. They sometimes may not seem like it because they become so embedded in our social norms and collective subconsciousness that they appear to be inevitable. But they're not. Whether intentionally or not, we ourselves have created them. That means that we ourselves also have the power to change them. Metaphor, no matter how useful, should not blind us to this reality.

As we begin to examine liberalism and its modern manifestations, we can identify two themes that are illustrated by the stories with which I began. The first is an ethic of radical individualism which, in the limited moral universe of the corporation, results in an attitude of grab and get. The other is the suppression of any impulse to care about the welfare of others.

LIBERALISM'S BASIC PREMISE

Liberal philosophy itself, which might be considered to be comprised of the two main plates of liberty and equality, is familiar to most of us and relatively easy to identify despite the ridges and valleys, the different emphases given to different aspects of it by different thinkers. These variations on liberalism are important because wrongly understood or taken as caricatures, they become its pathologies. Nonetheless, the core is common to most mainstream thinkers on the subject.

The main precept of liberal philosophy begins with an idea, made familiar to us by Thomas Hobbes's description of the state of nature, and that is the rough equality of all persons. This rough equality—whether resulting in Hobbes's war of all against all or giving rise to more peaceful deliberations among equals as imagined by the modern philosopher John Rawls—leads to the conclusion that all persons are equally autonomous, free and self-directed in pursuing their own ends. They are at the same time equally vulnerable to interference by all others in the pursuit of their own ends. Hobbes's solution to the inevitable war of all against all is some governmental authority that maintains each person's ability to set and attempt to achieve goals while at the same time restricting others from interfering with those pursuits. Rawls argues in favor of fundamental principles that are to serve as reference points for our laws and economic distribution. In both cases, and indeed in liberal theory generally, there is some higher authority to which we appeal in order to ensure the justice necessary to allow us to be free.

What makes the theories liberal — what differentiates them from older ideas that required us to submit to authority — is the fact that in each case it is the individual right of each person to choose to surrender some autonomy to the government, to choose the principles under which they are to be governed. And it is equally important in liberal theory to note that all of this is to a purpose: to ensure that each of us has as much freedom as possible to pursue goals of our own choosing. Finally, this freedom is necessarily limited by the freedom of others to pursue their goals. These are the ideas embodied in our basic constitutional structure based on equal rights and equal liberties; in our government designed to protect our individual boundaries so that our enjoyment of our liberties does not unduly restrict the liberties of others. Liberty is bounded by equality, and so we have equal liberty (or that, at least, is the goal).

A simple example will illustrate this function of authority in the service of freedom. You and I might want to drive our cars to the store at the same time.[c] Each of us is equally vulnerable to interference by the other; that is, you might drive your car in a manner that creates danger for me so that you keep me off the street or divert my course. Liberty would suggest that we are free to drive however and wherever we want. But if we do so, our independent goals might well be frustrated. I might prefer to drive on the right side of the road and you, coming from the other direction, might like to drive on the left. A head-on collision is all but inevitable. Or you might be in a hurry and attempt to beat me through an inter-

[c]Driving to the store is hardly the kind of value toward which liberal philosophy ultimately aims. But it is something we choose to do, and the example works well enough as an illustration, so I ask you to pardon what might appear to be a trivialization of a very important idea.

section at which we both must make turns but from opposite sides. In each case, neither of us will realize our goals; we are more likely to wind up in the hospital than make it to the store. The simple solution is traffic law, which mandates that we drive on opposite sides of the road and that we follow certain rules at intersections, typically regulated by traffic lights and stop signs. We each have sacrificed a portion of our liberty to drive as we would choose. But the benefit of that sacrifice is that we are equally free to drive to the store — free of the fear that the other will choose to do so in a way that harms us. In a paradoxical but very real sense, this modest sacrifice of liberty gives each of us greater liberty.

But liberalism is about more than mere restraint; it's about more than what we can't do. For while Hobbes may have emphasized the need for these restrictions primarily in terms of protecting us from each other, others have emphasized the affirmative side of liberalism, the right to self-determination; that is, the right to choose our life courses, free from others telling us what to do. In this aspect of liberalism, each of us is a naturally equal person, with the ability to determine for ourselves how we wish to live our lives, the goals we want to pursue, and the people with whom we want to pursue them.

The historical background against which this concept of liberalism developed — the world to which it was reacting — is the relative rigidity of premodern society. It is a background exemplified by the strict limitations of Athenian democracy, the English feudal system, and, in modern times, American slavery and the theocracy that is Iran. Each of these (and many other) social structures offers a unique rationale for the way it's designed, a different justification for the type of authority it legitimates, a different source of difference, but the central common fact of each is that every member of the society has a place that is more or less determined by the position of her parents at her birth, which itself is determined by the position of their parents, and so regressing back into time.

The liberal solution — the liberating solution — was to argue that among the natural rights of humans is the right to self-determination, an idea brought to its most famous articulation in the moral philosophy of Immanuel Kant but earlier described in both social and economic terms by John Locke, David Hume, and Adam

Smith, and later in the writings on liberty of John Stuart Mill. The basic idea is that you, simply because you are a person like every other person, are a self-governing being, and that gives you the right to choose a life course and pursue it, regardless of your parents' occupations or social stations. Indeed (and this is Kant) one cannot realize full personhood unless one is free to make these choices.

The flip side of this way of thinking is the restraint on liberty that I mentioned earlier; nobody can tell you how to live your life. Nobody can impose their values or goals or desires upon you. So we limit the necessary authority of society. We see the limits in our rights of free speech, assembly, and religion, we see them protected in the First Amendment to our Constitution. And we also see in American law a strong, almost rabid fear of imposing affirmative obligations on our citizens. We have no legal obligation to help others in distress, even if we can do it at no risk or cost to ourselves. All we really need to do is pay our taxes and serve in the military if we're drafted (though even the draft allows room for conscientious objection). So we also see our privacy rights protected (though by how much is the subject of vigorous debate) in the Constitution's Third, Fourth, and Fifth Amendments, and of course the Fourteenth Amendment passed following the Civil War.

The right of self-determination transforms into the idea of individualism, the idea of the self-made man, the hero, the free spirit. It is the cult of Warren Buffett, the icon of Michael Jordan, the damn-the-world freedom of Madonna. It is a feature of American social thought and mythology from the log cabin presidency of Andrew Jackson through the tales of Horatio Alger and the success stories of so many sports heroes and Internet millionaires. It is the idea that any American has the freedom to achieve any level of wealth or political or social or professional success just by virtue of being a person; it is the idea that every American is free to say what she thinks, no matter how unpopular; it is the idea that every American is free to practice any religion or no religion at all; it is the idea that every American is free to form intimate relationships with whomever he chooses; and it is the idea that no American can be forced to follow a path of life chosen for him by another or by the state.

Equality and freedom—equal freedom. These form the central and adjacent tectonic plates of American liberal thought. While they sometimes break and sometimes clash, while sometimes one is forced to give ground to the other, these ideals remain largely intact.

The clash of these plates can produce malformations, but they are malformations that, like mountain ranges, at least rise from the basic groundwork. There are times in our history when liberty has been emphasized at the expense of equality. Examples are the Gilded Age of the late nineteenth century and the Reagan era that began in the 1980s and continues to the present. At other times equality has been dominant, as illustrated by the civil rights struggles of the Reconstruction era and the early 1960s and the economic programs of the New Deal. The desire for equality can be seen in contemporary struggles for equal religious treatment and gay rights and in debates over universal health care and welfare reform. In every one of these and many other situations, both strains have been present but only one has been obvious. Usually they exist in an intricate counterpoint, seeking resolution through politics and adjudication but never quite getting there, like a fugue without end or a continent never completed. This continuous flux is most likely to be the perpetual fate of our democracy—it may in fact be the saving grace of our democracy.

Despite this constant search for balance, liberty has for some time been the dominant strain in American social and political thought. Of course liberty and equality are not entirely unrelated; as I've noted, frequently the claim for liberty is a claim for equal liberty. But Americans have become increasingly jealous of their liberties and correspondingly suspicious of equality. Equality requires interference with liberty: people are born equal in nature and in the eyes of God, but hardly so in economic and social circumstances. To improve the equality of the disadvantaged requires the state to interfere with the liberty of those more fortunate. Even so, we can for the most part see equality as a natural fact, with equality of condition as an aspiration—in this way of thinking, some measure of equality always remains.

But liberty is terribly fragile. Liberty is at risk whenever people put themselves under a government and laws, whenever they sacrifice some measure of their freedom to others, no matter how necessary that sacrifice may be to preserve the opportunity for all to enjoy most freedoms. Americans have become more sensitive to this fragility of liberty in recent decades, a fact as obvious in the social as in the economic realm. Americans of increasingly diverse backgrounds and views are fearful of losing their rights to pursue their ends to the pressures of more dominant groups.

The strong emphasis on liberty is evident in contemporary social life in the assertions by various religious groups of their rights, of homosexuals to marry, the rights of free speech and privacy on the Internet, and the right to die. It is manifest in what the legal scholar Mary Ann Glendon calls rights talk, the modern tendency of Americans to assert every desire in terms of their rights. It is also reflected in the strong assertions of economic liberty over the past several decades, which find their most popular expressions in the booming stock markets populated with speculators and day traders who have no concern for the companies in which they invest but are interested only in the maximization of their wealth. It is reflected in the political resistance to new and expanding social programs, in the defeat of affirmative action in public universities in Texas and California, and of course in the perennial opposition of so many Americans to increases in their taxes, especially to support social programs that promote equality.

The problem is more than simply political. It is also cultural, although I will have less to say about this aspect of the problem. Max Weber famously (if controversially) described the effect upon modern capitalist economic development of an ingrained Calvinist concept of the achievement of worldly success as evidence of predestination for salvation. More important, perhaps, is what Weber saw as the spirit of modern capitalism, the very rationality of modern capitalism, and that is the idea of acquiring wealth for its own sake, the idea of acquisition itself as a value, as an end and not as a means. It is an ethic that has come to form the core of American culture as waves of immigrant groups, some of divergent cultural norms and some coming from cultures that in some way had norms that oper-ated like Calvinist norms, assimilated and absorbed into American society.

Now look what happens when this ethic of acquisition combines with a strong disposition to regard liberty as the dominant political value. You have created a society in which people believe it is their right to get what they can and to keep what they get. You have created a world in which self dominates society, in which entitle-ment trumps responsibility. You have created what I have elsewhere called the selfishness surplus, that is, the difference between what the winners have today and what they would have if we cared more about equitable distribution and economic justice for others than we do, if we cared about equality the way we care about liberty; in short, if we cared about others besides ourselves. The selfishness surplus can be captured in a simple formula, SS = AS − CS, where SS equals selfishness surplus, AS equals autonomy society (or the society of rampant individualism), and CS equals caring society, based on principles of economic and social justice.[11]

The selfishness surplus is easy to illustrate. Imagine two boys playing ball in the schoolyard. One is tall, the other is short. The taller boy gets the ball and decides he is tired of playing. The shorter boy wants to play with the ball. The taller boy — and most of you have seen some version of this — holds the ball as high as he can and says to the shorter one something like, "You want it, take it." The shorter boy jumps and jumps, but he'll never reach the ball and will even-tually give up. The difference between the height of the ball and the highest that the shorter boy can jump is the selfishness surplus.

For those of you who prefer reality to metaphor, it is easy enough to put the selfishness surplus in concrete economic terms. In 1998 the average household income in Scarsdale, New York, was $280,049, with a median of $159,447 and a per capita average income of $89,483. The corresponding numbers in Compton, Cal-ifornia, were $41,471, $30,546, and $9,970. The selfishness surplus is something short of the differences between these figures, some-thing that would reflect a fairer economic distribution in which we recognized that it is only our social structure that permits great wealth (and great poverty) and that the one should be adjusted to account for the other.

Some of you will object. We deserve what we've earned. We pay our taxes and that should be enough. I've answered the first argument elsewhere. Deservedness has very little to do with anything. As to your taxes: Well, coupled with the fact that the United States has the lowest tax rates of any industrialized Western nation, paying your taxes is a fairly minimal obligation if that's all you've got to do. And it pretty much is.

How do the stories with which I began this chapter relate to the selfishness surplus? It's pretty easy to see in the Marriott case. The law (or rather Marriott's manipulation of the law) gave the corporation a permanent advantage over its creditors and allowed it to hold the ball so high that the preferred stockholders and debtholders had no chance to play—in fact it was their ball that Marriott's stockholders were taking. It's what Coke was doing when it laid off workers (who have almost no legal rights to their jobs) in order to save money to raise its stock price. Certainly AlliedSignal, while it got caught, was simply stretching the selfishness surplus to see how far it would go. And Unocal's Imle, in trying to distance the company from its responsibility for shutting its eyes to the use of slave labor, resorted to the law of contracts to protect himself. We didn't have a contract with SLORC, he said, and so we couldn't control them. We had no legal right and thus no legal obligation. But of course this ignores the fact that, as between Unocal and SLORC, Unocal had all the money—it had something SLORC wanted. It ignores the fact that Unocal could hold the ball as high as it wanted and that SLORC knew it. It ignores the fact that, like the taller boy in our metaphor, SLORC could get what it wanted only if Unocal chose to give it to them, and Unocal would choose to do so only if SLORC did what it wanted. The Unocal case is extreme. But it's only an example of the way the selfishness surplus works.

There's another side to American social and political culture — to American character. It is this side — or rather the lack of it — that is illustrated by the stories of General Motors' Malibu and Unocal's slave labor. That is the caring impulse, common to all people. But in contemporary America that caring impulse is submerged by the American obsession with liberty.

OUR CARING IMPULSE—
THE FLIP SIDE OF PATHOLOGICAL LIBERALISM

There is another aspect to the American character that is embodied in our political and social thought as well, an aspect that goes beyond the self-centeredness that is the pathological manifestation of individual liberty. It is the impulse that leads us to care about the equality side of the equation, to provide the social programs that we do, to give money to charities, to volunteer our time, and in countless other ways to join with other human beings to better our communities and help those in need. It is especially important to spend some time discussing this impulse because modern American society has all but buried it, and, as we will see in the next chapter, this interment exacerbates the corporate problem.

The caring impulse undeniably exists. The social programs I alluded to embody it; our redistributive system of progressive taxation, flawed though it is, reflects it. The caring impulse is the motivating factor behind laws like the Americans with Disabilities Act, the funding of Head Start, the appeal of the call to put people first. It is the reason George W. Bush felt it necessary to modify "conservatism" with "compassionate." It is the reason that so many Americans give money to charities and their time to causes like Habitat for Humanity and Big Brothers and the local soup kitchen. This caring impulse exists in all people, for it derives from a simple truth — that all of us are human, and as humans each of us can see the humanity in others. It is the mechanism described by Hume, whereby our common humanity leads us to identify with others who are — despite all of our differences — more like us than not, and that causes us to "feel their pain." And in feeling their pain, it causes us to want to help.

The way this motivational mechanism works is obvious if you take a moment to reflect upon it. How many times have you flinched in front of your television when another sensationalist news story shows the victims of disaster — or even when watching a violent movie? Why is it a natural tendency to look away when we see a severely handicapped person — even as we want to help? Why do we stop to make sure that someone who has fallen on the street is okay or to help a lost child find its parents?

The reason is that we can imagine ourselves in that same situation, in the same kind of pain. We know, at least at some deep intuitive level, that vulnerability is as much a condition of human existence as independence, that none of us is immune to tragedy or pain, that a fine line divides us in our current well-being from those whom we see suffering. It is this intuition of vulnerability, combined with the recognition of humanity in each of us, that leads us to want to help others. In a broader social sense, it is this understanding of the universality of vulnerability that leads us to create institutional and legal structures to help others, and then to support those structures.

But there is a problem with our caring impulse, one that applies even more strongly in the corporate context than in the broader social context. That is the problem of separation and distance. Hume noted this even as he developed the moral psychology that explains why we care, and it also is intuitive. We tend to identify most readily with those who are close to us. Notice that in the paragraph above the examples I gave envision face-to-face (or at least virtual face-to-face) encounters with other people. It is in these circumstances that we most easily identify with others — in short, that we most easily see them as people like ourselves. Most of us care about our families more than we care about our neighbors and friends, and we care about our neighbors and friends more than we care about those whom we don't know. And we tend to care more about those most like us — in religion, in class, in race — than we do about those who are different.

In a large and diverse society like that of America, most of us are only dimly aware of the existence *as people* of those outside our circles. We may see their faces in the workplace or pass them in the street. We might learn something about some few of them on television or in newspapers. But mostly we don't think about them at all. Because of this separation, our appreciation of their vulnerability, and our correspondent ability to care, becomes tenuous. That's why it takes much more dramatic misfortunes to make us think about them and care about them in the first place. We send money to aid the victims of natural disasters like floods and earthquakes not because we care about them more but because the dramatization of their plight makes it seem more human — and therefore more real — to us. We mourn with the victims of crime whom we see on television, we share their outrage, because we can attach the event to an individual face, an individual identity. Most of us don't share the same feelings of pain and outrage for the victims of inner city poverty or bad schools — we don't see them everyday, they are a nameless, faceless other. And while anyone can experience a natural disaster or fall victim to crime, if you're a relatively well-to-do American you don't expect to wind up homeless or impoverished in the South Bronx, and so the particular vulnerabilities and tragedies of the lives of those who do rarely reach our individual radar screens, rarely penetrate our caring mechanisms.

The point should be clear. Space and time separate us from others. They interfere with our caring mechanisms and allow us to focus only on those closest at hand — and that means ourselves and our loved ones. That's why it is so easy for Unocal's Imle to disregard — or choose to disbelieve — stories of atrocities committed on behalf of his company in Myanmar. He doesn't see the people; he doesn't see the pain. It's why he can fall back on the legal mechanism of contract to disclaim control and responsibility. For an unfortunate effect of one of the most important social mechanisms we use to protect our liberties — our laws — is to keep us a disinterested distance from other people, to limit our feelings of responsibility for them. So the contract Imle says Unocal didn't have with SLORC means, at least to him, that Unocal had no control; it had neither a cognizable relationship with SLORC nor any responsibility for SLORC's actions.

The effect of distance also explains why General Motors' executives can with seeming callousness sell cars they know are unsafe. The cars are to be driven by nameless, faceless others who, except in the rare case of litigation, remain nameless and faceless even in tragedies of GM's making. We would think of these executives as monsters if they willingly let their loved ones drive cars they knew to be unsafe.

Distance is also why it is so relatively easy for Coke's Daft to fire six thousand people. He doesn't know them. He doesn't have to personally experience the pain of looking them in the face and firing them. He doesn't have to hear the stories of the hardships he's caused, or see the faces of their spouses and children when they're told they have to go without, or experience the uprooting and separation from friends and family that may accompany the search for new work.

The problem is, as I've described it, not unique to corporations. It is a problem that commonly arises in a geographically vast and enormously diverse modern liberal society. It is what might be called the liberal perversion — the destruction of one tectonic plate by another, creating a malformation at the surface: the towering dominance of selfish individualism over caring. That is why I said that this problem offers only a foundation for the corporate problem, although even in this form — and before I describe the corporate problem in more detail — you can see how it becomes especially pronounced in the corporate context. But it also helps to exaggerate the problem in the corporate context, for if our caring impulse is so easily buried by flesh-and-blood humans enmeshed in the individualism of modern life, if it is so easily abetted by the laws of liberty that create the selfishness surplus, how much more so is it buried when we interpose an artificial person, that is, a corporation? That is the subject of the next chapter.

THE LIBERAL CORPORATION— THE AMERICAN CORPORATION

The bottom line is that the precepts of liberalism, as distorted as they are in modern American life, simply cannot be applied to the modern business corporation. Yet we have applied them in just this way. As a brief preview of the argument to come (and a bit of a summary of what I've said so far), the story goes like this: The modern American corporation was born into the liberal environment and has in many ways been at the forefront of our contemporary emphasis on liberty. Naturally enough, and given its largely economic nature, it has also been at the forefront of the liberal perversion: the idea that we are responsible only for ourselves, that we are to get what we can and to keep it from others. The consequence of this for modern corporate behavior and, to be fair, for our expectations of modern corporate behavior as well is irresponsibility, by which I mean the failure of responsibility, and unaccountability. This situation ultimately permits the corporation to externalize many of the costs of its profit maximization on groups who are affected by the corporation but powerless to change its behavior.

The corporation has always been acknowledged to be, in the words of Chief Justice John Marshall, "an artificial being, invisible, intangible, and existing only in contemplation of law." But despite this artificiality, despite the inhuman legal construct that it is, the law treats it as a person, endowed with virtually all of the legal and constitutional rights possessed by real people. To be sure, this is an odd application of rights provided by a constitution that was designed for a nation that perceived those rights to "life, liberty, and the pursuit of happiness" to have been bestowed by the Creator upon natural persons. But the obvious fact that the corporation is not a natural person didn't stop the U.S. Supreme Court from holding in 1886, without any discussion of the matter at all, that corporations were indeed persons as contemplated by the Fourteenth Amendment. And it is that Fourteenth Amendment that has proved to be the wellspring of so many of our individual rights, making corporations persons like any other for all practical purposes.

Yet the assumptions that underlie liberalism and ground our Constitution and our laws cannot sensibly be applied to the corporation. The corporation is nothing more than a legal device; in fact, it is nothing more than a piece of paper in a state secretary of state's office, where the certificate of incorporation is filed.[d] Thus the

---

[d]A more sophisticated statement would be that the certificate of incorporation embodies all of the corporate laws of the state of incorporation. I'll discuss those in subsequent chapters—but all of those laws taken together don't

corporation as a wholly artificial being lacks the motivational capacities of a real person as well as the ability, so fundamental to liberal theory, to choose and pursue ends for itself. It lacks the moral framework of a natural person. In terms of the regulation of its behavior, of the perceptions of guilt and shame that philosophers like Hume and Smith believed were strong motivators to moral (or at least socially acceptable) behavior, it has, in the words of an English jurist, "no soul to be damned, and no body to be kicked."

Wait a minute, you might object. Whatever the legal requirements of incorporation are, whatever the structure of the entity and the laws that govern it, it can be moved only by those real persons who are responsible for its operations: the board of directors, the officers, and the employees. Of course you'd be right. The problem is that when these people act within the corporation, they are acting as *corporate* people. Oz behind the curtain is mighty Oz. But when the curtain is pulled back, he's just a little man. These corporate constituents, although real people with real motivations and real souls, are straitjacketed by the legal structure of the corporation in the goals they direct it to pursue and the manner in which they pursue them. When they are acting for the corporation, the curtain remains closed.

Corporations are people. But as we've already seen, they are special kinds of people; people created not by God but by law and humans. As such, and in contrast to the Enlightenment vision of autonomous man, they have only the ends given to them by their creators. And the ends given to them by structure if not by doctrine are one: maximize stock price. This is the rule by which we have come to expect corporations to live, their revealed truth, their moral compass, their reason for being. Maximizing stock price is corporate self-actualization. Maximizing stock price is, for the corporation, the pursuit of the good which liberalism encourages. If there ever was any doubt that this is the truth of corporations, increasingly deregulated capital markets and the proliferation of speculative investment strategies, not to mention pressure from

---

change the essential fact that the corporation, although we treat it like a person, is artificial.

institutional investors (whose own goal is to maximize profit), have forced it to be so. Like Rabbi Judah Loew's *Golem,* a statue which came to life to protect the Jewish people once the right words were inserted into its ear, the modern American corporation knows only one thing. And, like the *Golem,* once loosed to pursue that end it cannot be controlled — or at least we seem to have lost the collective will to control it. So we have the paradox of having created an artificial creature with all of the rights of natural persons to formulate and pursue ends that give its life meaning, but without the ability to choose and pursue those ends.

Not so fast, you might say. What about those people you mentioned before who animate the creature — the directors, officers, and stockholders? Surely they are real live people who are capable of selecting goals and making personal, moral, and social commitments just as other natural people can, even as corporate actors.

True. But the limiting condition of the corporation is that while the directors, officers, and employees might well look and sound like the natural people of liberalism's ideal, the reality is otherwise. Instead of animating the corporation, the corporation animates them. It's like the soldiers of Troy who piled into the Trojan horse. Until they climbed aboard, they were soldiers with the responsibilities of soldiers but also free and independent people who could do as they wished, though they might pay a price for disobeying orders. But once inside the horse they collectively took on the horse's form and could go only in the direction the horse was designed to pursue.

The same is true of corporate actors. Outside the boardroom or the office they may be regular people, churchgoing, good parents, members of the country club, and respectable people in their community who balance their various roles and obligations in life against one another in ways they find both fulfilling and consistent with their systems of values. But once they act under color of their offices — once the magic words are placed in their ear, once they climb into the horse — they take on a single function, a single form: to cause the corporation to maximize its profits. They are obligated to do so even if that pursuit leads them to make decisions they wouldn't make in their quotidian lives, or if it means cutting corners on safety, or harming the environment, or laying off old Joe or thousands of old Joes who have been with the company for their entire careers but are simply becoming too expensive to employ when cheaper labor is available in India or Thailand or Mexico. They are no longer people but something else: directors, officers, and employees of a corporation. And as such they forego the capacity of people so prized by liberalism — the capacity for self-determination.

This might not be such a bad thing if we treated the corporation as the artificial legal construct that it is, if we understood it to exist for a narrow purpose and that the consequence of that limitation was that we carefully watched and regulated what corporations did, that we carefully watched and regulated the way their directors, officers, and employees behaved. But we don't. Directors, officers, and employees act in an artificial corporate context which takes away their individual capacities for self-determination all the while permitting them to act on behalf of an entity that retains all of the rights accorded to people who possess that capacity — and which are accorded to them only because they do possess it.

I'll take up this problem of cabined autonomy, of role morality, in more detail later. For the moment, there is another important aspect of the liberal problem that becomes exacerbated in the behavior of the corporation. That is the problem of responsibility or accountability. It is the problem of (dare I say it?) corporate morality.

THE MORALITY OF THE CORPORATE PERSON

We live in an age when people believe morality is a more or less relative thing. Maybe so. But my argument doesn't depend on your accepting any particular moral system or code or any particular form of morality. You may govern your life in accordance with revealed truth as you see it, or natural law, or a simple precept of not treating others as ends, or in pursuit of the good life of contemplation prized by Aristotle. You may believe that morality lies in doing the best you can for yourself and your children and giving something back to the community when you can, by donating your money or volunteering your time. You may think that morality is simply being responsible for your actions, avoiding harm to others when you can and compensating them for their pain when you cannot. You may think that morality is simply doing whatever produces the greatest good for the greatest number. You may, like certain contemporary thinkers, believe that morality is nothing more than maximizing your wealth.

You may believe any of these things. But chances are pretty good that you have some form of moral compass. You have some belief or system of beliefs that directs you in your daily life and in your contacts with others. Despite the sometimes contorted arguments of theorists, you have some limits to what you will do in pursuit of your self-interest. You have some sense that sometimes, at least, the ends do not justify the means, and that sometimes, at least, the ends themselves are not worth pursuing. That is all I need to make my point. For the corporation is different. The corporation has one end, and that is to maximize its stock price. And the directors and officers that animate it do so with that end in mind.

Again you might object. There are people, you say, for whom making as much money as they can is the pursuit of the good. Perhaps we disagree with them. But one of the hallmarks of liberal society is that each person is free to choose her own ends. So what right have we to judge? Again, I agree. But the difference between the corporation and a natural person is that when a natural person makes a decision and acts on it, she is conscious of actually making that decision, of choosing between alternative ends, and of being conscious both of that choice and her own responsibility for making that choice. And if the choice turns out to have bad consequences for herself or others, our natural person knows that she is accountable for those consequences, either because of legal sanctions or of social sanctions or even the sanctions of conscience. Few of us always behave in ways that we or others consider admirable. But when we fail we have souls to damn and bodies to kick. We have the capacity and usually the desire to repent for, and sometimes rectify, our mistakes.

Corporations have no such mechanism. Quite the opposite. As I have pointed out, the corporation knows one thing and that is profit maximization, regardless of the fact that it requires human beings to help it pursue that goal. The result is that corporations are able to act without morality or accountability for they are formed for a single purpose. As we will see in the next chapter, the device of limited liability compounds this by encouraging the corporation to externalize many of the costs of profit maximization upon people who have no power to protect themselves.

Add to this the rights of natural persons in liberal society, the same rights that corporations have been granted. What you get is a nonperson with all of the freedom of persons, an uncontrollable *Golem* that can never be called back, a machine that runs of its own logic, a logic not that of natural people. What you get is the modern corporation.

Now add back in the modern American obsession with liberty, the modern perversion of liberalism as the pursuit of self-interest. It is bad enough to encourage irresponsible behavior in real human beings — thinking, feeling people who have to interact with others and see the impacts of their actions on others, people who know they will be held responsible for those actions — people who will rarely act only selfishly because they still feel their common humanity, even if they've tried to suppress it in pursuit of their gain. Think about how much more severe are the consequences of setting a corporation, which has none of those qualities, freely into the world with a single given mission. And then think about a corporation which is structurally and legally organized in such a way that it responds with extraordinary sensitivity to every possible pressure to conform to that mission. It's a scary thought. The result is a corporation that has not only the right and the power but also the *incentive* to push the costs of its stock price maximization onto other people.

So there you have it. A society predisposed to excessive individualism, but one in which people at least retain their personal moral frameworks, models its corporations in its image without recognizing that the resulting structure lacks their moral framework. Indeed, it replaces that moral structure with constraints that encourage corporations and corporate actors to behave immorally. What you see is what you get.

In a recent, very bad movie, *The Deep Blue Sea*, scientists enhanced the brains of sharks in order to use their biological material in the treatment of human disease. The sharks became far smarter, far more skilled, far more capable of reason in pursuing the one goal they knew by nature: to kill and eat. As any teenaged boy would have predicted from the first scene, the consequence of this misguided, if well-intentioned, experiment is that the crew of scientists themselves were eaten and the sharks ran amok threatening anyone that might come in their path (and undoubtedly awaiting a sequel). Modern American corporations are those sharks. And they threaten not just American society but world society. In the rest of this book, I will explain why.

THE PERFECT
EXTERNALIZING
MACHINE

I began chapter 1 with some examples of what might generally be considered corporate misbehavior: Coke's disregard of its employees' well-being, Unocal's use of slave labor in Myanmar, GM's exploding Malibu, Marriott's theft of money from preferred stockholders and bondholders, and Allied Signal's tax evasion, all for the purpose of jacking up stock prices. In a general way, we then saw how the kind of thinking that led to the cavalier attitudes of these companies can be found in some basic truths about American culture, and how the corporate context exaggerates its effects. The rest of part 1 will focus on the more specific ways in which the laws governing the American corporation and the social thinking from which they arise can lead us to expect nothing other than corporate irresponsibility. It will explain why managers and workers are trapped behind this very structure — why they are Oz forced to remain forever behind the curtain.

GOOD BUSINESS, GOOD ACTORS;
BAD BUSINESS, BAD ACTORS

Not all corporations are bad. And even the bad ones don't necessarily mean to be bad. The *Financial Times* recently reported a fact that we all intuitively know: good behavior is good business. *Fortune Magazine* noted that most of the one hundred best corporations to work for in America are more profitable than average, and further reported in the summer of 1999 that companies that spend the money to hire, train, and retain minorities outperform the S&P 500. Various studies by organizations like Hamilton, Jo and Statman, Luck and Pilotte, and Covenant Investment Management have supported these findings. These corporations worry about the overall quality of life of their workers, behave as responsible citizens in their communities, produce good, safe products, and, in bad times, try to maintain these values. When Levi Strauss, a privately held company, recently was forced to lay off thousands of workers, it did so in a humane and careful fashion, offering substantial transitional help to its employees and thus preserving enormous goodwill for the future. In my own experience, the law firm for which I worked not only treated me with respect but also was quite helpful and supportive as I made the transition from lawyer to teacher; the result is that I encourage my best students to work there.

These stories show the benefits of good behavior, benefits demonstrated by recent managerial research like *The Loyalty Effect,* by the management consultant Frederick Reicheld. Basing his book on research and years of consulting experience, Reicheld describes how good and loyal treatment results in good and loyal treatment, whether of employees, stockholders, or managers.

Psychological evidence, too, supports the assertion that in corporate environments, as in other types of organizations, people who believe that decision-making processes are fair and that they are trusted accept the outcomes of those decisions more readily and behave in more trustworthy ways than people who don't.[1] The evidence is also clear that trusting people are themselves more likely to be trustworthy than people who are suspicious or less trusting, implying that environments in which trust and respect are fostered are more likely to be healthy and productive than those in which they are not.[2] By contrast, the structure and rules of corporate law (and the major premises of corporate legal thought) are based on the idea that corporate actors are not to be trusted. Such mistrust is evident in the push toward having institutional investors like large pension funds put pressure on corporate managers through increased monitoring, and goes all the way back to traditional methods of shop floor production, parodied in 1936 by Charlie Chaplin in *Modern Times* but based on the serious and widely accepted work of the efficiency expert Frederick Winslow Taylor.

While it is true that corporations are widely thought of as treating their employees better today, there is some evidence that the reality is otherwise. The consultants Patricia McLagan and Christo Nel report in their book *The Age of Participation* that 70 percent of the Fortune 1,000 polled had a worker participation program, but only 13 percent of their employees were involved in it.[3] I will have much more to say about this (as well as about all of the issues raised in the last paragraph) in chapter 9. For now it's simply worth wondering whether this apparently improved treatment is the result of a tight employment market or reflects a truly enlightened managerial style. I certainly hope it's enlightened management, but for reasons I'll discuss I suspect that as long as American corporate law remains in its current posture the reality is different.[4]

Billy Crystal's *Saturday Night Live* character Fernando was fond of saying, "It is better to *look* good than to *feel* good." But Adam Smith and the modern economist Robert Frank disagree. In order to look good, they say, you have to *be* good. Good people attract others. Good people beget loyalty from others. And, if we must be materialistic about it (Frank is), good people collect the rewards. But as Smith and Frank point out, you can't fake it. If you're not good and pretend you are, you might be able to get away with it for a while, but it won't last; people will eventually see through you.

The simple fact is that most corporate managers are good people who very much want to be good. Harris Research polling shows this, as does a recent study by the Malcolm Baldridge Foundation and the empirical work of corporate scholars like Myles Mace and Jay Lorsch. The proliferation of voluntary corporate codes of conduct like the Sullivan Principles, the MacBride Principles, the CERES Principles, and the Caux Principles are further evidence of business leaders' desire to look good. And to look good, they have to be good, especially in an age when we are sensitive to the problem of false consciousness, of being manipulated by the appearance of others acting for our benefit. So why is it that so many of our corporations behave so badly so much of the time?

The simple answer is that managers are trapped — or at the very least, that it is easier for them to feel trapped and succumb to it than to gnaw their legs off to get themselves free.[a] The trap is largely created by the financial and legal structures of the corporation, which themselves are grounded in the legal and social ethic described in chapter 1. The American corporation is structured to maximize its short-term stock price and to avoid long-term accountability, much as American legal and social thought encourage the irresponsibility of citizens. As the French executive and writer Michel Albert describes it, American companies, in contrast to European corporations, are "mere cash flow machines," obsessed with short-term profit.[5] American corporate law and practice give the short-term competitive edge to those who directly seek to maximize stockholder profit, regardless of the consequences. From Coke to Unocal to General Motors, from Union Carbide's Bhopal disaster to the Exxon Valdez oil spill that almost destroyed the magnificent and pristine Prince William Sound, from Bristol-Myers's Dalkon shield to Johns Manville's asbestos and Nike's treatment of its overseas workers, corporations more often than not use their special structure and privileges to increase profits by placing their costs of doing business on those who are vulnerable to corporate power. And they do so proudly, in the name of maximizing stockholder profit, the sacred watchword of modern American business faith.

Good behavior *is* good business, but the rewards of good behavior lie largely in the long run. And who knows quite how long that is? In the short run (from which we have more confidence we will profit), bad or at least indifferent may be better. The structure of American corporate law encourages most managers to focus on the short term.[6] There are a number of reasons for this, a few of which I will discuss here and the others in later chapters in which they become more relevant. Let's begin with a feature that sets the

[a]To be fair, corporate managers have readily succumbed to the trap. Average executive income has risen dramatically to about 475 times that of the average worker. It is terribly difficult to determine anything causally about this, but it does seem that the increasing ethic of stock price maximization has unleashed the worst tendencies in our executives.

trap by building an attitude of irresponsibility directly into the corporate structure: that is, the feature of limited liability.

LIMITED LIABILITY, OR NOT IN
MY CORPORATE BACKYARD

Just as evolution has made the shark a perfect eating machine, the device of limited liability has allowed the corporation to perfect its function, so much so that in one ridiculous bout of hyperbole Nicholas Murray Butler, Columbia University's towering twentieth-century president, described it as a more significant invention than the steam engine. The function perfected by limited liability is that of permitting corporations to externalize the costs of stock price maximization, that is, to push those costs onto others. The corporation is the perfect externalizing machine.

Defining limited liability is simple. It means that no matter how much environmental damage a corporation causes, no matter how much debt it defaults on, no matter how many Malibus explode or tires burst or workers and consumers die of asbestosis, no matter how many people it puts out of work without their pension benefits or other protections; in short, no matter how much pain it causes, the corporation is responsible for paying damages (if at all) only in the amount of assets it has. When Johns Manville faced legal claims from people harmed by asbestos far greater than the assets it had, it declared bankruptcy. It couldn't pay all of the claims, and it didn't have to. Bankruptcy law is beyond the scope of this book, but basically it provides the added advantage of giving the corporation an escape hatch, leaving the creditors to fight it out. You can't go after the stockholders for any more than they've invested. You can't go after the managers or employees except in limited and largely irrelevant cases. No matter what kinds of harms the corporation causes, and no matter what kinds of judgments a court may levy against it, it must pay only what it has.

Limited liability in American corporate life shouldn't come as a big surprise. In one sense, it is the realization of personal autonomy in the corporation, an important way of individuating the corporation and making it more like a person. In fact it may flow, at least in part, as a consequence of our thinking of the corporation as a person.[7] For while you can think of flesh and blood people as having unlimited liability — that is, they are legally responsible to others for all the harms they cause up to the full amount of their personal wealth (as well as their individual consciences) — in a real sense their liability is much like that of the corporation. You can't get what someone doesn't have, no matter what they've done to you, which is one major reason we have insurance requirements for activities like driving cars.

By itself limited liability doesn't appear terribly troubling. If the corporation is indeed a person, albeit, as I shall keep repeating, an artificial one, why should it be liable for more than it has any more than any other individual? If you can't get blood from a stone (or from a judgment-proof person), why should you be able to go after the stockholders of corporations that have become judgment proof? To do so is to ignore the corporation's legal personhood, to ignore its individual integrity as a person.

The answer lies, as the answer consistently lies, in the important divergences between a real-life person and an artificial person. And while those differences may themselves be enough to justify disparate treatment, the justification becomes all the more powerful when you add to the mix the highly limited moral universe of the corporation: the mandate to maximize stock price.[b]

The combination of limited liability and the ethic of stock price maximization is the ultimate realization of individual autonomy as understood in some prominent academic circles.[8] That is, it is the ultimate realization of the perversion of liberal autonomy that sees that ideal as satisfied by the pursuit of self-interest. But it is a realization that is deeply immoral for the same reasons that the theory of radical autonomy I earlier described is immoral for individual human beings: it permits the corporation to behave as if other people didn't matter.

But there is a difference between real people and corporations. At least when we're dealing with individuals, even if they act in the pursuit of self-interest, they are sufficiently complex as to have

[b]I'll explore this moral universe in detail over the next several chapters.

other attachments and concerns that put limits on what most of them do. Even in the crude and dehumanizing economic terms in which this idea is sometimes described, you take other people into account — that is, you act as if you care — only as something which serves your self-interest. (The theory doesn't actually *require* you to do this — you only have to do it if you want to.) But at least it's there, and most of us would take some advantage of it or life would be awfully lonely.

The situation in the corporation is different. One important difference is natural. Suppose that it is theoretically possible to get more from a natural person than he owns, by making him buy insurance, for example, as we do for specified activities like driving. Life would be complicated if we made people take out insurance for everything they do. Instead, we rely upon their sense of responsibility to others to regulate most of their behavior. Limited liability for a person is natural — when we demand insurance we create a constraint on nature. Limited liability for the corporation is not in the least natural — it is constructed from the beginning. And, unlike a person, a corporation has no sense of responsibility on which we can rely. This combination makes the corporation potentially very dangerous.

SPARE THE ROD AND SPOIL THE CHILD

Assume you have a child whom you have raised to believe that she can behave however she likes; she doesn't have to clean up after herself, she doesn't have to do her homework; she can stay up as late as she likes; and whatever the consequences of her behavior might be, you will not punish her or hold her accountable. If she leaves a mess, you or someone else will clean it up; if she damages someone's property, you will pay for it, and if she damages her own property, you'll replace it; if she fails to do her homework, you will pressure her teachers to excuse her and to grade her as you demand; if she stays up too late, you will let her sleep as late as she likes, and if she suffers at school or in her activities you will somehow make it right for her. If in the long run she doesn't succeed as she might, you will continue to support her. You don't need to be a behavioral expert or child psychologist to realize that you are likely to have raised an extraordinarily irresponsible child. Nor do you need to be especially perceptive to see that your child will probably never feel accountable for her actions. You have, in a very real way, limited her responsibility and accountability by limiting her liability. The child can act however she likes and never have to pay the price. An economist would say that she never has to internalize the costs she imposes on others or, conversely, that she has externalized the costs of her behavior onto others.

Imagine now that you behave like that child. You drive recklessly, are abusive toward others, refuse to help your coworkers, push your way ahead in line at the store, take advantage of others' generosity, ignore your friends when they need your help. You do all of this, you say, not because you are a bad person, but because consideration for others takes time, it gets in your way, and you are simply trying to maximize your self-interest.

Assume that most other people don't act the way you do (all you need to do is spend a day watching people around your town to confirm the validity of this assumption). People aren't going to like you. In fact, chances are you'll be shunned and treated as a social pariah. The reason of course is that normal people, that is, people who are normally socialized, don't act this way. They don't impose the consequences of pursuing their self-interest on everyone else. They drive according to the traffic rules, repay others' generosity, wait their turn in line at the store, and treat their friends the way their friends treat them. When you behave the way I described above, you, like your spoiled child, are externalizing costs. You are imposing the consequences of pursuing your self-interest onto others.

Generally we consider externalization to be a bad thing; as a social matter, we expect you to bear your own costs, at least unless you make other arrangements with those with whom you deal. If you fulfill these expectations, you are internalizing costs, which is the desirable economic result. Economists from Arthur Pigou in the early twentieth century, who advocated taxation as a means of forcing corporations to internalize their costs, to Ronald Coase later in the twentieth century, who argued that bargaining, under certain conditions, would lead to the most economically efficient result believe that your costs should be internalized, that you should bear them yourself.

The doctrine of limited liability reduces the likelihood that the corporation will internalize its costs. For the consequence of limited liability is to permit, if not encourage, the corporation to externalize the costs of its profit making upon others. Take the following classic example drawn from Coase's famous work.[9]

A railroad runs through cornfields. Because of the friction created by steel wheels on steel rails, the trains produce sparks when they run. Periodically, the sparks ignite the fields and burn the farmers' crops. The crop burning is an externality created by the railroad; in the absence of a legal device or other incentive to make the railroad accountable to the farmers the railroad will have no incentive to prevent the burning. It will have no incentive to encourage it to develop ways to prevent the problem. It could, for example, buy up rights-of-way from the farmers for a sufficient distance from the tracks to clear the fields or develop less incendiary technologies like rubber wheels. The externality would exist whether or not the railroad is a limited liability corporation. The fact that it is one simply means that the railroad's financial exposure to the farmers will be limited, that its stockholders will profit from the railroad's ability to evade responsibility or, to put it differently, from the farmers' losses.

Or take a more contemporary example, like the General Motors story I described earlier. In that case, the cost-benefit analysis that resulted in GM's decision not to redesign the car and recall cars already sold was a conscious choice to place the costs of keeping corporate profits and stock prices high onto the drivers of the cars. Certainly as the legal judgment in that case showed (and as tort law in the farmers' case might show), we do have laws that force some internalization of the costs. People harmed can sometimes sue and recover damages. But those laws are insufficient and incomplete. Even in a regime in which the farmers could successfully sue the railroad, they would incur significant costs, including the time value of their lost profit, in recovering their losses. And even though crash victims successfully sued General Motors, no amount of money could compensate them for the physical and emotional harms they suffered. Moreover, there are thousands of other people driving unsafe cars for whom the cost of replacement is prohibitive or who, for one reason or another, simply are unaware of the problem. Either they live with the fear of explosion, which clearly is a cost, or they might actually suffer serious harm one day.[c]

These examples are troubling. And of course there are plenty of others. Just to stay with the same corporation, when GM closed its huge Willow Run plant in 1991, it left the town of Ypsilanti, Michigan, devastated. Ypsilanti had grown to rely upon the factory, so much so that it had negotiated with GM to rebate certain tax burdens in order to keep the plant there in the first place and to provide jobs for its citizens. But GM had a better idea: after sixteen years of accepting generous tax abatements and a variety of other tax advantages, and after thirty-eight years of operating Willow Run, years during which the town grew dependent upon the plant not only for its economic base but for general community support, GM decided it was cheaper to make its cars elsewhere and closed up shop and moved. The economic and social dislocation this caused was enormous, and while the town was victorious in a lawsuit in the trial court, it lost on appeal because the court decided that Ypsilanti's government was unreasonable in relying upon GM's promises to stay; that is, they were unreasonable in trusting GM, even

[c]Of course I am aware of the argument that there is a social benefit in lower-priced cars. But the cost of many safety improvements relative to the cost of the car is fairly minimal. For example, General Motors estimated that relocating the fuel tank to make the 1973 model safer would have cost a mere $8.59 per car, and there was evidence at the trial that General Motors refused to install safety features costing as little as $2.40 per car. Michael M. Weinstein, "Cost of Life Issue in GM Suit Lost on Price of a Part," *(Oklahoma City) Journal Record*, August 13, 1999. A study in 1999 showed that 95 percent of child safety seats in American cars are incorrectly installed, a problem that can be fixed by auto manufacturers for $10 per car by providing a Universal Child Attachment System. Elaine Morgan, "Seat of Knowledge," *Tampa Tribune*, February 13, 1999. And even if a multiplicity of safety devices or a single device increases cost to the point that some consumers might not be able to afford a particular car, this does nothing to diminish the moral priority of human life to profit. I suspect that most people would chose life without a car than death in a car.

when they had given the company substantial financial benefits.[10] So the result was that GM successfully externalized the costs of increasing its stockholders' profit onto the citizens of Ypsilanti.

Limited liability means never having to say you're sorry—or at least feel the pain of sorrow. It means the corporation can, in effect, draw in its wagons and pay attention only to those people to whom corporate law says it's responsible, namely, stockholders. And the responsibility it has to the stockholders is to maximize their stock prices. As long as the corporation, through its directors, officers, and employees, is performing this function, it is doing everything that we expect of it. And because this is the limited responsibility of the corporation, because we can't chase after these people if they hurt us while doing their jobs, they are able to push off the costs of maximizing stock prices on all of the rest of us; that is (in economics talk), they are able to externalize the costs of stock price maximization on the rest of us.

Now this is perfectly consistent with the modern economic views discussed in chapter 1. In fact, many economists would say this sort of behavior is actually economically efficient; and in honest moments most of them would say economic efficiency is a good thing. In a liberal society in which every person, including the corporate person, seeks to improve his own self-interest, we would expect the corporation to maximize stock price this way. This doesn't mean that other people are unprotected; they can, after all, enter into contracts with the corporation in order to share the costs or shift the costs back onto the corporation. And it's even good to have this potential problem regulated by contract because in a liberal society contract is the principal legal means through which people come together to express their preferences and strike economic bargains that maximize their self-interest. Sometimes laws shift costs, too, like the Superfund law, which requires corporations to pay for the cleanup of the messes they've made.

But there's a problem with this way of thinking: in order to strike an efficient bargain, you need to have the bargaining power to do it. In order to pass laws, you need specific problems of sufficient size and effect to force lawmakers to act. Many of those who deal with the corporation, like the town of Ypsilanti and GM's employees, clearly do not have bargaining power equal to that of the corporations on which they rely. Many of the problems corporations cause are local and diffuse and don't lend themselves to legislative solutions. When such conditions prevail, the justification for limited liability fails. People can't bargain as autonomous equals with the corporation. Laws can't control it from the outside because we've already created the corporation with a consciousness that will let it evade laws and legal detection — and allowed it to acquire and use political power to prevent legislation when problems are too obvious to ignore. Limited liability has cast the corporation in the image of the spoiled child.

LIMITED LIABILITY AND THE LIBERAL PERVERSION— LOOKING OUT FOR NUMBER ONE

There's another problem, too. Even if corporate limited liability is, technically speaking, the same as liability for ordinary human persons (you can give up only what you have), does corporate limited liability enable corporations to escape responsibility in a way that is different from flesh and blood people? Does limited liability create what economists call a moral hazard, that is, an increase in the risk of bad behavior because the costs of that behavior are shifted onto someone else? Even to ask the question this way is to presume that the corporation is capable of the kind of moral action that, as we have already seen, law and corporate structure deny it.

The corporate scholar Theresa Gabaldon has framed an interesting way of looking at the issue of limited liability, one which relates directly back to the liberal perversion I described in chapter 1. As she points out, "Limited liability is about imposing risks that someone else must bear. Liability limitations artificially distance individuals from the real life effects of the enterprise in which they invest, thus decreasing their acknowledged personal responsibility."[11] Of course this is the broader point that I am making about corporate law generally, but the focal point of limited liability helps to place it in a concrete context. Moreover, as Gabaldon perceptively observes, limited liability as a legal doctrine can produce a harm beyond that simply caused by corporate law. Because it exists, because it expresses social approval of a certain kind of conduct, it can help to shape social values and realities. The particular harm it creates is passivity and irresponsibility, the sense that you needn't care and won't suffer any of the consequences if you don't. It is not only in line with the selfishness surplus and the suppression of our caring impulse, but helps exaggerate them.

Limited liability is one of the ways we let our corporations evade responsibility for their actions. For present purposes it is enough to note with Gabaldon that limited liability goes a long way toward separating corporate decision making from the effects of those decisions and their consequences to others. Thus it helps to replicate the corporation as an asocial being, with its morality severely constrained by the goal of maximizing its own profitability. Like our amoral actor (or the aforementioned shark), it looks out only for itself and grabs whatever it can get in the process.

Now of course there are arguments in favor of limited liability, and I don't mean to ignore them. One argument says that limited liability makes investments in corporations rational, which in turn makes the economy function by providing capital. It does so by allowing stockholders to engage in the sensible activity of diversifying their stock portfolios and thus reducing the risks of their investments. Why? Because limited liability lets you ignore who the other stockholders are. Since nobody can come after you for corporate debts, it doesn't matter whether you are the richest stockholder — the deepest pocket — or the poorest. So you can invest in a lot of corporations and not pay attention to any of them. The only risk you face is losing the money you invested. And you lessen the risks of that by diversification.

The virtues of diversification as a financial matter hardly need extended discussion in an era in which the stock market is a major topic of social conversation. But the idea is that one reduces the risk of investing by holding a reasonably broad portfolio of securities (hence the rise of mutual funds.) If limited liability didn't exist, people would be afraid to diversify because diversifying your portfolio also means diversifying your attention away from any particular corporation. You'd have to put all your eggs in one basket and, in the words of Mark Twain, "watch that basket" because the risk of personal liability beyond your investment would be too great simply to let it ride. You'd want to watch the managers, to look over their shoulders to be sure they weren't taking too many risks. You'd want to find out who the other stockholders were because if the corporation came tumbling down and the creditors started chasing after you, you'd want to know that they were able to step up to the plate for their share of the liabilities. If limited liability didn't exist, corporate shares wouldn't be so freely tradeable because the risks of investing in any given corporation would depend very much on who else was investing in that corporation. This fact would complicate the information available in the securities markets and make it much more difficult for stock to trade smoothly, thus destroying secondary market liquidity and hampering the market's ability to move capital to its highest-value use. So limited liability serves a purpose.

But not so fast. For the argument I just laid out assumes that diversification is the only rational strategy and that inattention and passivity are legitimate and reasonable consequences for us to bear for the privilege of having efficient markets. Is this assumption necessarily correct? What would the world look like without limited liability?

Well, for one thing, investors would learn a lot more about the companies in whose stock they were investing. They would want carefully to study their financial positions, to be sure, but they also would want to learn a lot more about their management, their behavior, and the risks that they would incur liability beyond the stockholders' investments. Not only that; once you invested in the stock you would carefully watch the way the corporation behaved and might even take the time to return your proxy card or attend the annual meeting to try to influence the corporation's direction. You would demand more information, such as whether your corporation was employing slave labor in Burma or cheating on its taxes or destroying whole communities. You would care about these issues, at least in part because you would be concerned about your own liability. But you would care about them for another reason as well.

THE PERSONAL TOUCH AND THE
EXPERIENCE OF RESPONSIBILITY

The reason you would care is that it is characteristic of us as human beings, as part of our moral and psychological makeup, that we come to identify with those things and persons who are closest to us, with whom we have relationships. The justification I gave for limited liability assumes that you have no relationship at all with the corporation other than to pay your money and watch your portfolio rise or fall. But imagine if you were investing not in Microsoft but in a small software store that you incorporated and of which you were the sole stockholder.

You probably don't want to do all of the work yourself, so let's say you hire two people, Jeff and Sarah, to work for you. Jeff is right out of college and doesn't quite know what he wants to do with the rest of his life, but you've explained to him that you might want to grow the business into several stores and that he has a future as a manager and maybe even as a partner. Sarah is the divorced mother of two small children who needs to take on extra work to supplement her child support payments and the income from her first job; she is attracted by the regular hours and reasonably stressless nature of the work. Your customers come from all walks of life, but you have a sizable component of adolescent boys who regularly buy computer and video games with hard-earned paper route money or allowances.

Let's say business is good for the first several years. Although you often leave Jeff or Sarah in charge of the store, you spend quite a bit of time there yourself, and you become friends with both of them. You have lunch with them and sometimes invite them to your home for dinner. You get to know Sarah's kids, both of whom are into video games, and you spend a lot of time talking with Jeff about his future in business and your plans for expansion. You start a modest pension plan and make contributions for your employees. They come to rely on you as a source of advice as well as a source of income and future financial security. You also get to know your young customers pretty well, since most of them come by regularly to see what's new in stock and to window-shop, as well as to play the sample games you set out and to buy new games.

But after a while business goes bad. A recession occurs, coupled with a new interest in old-fashioned board games. You're having a little trouble meeting your expenses, and your profits decline by 10 percent. You know you could easily recoup the profits by firing either Jeff or Sarah and working more at the store yourself. You also know that you could start cutting back on inventory and stop supplying your sample play stations with new games, and that would save you money too. You figure you can ride out the recession by cutting costs and believe that board games are a fad and that video games will soon be back. But you need to watch your costs. Do you do any or all of these things? in what order do you do them? Or do you simply swallow the decrease in profit and keep your (temporarily) less-profitable business running? If you do make adjustments, do you consult with Jeff and Sarah to seek their advice and cooperation? or do you simply decide to keep your own profits up?

Well, chances are you at least consider working with your staff to ride out the problem. The reason is that you know them as people, you have relationships with them, and you see them as more than simply a business expense. As a result, you are unlikely simply to fire Sarah, who has come to depend on the income, or to disappoint your customers, whom you've come to know and like (in addition to having created good will with them that you don't want to destroy). You've come to appreciate the human element in your business.

Stockholders in public corporations don't feel the same way. At least not all of them do — some do, as evidenced by the rise in so-called social responsibility mutual funds, which captured approximately 2 to 3 percent of the dollar value of the mutual fund market in 1999 (I'll discuss the limitations of these funds in chapter 7).[12] Public corporation stockholders don't feel the same way because the disassociation from the corporation which limited liability makes possible allows them to distance themselves from the human effect of the corporation's behavior to the point of having to pay no attention to it at all, a subject I'll take up in more depth in the next chapter. In short, limited liability breeds irresponsibility. And the detachment from the consequences of corporate behavior is equally true, although for different reasons, of corporate boards of directors, a subject to which I'll now turn.[d]

[d]There is also a legitimate question of the practical consequence of eliminating limited liability, at least for large corporations. (We might want to keep it at the formative stages of business to protect risk-taking entrepreneurs, although there are good arguments against this as well.) An example will illustrate my point. As I write this, Microsoft has 5,355,377,000 outstanding shares. Now let's assume that Microsoft goes bankrupt and not only loses all of its current value but is left with debts and liabilities of $5 billion — a fairly substantial amount, I'm sure you'll agree. If we had no limited liability, and each shareholder were liable only for their pro-rata share, then each shareholder would owe only one dollar a share to Microsoft's creditors. Double the amount to an astounding $10 billion deficit and each would owe two dollars a share. It's at least worth asking whether this is too high a price to pay for the elimination of limited liabilty if in fact the result would be more responsible, long-term corporate behavior.

**CORPORATE PSYCHOLOGY 101,
OR ALL THE CORPORATE WORLD'S
A STAGE: THE CONSTRAINTS OF
ROLE INTEGRITY**

Limited liability forms the background structure of the problem. But the issue is not just limited liability. There are other ways in which we have built the corporation to be irresponsible. The legal constraints we've constructed around modern American corporations are completely inconsistent with prevailing psychological understandings of free moral development, whether as described in the work of Jean Piaget and Lawrence Kohlberg or in the feminist revision of those theories made so influential by Carol Gilligan.[1] These constraints take two related forms: one is the combination of law and structure that narrowly constrains the corporation in the ends it is permitted to pursue, which I've earlier described as the mandate to maximize stockholder profit. The other is the limited and morally stunted role that corporate actors (directors, officers, and stockholders) are required to play in directing the corporation to achieve this goal. More directly, the structure and laws of the modern American corporation impel (if they don't absolutely require) corporate actors to make these goals their own. In so doing, they have helped to exaggerate the liberal perversion in the corporate context.

Let me give an example and then explain the effects of these constraints in turn. The Car Corporation of America (CCA) manufactures and sells automobiles. As part of its ongoing study of automotive safety, the National Highway Traffic Safety Administra-

66

tion (NHTSA) begins to hold hearings on the advisability of requiring all car manufacturers to install airbags in their cars within five
years at the latest. CCA asks its engineering and sales departments
to study the issue, and they report that adding airbags would increase the sales price of cars by 8 percent. Although the regulation
would apply to all car manufacturers and the price increases would
thus occur across the board, CCA's sales experts conclude that the
consequence of increasing prices, even for a safety feature, would
lead people to keep their cars for two years longer before trading
them in. As a result, sales would decrease by more than the increase
in revenues. Car companies, including CCA, will lose money as a
result.

At the same time, the NHTSA staff has determined that mandatory airbags would dramatically decrease traffic deaths. CCA has
two alternatives. If it is constrained by the current legal precept that
the purpose of the corporation is to maximize stockholder profit,
its board of directors could legitimately fight the regulation. If, on
the other hand, the directors are free to act as moral human beings,
balancing the need for corporate profit against the increase in
safety that airbags would provide, the board might decide to accept
the regulation or perhaps to work with the NHTSA in achieving
some kind of compromise. Certainly each director would be required to consult his or her conscience in deciding how to vote, and
because of the moral freedom enjoyed by the board they would be
accountable for whatever decision they make.[a]

The example illustrates both kinds of constraints, which although related in that they produce the same effect are nonetheless
different in operation. The first is the legal constraint imposed
upon the corporation itself, the narrow moral universe that mandates that the corporation maximize its profit.[b] The second is the

[a]In fact the American auto industry fought airbag regulations for sixteen
years.

[b]Note that I say "maximize corporate profit." The law has never demanded, except in one rare circumstance, that the corporation maximize *stock
price*. (In fact it is questionable whether the law has actually ever demanded
that the corporation *maximize* profit.) That, however, is the way we've come to

constraint under which corporate directors and officers operate, limiting if not obviating their broader moral selves in order to function within the roles that the ethic of stock price maximization creates for them.

Now constraint in both cases is a problem: it inhibits the freedom of the corporation and its directors to act in the manner they think most consistent with the behavior of a full moral person by erecting walls around the scope of their considerations. By itself, this constraint wouldn't necessarily prevent the corporation and its directors from acting morally, even within limits. The reason is the legal scope of directorial action, which is governed by a legal doctrine known as the business judgment rule (BJR). The BJR, in its classic formulation, is a legal presumption that in making corporate decisions the directors have acted with due care, in good faith, and in the best interests of the corporation. Because it is a presumption that is difficult to rebut, it gives the board a great deal of latitude in deciding how to pursue the goal of profit maximization. Thus one could argue that directors need not leave their moral compasses behind, they need not guide the corporation to behave irresponsibly, because the BJR permits them to bring issues of morality and responsibility into their decision-making process. In other words, one could argue, the ends are given but the means are not. Looked at this way, it's not terribly different from the natural law of St. Thomas Aquinas, which sees the end (of return to God) as a given, with the means to be determined by human reason in accordance with that end; or Aristotle's conception of the end as being the good life, with the means to achieving it also to be determined by reason.

But the answer is not that simple. In the first place, even if we take the position that the ends are given but the means are not (and thus that the means can be morally determined), the given end is not the elevated one of a return to God or the contemplative life but rather the less lofty one of stock price maximization. That is to say, even if the means are undetermined, we must still defend the end itself. Now one could argue, I suppose, that stock price maximi-

---

see it, and, as I will discuss in part 2, it is a logical result of our corporate legal structure.

zation is as morally justifiable as redemption. But I don't think it's obvious on its face — it needs a defense.

Second, the moral judgment of directors acting under the constraint of stock price maximization (or corporate profit maximization), even with the latitude provided by the BJR, is a contingent morality. That is, even if we assume that the BJR gives the board the freedom to make morally defensible decisions, the moral freedom of the board extends only so far as it is consistent with the end goal of the corporation, the end of maximizing stockholder profit. When moral, or, if you prefer, responsible, behavior conflicts with this end, responsibility must take a back seat to profitability.

A brief example will show what I mean. Presumably GM, in designing the Malibu, built what its engineers considered to be a reasonably safe car. We would expect them to do this if for no other reason than that they wouldn't be able to sell cars that were known to be dangerous. But we might also expect them to feel some moral responsibility to their customers to build safe cars, even if this meant a slight reduction in profits, which it may or may not have caused. The company's decisions not to install an inexpensive safety device that would have prevented the Andersons' harms and not to recall the cars illustrate how corporate morality is a marginal morality. For the company decided that the cost of doing either of these things far exceeded the financial benefit, measured in terms of likely damages awards in litigation. On the margin, profit maximization trumped morality. This is what I mean by contingent morality: moral behavior is contingent upon its financial rationality.

The prestigious American Law Institute grappled with the issue of corporate morality some years ago in attempting to codify and, to some extent, expand the ability of directors to act responsibly. But it fell woefully short. Section 2.01 of its Principles of Corporate Governance, which sets out the rules of proper corporate conduct, only went so far as to suggest that the corporation, even if corporate profit and shareholder gain are not enhanced as a result, (i) must act in accordance with law like a natural person; (ii) may devote "a reasonable amount of resources" to charity; and (iii) "may take into account ethical considerations that are reasonably regarded as appropriate to the responsible conduct of business."

Now if there's going to be room for real moral action, it's going to be in this last consideration. But note the limitations: while the institute's principle requires that corporations comply with law (the minimum obligation of any citizen), charitable giving and ethical behavior are not required but only permitted. And ethical behavior is permitted only within the bounds that such conduct be "appropriate to the responsible conduct of business," whatever that means.

As far as the permissive rather than mandatory nature of this flexibility goes, one first has to consider the likely behavior of a corporation and its directors in an environment in which profit maximization is the norm. In this environment, in which corporations are competing with one another to survive, the corporation that can best maximize profits will be the most likely survivor. The market will vote the others "off the island."

How does the corporation maximize profits? Of course it could make a better mousetrap. But another way is to reduce expenses. Ethical behavior, responsible behavior, is costly. In fact, ethical and responsible behavior is ethical and responsible precisely because it is behavior that we would not ordinarily undertake if our own purpose were to serve ourselves; it is behavior that we would prefer not to undertake. We would prefer not to do so because it is in some way costly to us. Otherwise it wouldn't be ethical at all, but rather merely a means of satisfying our own desires; we would do it simply because it served our interests.

The corporation that behaves ethically and responsibly is a corporation that incurs greater costs than corporations that choose to comply only with the minimal requirements of law. It is possible that our ethical corporation will generate greater revenues because its ethical reputation may garner more good will for it and thus a larger, more loyal customer base. But this last result is hardly obvious on its face, and in any event that corporation's costs would be higher and would offset at least some of the greater revenues.[c]

[c]It is no accident that one of the most ethically admired corporations, Levi Strauss, is a privately held company, or that the publicly held Ben & Jerry's, with its famous commitments to small local suppliers and charities, felt the need to sell out to a large public conglomerate.

Thus the American Law Institute's granting permission (which doesn't go beyond the BJR) to corporations to behave ethically is no change in current law. It is unlikely to result in an outpouring of responsible corporate behavior. The competitive environment in which corporations can irresponsibly externalize their costs (and thus gain an advantage) without being held accountable discourages good behavior. In order to see this, you don't need to go further than the stories with which I began.

Constraint is harmful in a broader sense as well. Developmental psychology has something to tell us here. The theories I will be relying on, principally those of Jean Piaget and Lawrence Kohlberg,[d] were developed by studying and theorizing about individual human beings, and so they do not offer a perfect parallel with corporate constraints. Thus I am mainly using the structure of their argument more than its specific content to evaluate the morality of the corporation. Yet they are relevant not only by structure and analogy but for two other reasons: both Piaget and Kohlberg saw implications for social organization in their work, and corporate directors and managers are individual human beings to whom these theories can directly apply. In any event, the claim I want to make is not overly strong: it is simply that in an atmosphere of legal and practical constraint such as I just described, neither the corporation nor its directors and managers can be expected to behave responsibly and accountably. They don't have the freedom to do so, and we don't hold them accountable for failing to do so.

THE MORAL JUDGMENT OF THE CORPORATION

The argument of developmental psychology is an argument about the development of moral autonomy, that is to say, moral

[d] I realize that Piaget and Kohlberg have been accused of gender bias in their studies, see Carol Gilligan, *In a Different Voice* (Cambridge: Harvard University Press, 1982). My critique is entirely consonant with certain approaches to cultural feminism, so I am perfectly comfortable relying on their studies because my argument will begin with them (as does Gilligan) and then take them beyond their limitations in attempting to understand their relevance to the problem of corporate responsibility.

freedom. At this point, you might fairly ask why I am talking about moral autonomy when I began this book with a critique of liberal autonomy and grounded the problem of corporate responsibility in that very critique. The answer is not difficult. It is that the problem of autonomy with which I began is one of a radical perversion of the Enlightenment concept of autonomy, which has produced a social understanding of autonomy that holds that each individual ought to serve only themselves. One of the two major observations of the critique I have developed here and elsewhere is that this perversion of autonomy denies caring and community. It is similar to, if broader than, the critique that Robert Kuttner in his book *Everything for Sale* has leveled at modern American society, namely, that this perversion turns everything we value into a market commodity.[2] It is not an argument that autonomy in the original Enlightenment sense is intrinsically bad, only that we have made a fetish of individualism to the point where it has suppressed the intuitions that lead us to care about one another and our larger communities.[3] That caring itself is the result of a healthy moral development, and indeed that moral development is the development of our maturation in a caring manner. Thus the argument I am making here is that corporate moral development, which means the free moral development of corporate actors as corporate actors, is a precondition to responsible, accountable corporate behavior.

I recognize that in making this claim I am putting a particular spin on moral development. One could, for example, argue that moral development means deontological moral development, which is the morality of intentions regardless of the consequences. In this way of thinking, outcomes don't matter; what matters is that you mean to do the right thing. If I mean to help an elderly lady across the street but a bus blocks my way and she crosses before I can get around it, I have behaved morally even though I did not achieve the result I intended.

This deontological, or nonconsequentialist, morality is the morality of Immanuel Kant. It lies in the duty of each individual to act as his own moral rule giver. It is the duty of every person to act in accordance with abstract moral principles that require you to universalize your decisions for the purpose of making your actions internally consistent with a general governing principle, like Kant's categorical imperative. Consequences don't matter; you don't have to achieve what you intend, as long as your intentions are good and are based on a principle that everyone could follow. One of the most important principles Kant identifies is that of treating each person not as a means to the fulfillment of one's own goals, but as an end in herself.

To think in this way is to strip moral action of context and consequence and to make it a matter of pure intention. While I, along with many others, reject the idea that consequences don't matter, my argument is not really inconsistent with a broader understanding even of Kantian morality because it, like Kant's own theories, winds up requiring that corporations and corporate actors treat others as ends and not as means; that is, it ends up arguing that corporations and corporate actors are not allowed to use others for their own gain. This is somewhat the same argument I made earlier in the context of limited liability, that corporations not be allowed to externalize the costs of stockholder profit maximization onto others. And so I return to the point I made in chapter 1, that the specific moral theory one adheres to is not especially important as long as you understand that *no* moral development can take place within the constraints imposed upon the corporation.[e] It is that structural point, and not the particular content of morality, I want to emphasize. The opportunity to freely make moral decisions is

[e]It may be that my argument is inconsistent with a broad social morality based in utilitarianism. I have elsewhere argued against utilitarianism as an acceptable moral alternative and will not rehash those arguments here. I simply observe that for utilitarianism to be a workable moral framework it has to be widespread within the society itself — it only really works on an individual level in the perverse form articulated by the neoclassical economists as the individual pursuit of wealth maximization (although even that perversion is developed on a social scale). It may be that individual directors, corporations, or boards act to maximize their utility; but in a regime in which corporate moral judgments are made the responsibility of the particular corporation and its board in contrast to the current American system, which provides the profit-maximization defense, corporate decisions made to maximize corporate profit or utility need to be accounted for by the board that makes them.

what is required; the actual moral framework for making those decisions is, for the moment at least, unimportant. As I have noted elsewhere, "Constraint is the enemy of moral development."

I won't belabor the argument (and so I take the risk of over-simplifying it, but I think the major outlines are clear enough). Psychologists believe that for a child to develop as a free moral actor, he needs to be able to see himself as part of the process of rule making. Such understanding develops over time, with children beginning their moral development under the severe constraints of parental rules and the rules of games. Children take the rules as given and behave accordingly, first imitating the rules alone in a form of codified behavior, then cooperating with others in games, complying with the rules in order to win, and finally participating in the process of rule making. In fact Piaget observed boys in this latter stage as arguing about the rules and learning to reach agreement. He concluded that this process is a central aspect of moral development. It is through this process that the child comes to see himself as having a role in the creation and development of rules and acquires a sense of his moral autonomy.[f]

Note that this is an argument that a given process will produce a desirable outcome. In order for moral development to occur, children must be free to cooperate with one another in the development and modification of rules and the resolution of disputes over the rules. By the way, the freedom to cooperate is at least as important in Gilligan's evaluation of girls' moral development because

[f]Gilligan doesn't take serious issue with this in her attempt to correct for the gender bias of this work. Rather, she sees the "rules" by which girls come to their complete moral development as contextual and relational, more in the nature of broader principles which are adaptable to circumstances and in which relationships take priority over winning. The jurisprudential distinction between rules and principles is an important one and is central to the work of liberal theorists like Ronald Dworkin, who challenge the perceived rigidity of positivism, and John Rawls's articulation of principles of justice against which specific contextual rules are to be measured, as well as legal pragmatists (or realists) like Karl Llewellyn, who saw almost all legal decision making in context.

that very development originates in a cooperative, consultative, and contextualized ideal of morality in contrast to boys' more competitive ultimate ideal (although of course that competition itself requires cooperation).[g]

Process itself can be constrained. In fact some kind of constraint is necessary for process to exist. Think for example of the process of a criminal trial which, while designed on principles of procedural fairness, follows a formal, stylized approach. While the procedures may have developed from a process of moral reasoning about what a fair trial requires, this won't do for moral development itself; that requires an unconstrained ability to experience the freedom that Kant assumed was a precondition of moral behavior and that developmental psychologists see as essential to moral maturity.[h] So while one might argue that the corporation has some process opportunities — to participate in the passing of corporate legislation, through the requirement of stockholder voting, through the compliance by directors and officers with corporate bylaws — this is really little process indeed (as I will argue in greater detail later) and in no way frees the corporation to determine its ultimate end. And that end of course constrains all corporate actors in their behavior through whatever governance processes are provided for the corporation.

This last observation requires me to repeat one point; there are perfectly respectable moral theories in which ends are taken as given, from Aristotle's ideal of the good life to Aquinas's goal of redemption to the utilitarian notion of the greatest good for the greatest number. In an important sense, though, each of these theo-

---

[g]I want to be clear that I reject the essentialization of gender types that has been drawn from Gilligan's work. Although she contrasts boys and girls as a general matter in her study, it is clear that boys are as capable of "female" moral development as girls are of "male" moral development. I, for example, consider myself to have a moral character far more like that of Gilligan's girls than Piaget's boys, and my scholarly work has reflected this. So has the work of many critical scholars.

[h]In fact, this very criminal process can itself be seen at least in part as the outcome of moral decision making.

ries begins with a principle of morality that justifies the end and works toward that end. And, as I noted earlier, each of these ideals ultimately serves a purpose that goes beyond narrow egoism — it goes beyond mere self-satisfaction. The corporate end of stock price maximization does not do this. It is an ethic of pure self-interest. Moral behavior — whatever your moral theory — is different. It is behavior that by definition takes account of the concerns of others. It's also a precept of every major religion. Corporate constraints retard, if they don't completely block, the development of such attitudes. As an end state of moral development, the current state of affairs simply won't do.

THE PLAY'S THE THING

A second level of constraint related to the first is that imposed on corporate actors when they are acting in the name of and on behalf of the corporation. This brings us to the problem of role morality.

The term "role morality" might not be readily recognized by all readers, but it is a concept familiar to all of us. Role morality simply means the rules of behavior and social expectations we have of people who perform specific functions in the course of performing those functions. One hotly debated role which carries with it a particular kind of morality is that of a lawyer. In the American system of jurisprudence, lawyers are supposed to vigorously defend their clients to the best of their ability and without consulting their own feelings about the client's behavior or purpose.[i] Recent examples of this in the public eye include the O. J. Simpson trial. The question of whether or not Simpson actually murdered his wife, Nicole, and her friend Ron Goldman was not one which his lawyers addressed; their obligation was to attempt to create a reasonable

---

[i]This is an oversimplification. There is an active debate over whether and when a lawyer ought to consult her own feelings about a matter in representing a client, and there are of course rules of ethics that limit how far a lawyer can go in that representation — avoiding fraud, for example. But the statement is generally accepted to be true, and the arguments are on the margins of conduct, not with the central premise.

doubt in the jurors' minds about whether Simpson actually did it and to use the rules of evidence, procedure, and constitutional protection to evade facts tending to show that he did.

I was recently listening to two of Simpson's lawyers, Barry Scheck and Peter Neufeld, talking about the trial with Terry Gross on National Public Radio's *Fresh Air*. Gross asked them directly whether they in fact believed that Simpson had not committed the murders. Scheck responded, with a tone of surprise, that in effect they had never asked Simpson the question; he said he hadn't done it and as his lawyers their job was not to verify his denial but to gain an acquittal.[4] The question of whether Simpson had actually murdered two people wasn't even on the table as far as they were concerned.

This kind of conversation bothers many people. And criminal defense lawyers have ready answers, including the central answer that their job as lawyers is not to sit in judgment of their clients but to convince juries to acquit within the procedural rules of the legal system. After all, a verdict of not guilty doesn't necessarily mean that the defendant didn't do the act with which he was charged; it only means that the prosecutors haven't proved it beyond a reasonable doubt. That is the role our legal and social systems creates for criminal defense lawyers. While we might not want to do their job precisely because we don't like having to be in the position of defending people we suspect might have done bad things, and while the very need for this role might make us uncomfortable, we accept the lawyers' defense of themselves as morally adequate because we have agreed to create the role for a purpose that, all things considered, we believe to be worthwhile.

But it isn't just about lawyers. There are lots of socially constructed roles, each of which has its expected norms of behavior. Because we have agreed to create the roles, the norms of behavior that go with them provide an adequate moral defense for those who are acting within them. So, for example, doctors, clergy, parents, policemen, spouses, and friends all have roles that carry with them rules and expectations. Of course so do mafia bosses, drug kingpins, prostitutes, and terrorists. The difference between the first and second set of roles is that we have collectively decided that the first are socially desirable and need the set of rules that define them in order to fulfill their function, whereas the second are socially undesirable and therefore the rules that define them and constrain them are illegitimate (and generally illegal). This doesn't necessarily mean, as the criminal defense lawyer example makes clear, that each of us as an individual approves of what the role requires — in which case we each have the choice of refusing to take on the role in the first place. Nor does it mean that we don't argue about the limits of what the role requires — clearly we do. But the core of the role and the rules are things that we take as acceptable in order to make our society function in the way we deem best.

So let's look at the role of the corporate director. In the first place, it is important to remember (for reasons that will soon become apparent) that corporate directors act on behalf of an artificial person. Is the role of a person whose sole objective is to maximize stockholder wealth a legitimate role, especially if it means imposing substantial costs on other people and society and getting away with it?

This is a question about which reasonable people might disagree. So first let's contrast it with the criminal defense lawyer's role and several other socially accepted roles as well. Then, in the next chapter, I'll look at the legitimacy of stockholder wealth maximization as a moral construct in itself.

THE NATURE OF THE BEAST—TYPES OF ORGANIZATIONAL MORALITY AND THE CORPORATION

In order to make the appropriate contrasts, let's begin with the point I made just above — that corporate directors and other corporate actors have roles that are organizational, not individual. In order to analyze these organizational roles, in order to see whether they are morally justified, we first need to examine exactly what the nature of the corporate organization is to determine whether we approve of it as a role-creating institution.

There are two basic types of organization. In one the participants have a common goal. A symphony orchestra or string quartet is a good example: each member of the organization does something individually, but their common goal is to play music as beautifully as possible. A team of surgeons and nurses is another: their goal is to make a patient well. The point is that while each of the members of the organization has a given role, that role is designed to work in concert with those of the others to achieve a common end.

In the other type of organization, people come together to fulfill their individual goals but need the cooperation of others to do so. A stock brokerage firm is a good example. Each stockbroker wants to make as much money as she can. Each can accomplish this goal alone, buying a seat on the New York Stock Exchange or working over-the-counter, performing her own research, and hiring her own office staff. But there are synergies in stockbrokers working together that benefit all of them in the pursuit of their individual goals. It is far cheaper for the firm to have one member with an exchange seat, a common research department, and a common legal compliance staff and back office. Each broker has her own clients, however, and the work of one broker does not depend in any important way on the work of the other brokers. While they work together, they do not in any meaningful sense work as a team. It is clearly a very distinct kind of organization from an orchestra or surgical team.

The principles that bind these teams are also importantly different. The legal philosopher Lon Fuller described what he called two principles of human association.[5] The first principle is one of shared commitment and binds the members of the organization by their common goal. Organizations of this type can be expected to share a strong sense of community and close relationship, for each of the members needs the others to achieve her goal. Thus religious institutions, universities, even country clubs can exhibit this principle.

In contrast to these are organizations which Fuller describes as bound by the legal principle. These are organizations which are held together by formal rules, rules which set out the rights and duties of the members. These organizations tend to be more formalistic and procedural in operation and, while the members may share the same goals, they are characterized more by the individual claims each has on the other (and on the organization) in the pursuit of those goals than associations based on the principle of shared commitment. So if one stockbroker decides to play golf more frequently than he spends time in the office, the other stockbrokers are unlikely to get too upset, as long as the leisure-loving stockbroker is paid according to his effort. They may sneer at his laziness, or they may be envious of his ability to enjoy life, but they are unlikely to feel betrayed. If, however, the principal bassoonist fails to practice, the entire orchestra will be embarrassed in its performance of the *Rite of Spring* and will justifiably feel she has let them all down.

While not exactly parallel, it should be clear that organizations in which the members share a goal are more likely to be organized along the principle of shared commitment, and organizations in which the goals of the members are more individual are more likely to be organized around the legal principle. The forms of organization and their organizing principles are not pure — most human associations exhibit characteristics of both. Yet as the examples of the orchestra and the brokerage firm I described above exemplify, there are important differences.[j]

Perhaps the most important difference is in the roles of the members. In organizations that are based on common goals, the members are more likely to subordinate their individual interests to the good of the group in achieving their goals. The bassoonist may not feel like practicing — in fact she might feel like playing golf. But with a performance coming up, she feels an obligation to the entire organization that leads her to forego her pleasure for the benefit of the group. In organizations like the brokerage house that are based on individual goals, members are less likely to worry about interfer-

[j]Fuller recognized the reality of American society that the legal principle appears in almost all forms of human organization and bemoaned the fact that once it took hold it had a colonizing tendency, leading to the greater formalization, proceduralization, and legalization even of organizations based on the principle of shared commitment. While I join Fuller in regretting this observation, it is only tangential to the purpose for which I share his argument.

ing with common goals the organization may have to the extent that their own interests are impeded in some way. It's hard to imagine a stockbroker sacrificing some of what she perceives to be her fair share of profits in order to make the other brokers better off. Or to forego playing golf in order to help everyone earn a few cents more in the company profit-sharing plan. The extraordinary mobility of brokers among firms, with brokers regularly leaving their firms for the highest bidder, is evidence of this. (Regrettably the same tendency has become quite pronounced in law firms, in which the sense of common goal seems largely to have been supplanted by that of individual goals. The same tendency is observable even in universities, where star scholars hop from appointment to appointment in search of the best deal.)

Now what kind of organization is the corporation? Clearly modern American public corporations, as legal creatures, are organized along the legal principle. Corporate law goes to great lengths to establish the rights and obligations of the members and to define who is included and who is excluded from whatever community of interests the corporation is. In fact, as I have demonstrated at great length elsewhere, the tendency of corporate law over the past century has been consistently and markedly to replace any sense of common purpose with a very individualized concept of competing legal rights and duties. And this trend has been aided in recent decades by neoclassical economists who have argued that the corporation is really nothing more than a collection of individuals pursuing their self-interest and bound together by a set of loose, contractually based rules — a free market within a shield of limited liability, if you will.

But the corporation also exhibits characteristics of the other type of organization as well. For the modern American corporation has one goal, and it is the goal toward which its members are bound to work; that is the maximization of its stock price. In this respect it is like the orchestra. Unlike the orchestra, however, in which the members presumably also have individual interests which they subordinate to the common good (golf or side gigs in wedding quartets, for example), corporate law presumes that individual interest can, if unrestrained, trump that common interest, and so the legal rules are tightly constructed to attempt to prevent this, to keep the members within their appropriate roles.

THE LEGITIMACY OF THE ORGANIZATIONAL GOAL

With this in mind, let's focus again on the legitimacy of the corporate goal and of the role it creates for corporate actors. The criminal defense lawyer, as we noted, has a narrow goal and a broad goal. The narrow goal is to defend her client to the best of her ability. This narrow goal is individualistic: it is the responsibility of each criminal defense lawyer to each of her clients. But this narrow goal is incomplete without the broad goal. That broad goal is a societal goal and transcends the goal of the individual defense lawyer. In fact it cannot be accomplished without the entire community of criminal defense lawyers and indeed the entire criminal justice system. That goal is to ensure that justice is achieved.

Now you might object that this is also the role of the criminal defense lawyer individually, to achieve justice for her individual client, and there are respectable arguments to support that view. But it is a disputed view, and one that may be at odds with the rules of professional responsibility that the criminal defense lawyer is obligated to follow. If you asked criminal defense lawyers (at least those who stay in business), and especially if you asked their clients what their role is, I suspect the answer would be to gain acquittal for the client within the rules of the system. In any event, this is not a debate I choose to enter, nor is it necessary that I do so, for the contrast is clear enough. Nobody, I think, could legitimately argue that the goal of criminal defense, as an integral part of the criminal justice system, is to obtain acquittal for every defendant — there are, after all, people who ought to spend time in jail. Looked at as a role in an overall social system, it is instead to protect persons accused of crimes from the unjust use of state power, to act as part of a system geared toward doing justice. That is why we have the criminal justice system and the practice of criminal defense as an integral part of that system.

There are other roles in which the individual and societal roles are the same, or at least overlap. The role of parents is to provide for, nurture, and raise their children. The role of teachers is to educate. The role of doctors is to cure their patients. Each of these roles, like that of the criminal defense lawyer, is designed to achieve a goal we decide is valuable. Each of these goals, and therefore each of these roles, seems defensible on its face. The persons who perform these roles do so with an eye to the good to be accomplished.

The single role of the corporation as it is understood in modern America is to make money for the stockholders. Like the role of the criminal defense lawyer, this role really can be played out only as part of a system, in this case as part of the market system which allows the corporation to purchase inputs and produce outputs from suppliers and for customers. The systemically justified goal is to increase overall societal wealth. And as we have structured the corporation, it also, like the criminal defense lawyer, has an individual role, namely, to increase the wealth of its stockholders, without regard to the wealth of others (and protected in this endeavor, as I discussed earlier, by the mantle of limited liability). Is the creation of stockholder wealth a defensible role? In order to evaluate this, we need to know whether the pursuit of wealth itself is a legitimate goal.

IS WEALTH
A VALUE?

If our defense of the role of the corporation and its directors and managers is to rest on our approval of the purpose of that role, we must first determine whether the goal of the corporation is one of which we approve. That goal is stock price maximization. Put more directly, the goal is to create wealth. So the question is whether the pursuit of wealth is a legitimate goal.

At first blush (especially in turn-of-the-century America), the answer appears obviously to be a resounding yes. Wealth is good; more wealth is better. Money makes the world go 'round, and with it we can do great things. Even to ask such a question seems to blaspheme our national faith. And in the context of the corporation it appears almost silly: Why do we have corporations if not to create wealth?

But the answer is not so obvious. In the first place, corporations do important things like produce goods and services we need and create jobs for people, not only to allow them to earn the bread they need to live but to provide some sense of personal fulfillment (although obviously work is not the only way in which people find fulfillment). But there's more: The pursuit of wealth for its own sake, an activity we have directed the corporation to engage in, is an empty mission. More wealth doesn't mean a better society or better lives. In order to give moral meaning to the accumulation of wealth, we need to understand why it is important. Wealth in itself has no value. But it is the value by which the corporation lives.

The philosopher Ronald Dworkin provides an interesting analysis of whether wealth itself is a value.[1] If it is, then the role we have given corporations (and by extension corporate actors) clearly is a defensible one, and our only concern is over the rules that guide them toward this end. If it is not, then the defense of corporate behavior is illegitimate, and the role morality of corporate actors is in fact a form of immorality.

So is wealth a value? Dworkin says no, and I agree. He begins to answer this question by describing a view that characterizes an influential strain of modern economic thinking, that maximizing social wealth is a valuable thing to do. In reaching his conclusion, he goes through a series of arguments by which one could reach the opposite result. One set of arguments treats wealth as an end in itself. Social wealth is part of social value, either because it *is* social value or because it is in itself *part* of social value. A second set of arguments turns on the effect: that wealth is a *tool* of social value, either because it *causes* other kinds of social improvements or because it may be *used to bring about* other improvements. A third kind of argument is that wealth is "a surrogate for social value" because the maximizing of social wealth would produce other things we care about, like overall happiness, more effectively than if we aimed to increase overall happiness directly.

The first set of arguments, that wealth is a component of social value, must rest on the value of wealth itself. This class of argument is different from instrumental arguments—it doesn't claim that wealth will lead to other things; rather it argues only that a society that has more wealth is better than a society that has less wealth simply by virtue of the fact that it *has* more wealth.

Here's an example. Let's say you would like to have my beat-up old Volvo wagon because you think it is a classic. I would sell it to you for five thousand dollars, and you, who really must want it, would pay six thousand. If the government simply took the car from me, thus saving us the costs of bargaining and writing contracts, and gave it to you, that would increase wealth. It would move the car from a lower-valuing user (me) to a higher-valuing user (you). The car is worth six thousand dollars to you and only five thousand to me. Thus overall social wealth would be increased. As a matter of increasing social wealth there would be no point in forcing you to pay me anything because five thousand dollars of the value — the five thousand you would pay me — would simply cancel out, and the remaining one thousand dollars rests with you because you value the car more highly. Society is wealthier by one thousand dollars. Of course I'm out five grand, but my own situation isn't important when we're talking about the wealth of society as a whole.

But is society really made better off because of this increase in overall wealth? Dworkin thinks not, and I agree — for we have to ask what it is about society that is better. We can immediately see that there is something worse about it, and that is the practice of confiscating property from some people and giving it to others. Surely this seems unjust in a society that values private property, at least without more justification. Is that justification provided simply by the increase in societal wealth? Is the society better as a result of this transaction simply because it is wealthier?[a]

Dworkin is careful to clear away the possible answer that the society is better off because overall *utility* is increased; that is, because you would derive greater satisfaction from the Volvo than I do. We've said nothing about who derives more satisfaction from the car, and because we have no way of measuring satisfaction objectively we can't. The question of utility, which utilitarianism defines very broadly as satisfaction, is not the same thing as the question of wealth — that is, money. So we must answer the question of whether the society is better off only on the basis of whether more money in itself makes the society better.

If your answer is yes, then you must explain why. Remember first that we are talking about the wealth of a society, not of its individual

[a]Dworkin persuasively shows how rules that require that you compensate me by assigning one of us the rights to the car are only instrumental to the goal of increasing societal wealth — in other words, the question of whether a society that has more wealth is better than one with less wealth is a philosophical question independent of how one gets there.

citizens. So why does an overall increase in wealth necessarily make the whole society better off? Even if the increase in social wealth means an increase in the wealth of every one of its citizens, does it make the society better off? If so, why? Is it because wealth leads to greater happiness? Not necessarily. Go rent *Citizen Kane* at your local video store and watch it for proof to the contrary. If wealth increases happiness, it is only because of what it can do for you. Everybody knows that a room full of cash doesn't make you happy simply because you possess it.

But what about the second argument in this class: social wealth is only one component of social value? That is, there are many things that make a society better, and more wealth is one of them. This requires us to look at all of the components of social value and ask whether it makes sense to think of trading off certain components of greater value for more wealth. Dworkin uses the example of trading off some measure of justice for an increase in wealth. If we think that taking the Volvo from me and giving it to you is unjust, is it justified by the fact that it increases social wealth?

Before going on with this line of argument, let's look at what it implies. To say that one can trade off one social value like justice or fairness or equality or liberty for another, like wealth, implies that each of these social values is merely a preference, like that of a child in the school cafeteria who trades his Oreos for his friend's potato chips. To accept the idea that social values are nothing more than preferences — like potato chips over Oreos — is to say, in effect, that morality or justice or liberty or whatever is nothing more than mere taste. Indeed, some economists have said exactly this.[2]

But casual reflection, I think, demonstrates the error of this way of thinking. As I've noted, people behave in ways they consider to be moral because they think they should, not because they want to. It is part of the concept of morality itself that when you do something for reasons of morality you do it despite the fact that doing something else would better satisfy your immediate desires. Otherwise, behaving morally would simply be another way of gratifying your urges, and we wouldn't need norms of morality to direct your behavior in circumstances in which you have conflicting selfish interests.

To complete the argument, then, the idea that we can trade other social values for increased wealth makes no sense on an aggregate societal level because no individual would rationally agree to do this (and if no individual would rationally do it, neither would society, which, after all, is composed of individuals). The reason you wouldn't do it is that you wouldn't have any guarantee that an increase in social wealth would increase your wealth — remember, we are talking about increases in social wealth without regard to how that wealth gets distributed. Moreover, you would know that you might well suffer by the loss of whatever it was that we traded to increase others' wealth, just as I suffered from the confiscation of my Volvo to make society richer. If you wouldn't rationally do this, there is little reason to think that we would collectively choose for society to do it. So maximizing social wealth is again off the table as a defensible value.

But then there is the second class of arguments, the instrumental arguments: that by increasing social wealth, for example, by trading off some other component of social value, like justice, for greater wealth, we increase those other components (like justice). In other words, you might think that increasing social wealth might somehow also increase the amount of justice in society. But this argument is intrinsically incoherent. Justice is an end. Wealth, in this instrumental class of argument, is only a means to that end. It seems incoherent to say that you would trade off more ends for greater means. Why would you diminish the ends for more means if it is ends toward which you are aiming?

Dworkin addresses the instrumental arguments — that a society that has more wealth can thereby achieve other goods — head-on. He focuses on what he calls the strong claim, that increasing social wealth will improve other social goals, like achieving justice or ameliorating poverty. But in order to make this argument, we first need to know what our other goals are, what goals it is that increasing wealth will achieve. Simply increasing wealth doesn't answer this question. What does?

One argument is that a society that aims to increase wealth breeds greater respect for individual rights because in order to maximize wealth we need some initial assignment of rights, like the right to my Volvo. We do, after all, have to know what someone owns before we know what someone is willing to pay to keep that property or what someone else is willing to pay to buy it. But a society that specifies rights is not a better society by virtue of that alone. Antebellum American law provided the right of one person to own another. A more efficient assignment of individual rights does not by itself produce a better society without reference to what those rights are.

Those who advocate maximizing social wealth would argue, however, that rights should be assigned in a way that results in maximizing wealth. This, as Dworkin points out, is circular and doesn't answer anything. It only says that you should have the right to my Volvo without giving any reason other than that it maximizes wealth. We need some independent reason to justify the assignment of rights in the first place; maximizing wealth simply won't do unless we can explain why we want more social wealth.

Even when we assume an independent basis for rights — say, the right to self-ownership — the idea of wealth maximization doesn't provide an independent value. For, the argument goes, once rights are in place we ought to arrange society in a way that the subjects of those rights wind up in the hands of their highest-value user. This, as I noted earlier, is measured by the amount someone is willing to pay for those rights — your willingness to pay six thousand dollars for my five-thousand-dollar Volvo. But, as Dworkin rightly points out, your willingness to pay depends on your ability to pay. You might be *willing* to pay six thousand for my Volvo, but you might not have the money. Questions of wealth distribution are logically prior to questions of social value. Thus it is not at all clear that pursuing wealth maximization serves other important social values.

Dworkin also addresses a well-known influential argument in American culture familiar to most of us as trickle-down theory. The theory holds that a society that maximizes wealth will encourage the individual members of that society to maximize their own wealth, which in turn will lead them to produce more for others. They do this by virtue of the mechanisms of market exchange, whereby we assume that people engage in such exchanges only when it increases their wealth. (They may also choose to give wealth to those they care about—although of course they don't have to give any of it away at all.) Thus, wealth maximization produces beneficence, as free exchange in pursuit of your own interest makes everybody better off. Note that if other people benefit from our maximized wealth, it is not at all because we intend for them to; their improvement is a by-product of our own pursuit of wealth. Thus, assuming trickle-down works at all, the type of beneficence such society creates is not a virtue at all but rather a happy accident.

Dworkin also addresses the argument that a society of people who maximize their wealth has the valuable result of achieving a more equitable distribution of wealth. But nothing in the theory assures this. Nothing says that we have to distribute that wealth in anything resembling an equitable way, and recent evidence makes it clear that in these terms modern America is just about the most unequal society in the world.[3] More fundamental is the question of what a just distribution of wealth is. This cannot be answered simply by referring to the value of maximizing wealth, but must instead be independently determined on the basis of our ideas of what constitutes a just distribution of wealth. We can reach this conclusion only by referring back to other values.

I think I've spent enough time on Dworkin's argument, but the answer to the question should be clear enough: Maximizing wealth can be defended as a value only by reference to other values. The argument that wealth maximization is itself a good fails because there is no plausible reason to think that a society that maximizes its wealth is, for *that* reason alone, a better society than one that chooses not to maximize its wealth, any more than an individual would be. And as a non–wealth maximizing law professor who gave up a wealthy life in the trenches for a more modest ivory tower existence, I can assure you he's right! I think I've said enough now to apply the analysis of wealth maximization to the role morality defense of the modern American corporation.

WEALTH AS THE CORPORATE TELOS

If wealth is not a value, then the argument that the sole legitimate goal of the corporation should be to maximize its stockholders' wealth falls. The game is over, and we can continue on and think about how to change things. But in order to reach this conclusion, we must consider a further argument.

You might say that the argument we just examined — even if it is right with respect to individual human beings and even if it is right with respect to an entire society — doesn't work when you apply it to the corporation. The corporation is, after all, only a tool in a broader social system. It doesn't have the moral framework of individual human beings (which of course is part of my point), nor does it represent society as a whole. Instead the individual corporation, looked at individually, is kind of like the criminal defense lawyer whose individual role is to make sure that his client is acquitted. It is not like the societal role of creating an entire system of criminal justice. The appropriate way to think about the corporation, then, is not in this broad societal way, but only as part of a system, namely, the capitalist market system, in which each corporation is just one actor, like the individual criminal defense lawyer is one actor in a more complex system of justice. In the more complex economic system, each corporation maximizes its profits in competition with other corporations and other forms of business enterprise, each of which is seeking to maximize its own wealth. You might argue that competition within the system of free bargaining checks the individual corporation's ability to run roughshod over society, much in the way that the adversary system checks the criminal defense lawyer in his zealous efforts to seek acquittal. You might conclude that, looked at systematically, there is nothing wrong with the corporation's pursuit of maximum stock prices.

Not bad. But not right. Before I answer this argument, let's turn to the systemic level to see if there's a defense of the corporate system there as well. I might respond to your argument by saying that even if the individual corporation serves a legitimate role that is kept in check by the need to compete and cooperate in a variety of markets, the corporate system itself is flawed because, unlike the criminal justice system, the goal of which is justice, the corporate system is designed to maximize stockholder wealth. And wealth is not a value. So its maximization cannot be a legitimate defense.

But again you have an answer. The corporate system, you might respond, itself is only a part of a broader social system. The role the corporation plays in this society may be narrow and not intrinsically valuable but taken together with everything else serves an important function. It's hard to disagree with the idea that a society needs a certain level of wealth to survive. We have chosen the corporate system as the principal way to generate that wealth. There are other systems, other social institutions, that pursue or facilitate our pursuit of values we hold to be truly important. Certainly the criminal justice system pursues such a value; our educational system is designed to aid students in the pursuit of knowledge; our medical system is geared toward ensuring adequate health care; religious systems take care of the spiritual needs of people; our system of taxation is designed not only to supply the funds to protect all these others systems but also to result in a mild degree of income redistribution. So what's wrong with having an institution like the corporation that pursues only one narrow goal? To borrow an idea of the philosopher Michael Walzer, the corporation exists in its own sphere and should be evaluated on its own terms and in terms of the way it fulfills its role in the larger system.

So now I have to answer these very perceptive objections. And the answer might be surprising — at least based on what I have said so far. There is nothing especially wrong with viewing the corporation this way, *as long as it is kept in its own sphere.* Recall that the problem with which we started was the problem of corporate autonomy, of the personification of the corporation and the attribution to it of essentially all of the rights and liberties our constitution guarantees, all of the basic liberties designed to fulfill the goals of Enlightenment humans. And recall that the corporation is an artificial person, constrained in ways that natural persons are not. By treating the corporation as if it were a natural person we allow it to run loose in society without the normal moral restraints individual human beings feel, without the balance of values and ends that human beings choose to pursue. Instead, we have set it after a nonvalue (at least when taken on its own) and given it the power of humans with which to pursue it. We have thus forsaken our power to regulate the corporation, from within as well as without, much in the way that Enlightenment theory leads us to reject the legitimacy of regulating human beings. But corporations are not human beings, and they do not pursue human values.

If we were to exercise our dormant power to regulate the corporation, to use that power to compel it to internalize its externalities, to cause it to behave responsibly and be accountable for its actions, to loosen the constraints of the corporate role and the roles of corporate actors, then the foregoing defense might be enough. Let the corporation maximize stockholder wealth and use other institutions to keep it in check. This might not be practically possible because of the speed and fluidity of business. But surely it is theoretically possible. And that theoretical possibility gives us a defense.

Maybe. But not quite. The reason the defense is incomplete is because it ignores a simple fact about the corporation that my reification of that institution in the preceding discussion ignored: it is fundamentally a human institution. That point is obvious. But it's more than the fact that the corporation is a human institution that destroys this argument. It is the fact that it is within the framework of that institution that a vast proportion of our population spends a vast amount of their lives, and it is within the framework of that institution that norms are formed and shaped, values are developed, and individual and collective goals are chosen and pursued.[b] And that makes all the difference.

The argument is somewhat similar to Robert Dahl's observations in his important *Preface to Economic Democracy*.[4] There Dahl argued that the modern American business corporation was highly socialistic, a hierarchical institution that internally replicated a command and control economy and in which the opportunity to develop civic virtue was constrained to the detriment of our larger democracy and its values and processes. Now I know that some readers immediately will note that corporate management structure has changed in recent years, that team production and total quality management and outsourcing and corporate networks and workers' councils and the like have flattened the hierarchy and ameliorated the problems Dahl observed. I will explain why this response is inadequate in chapter 9, even to answer Dahl's argument. For now, I want

[b]I'll explore this point in more detail in chapter 9.

to make a somewhat different argument that starts from the same concern.

Even if corporate management structures have changed sufficiently to address Dahl's concerns about democracy and civic virtue, the simple fact remains that the corporation is designed solely for the maximization of stockholder profit. That is its telos, its end, the goal toward which it drives. Even if corporate employees and managers have greater participation in corporate governance than they did when Dahl wrote in 1985, the participation they have is to make the corporation better at maximizing stock price, and they do so shielded by the doctrine of limited liability. We thus have created a corporate society in which most people spend most of the time engaged in the maximization of wealth. From the perspective of our earlier discussion, it doesn't matter that they may have a greater say in how the corporation maximizes wealth. The relevant point is that we have created a society in which most people spend most of their time in pursuit of something which in itself is not a value.

This is the role of the corporation; this is the role of corporate actors. The structure and laws governing the corporation create a situation in which the American citizenry learns to maximize profit, to make its decisions in reference to the maximization of profit, and to hone its skills primarily in the pursuit of maximizing profit. How can we reasonably expect responsible, accountable, and moral behavior from the enterprise in which this takes place? We have already structured and constrained its morality.

There is a broader point here as well. Even if we were willing to accept the narrow goal of wealth maximization for the corporation, the fact that it has become the breeding ground for so much of our social outlook can't help but affect the way we behave in our daily lives. It can't help but inculcate within us a sense that maximizing wealth is a worthy goal. It can't help but affect the way in which we see others, relate to others, situate others within our lives. It can't help but exacerbate the radical autonomy and pursuit of self-interest that already characterize turn-of-the-century America. The corporate goal of stockholder wealth maximization not only destroys the corporation, as I shall show; it also destroys our social fabric.

II

STRUCTURAL TRAPS
IN THE NAME
OF THE LAW

CORPORATE MANAGERS: DR. JEKYLL OR MR. HYDE?

Corporate misbehavior is not especially the fault of corporate managers, stockholders, and employees. As I have shown, it is the result we should expect from the legal structure and rules we establish to create the corporation. And the legal structure and rules we create for the corporation derive importantly from America's broader legal and social culture of radical autonomy. The corporation's legal structure and rules result in the dictum to maximize stockholder profit within the confines of limited liability, a dictum which not only gives managers, stockholders, and workers the excuse to behave badly, but also encourages them to do so. Having made the point in general terms, I turn in this part 2 to the details of the laws and specific examples in order to flesh out the argument.

Recall Robert Louis Stevenson's story of Dr. Jekyll and Mr. Hyde, a single person with two natures, one mild and gentle and the other the embodiment of evil. This comparison may slightly exaggerate the reality of corporate managers, but this classic story offers a useful metaphor.

Consider a corporate director, John, as Jekyll and Hyde. John is a person of good moral character who enjoys a distinguished reputation in his community. He has a family and is a good father and husband. He belongs to civic and religious organizations. He loves his mother. But when he enters the boardroom he abandons the values of his daily life and takes on an entirely new personality, that of the corporation. As I have described it, this personality or role of stockholder price maximizer to the exclusion of all others is a role that we would consider pathological if it described a human personality. Yet this is the personality that American corporate law creates for John and other corporate directors, the role that the structure of the modern corporation reinforces. Not only have we chosen to make our directors Mr. Hyde, but we have protected them in that role by absolving them of responsibility and accountability for their actions. Even more, we have given Mr. Hyde a competitive advantage over Dr. Jekyll. Absolving Mr. Hyde of accountability permits him to reduce his corporation's costs of production by shifting them outside the corporation onto those most vulnerable, the workers, the environment, the consumers, and the community. In this chapter I will show how the role would derive from corporate structure, even if social and economic norms of stock price maximization did not exist.

Let's start with the real world. Consider the story of Jack Welch of General Electric, widely considered to be America's best CEO (he was recently awarded a seven-million-dollar advance by TimeWarner Books for a book about business). Although there is no question that GE's stock price has climbed throughout his tenure — in fact, it's increased 1,200 percent[1] — he has laid off or displaced through divestiture approximately 120,000 workers, many of whom had been loyal GE employees for decades. And besides its well-known dumping of polychlorinated biphenyls (PCBs) into the Hudson River and the widespread health problems caused by its Hanford, Washington, nuclear plant, GE tops the federal government's Superfund list as "potentially responsible" for fifty-one toxic waste sites. Welch's defense? Maximize stockholder profit.

The federal government found that May Department Stores sold clothing made in California by Thai workers paid fifty cents an hour and held to their work by threats of rape and murder. What could be the defense? Maximize stockholder profit. And as long as we give corporations this defense, we have no right to complain when their managers behave accordingly.

Corporate directors and managers (to whom I will refer together as managers) generally want to behave well. This is the conclusion of the empirical work done by scholars like Myles Mace and Jay Lorsch. But, as one board consultant I know put it, "Almost every director I talk to feels trapped." And the trap they feel is the imperative to maximize stockholder profit, a logical outgrowth of the legal structure and rules of corporate law.

THE STRUCTURE OF THE CORPORATION— THE PUSH TO PROFIT

I think I've said enough about the way the concept of stock price maximization creates a serious constraint on the moral behavior of corporations and their directors and officers. But even if we didn't have a norm of stock price maximization, we would still have the basic structure of American corporate law, which by itself is sufficient to create almost insurmountable incentives for corporate actors to look primarily, if not exclusively, to maximizing stockholder wealth in performing their functions, and to make any more balanced concept of their roles extremely difficult to pursue. This same structure has, I believe, led judges to assume somewhat unreflectively that the purpose of the corporation is to pursue stockholder wealth, even in the absence of any clear legal rules or doctrine to support that idea. The reason is that the structure of American corporate law is geared directly toward stockholder interests.

There are three supports to this structure: voting, derivative litigation (which is the right to sue directors for breach of their duties), and sales of control. Each one of these is the province of the stockholders, and the stockholders alone.

THE CORPORATE FRANCHISE

Only stockholders can vote. That is the basic premise of corporate democracy. As virtually every state corporation statute provides, directors are to be elected annually by the stockholders. Stockholders get to vote on some other things too, like amendments to the certificate of incorporation, mergers, sales of all of the corporation's assets, and dissolution. This set of voting rights, which leaves the directors in control of everything else, is pretty limited.

But the fact that stockholders get to choose the directors is still a basic legitimizing premise of the corporation by which nonowner directors manage on behalf of owner-stockholders. As the highly influential former Delaware chancellor (now law professor) William Allen wrote in one case, "It is clear that . . . [stockholder voting] is critical to the theory that legitimates the exercise of power by some (directors and officers) over vast aggregates of property that they do not own."[2,a]

So stockholder voting legitimizes the entire system. But it does more than that, as a brief analogy to political democracy should make clear. Politicians are responsive to their constituents — and, as Tip O'Neill so famously understood, the more local, the more responsive. Campaign finance reform is a perennial issue, at least in part because there is some clear evidence that the biggest donors get the grease. *Mother Jones* magazine regularly publishes a list of the biggest political donors, the identities of those to whom they have given money, and their business interests. Only an ostrich would ignore the power of voting (and the ability to influence voting) on the behavior of politicians. Only that same ostrich would disregard the structural importance of stockholder voting to the locus of interest of corporate directors.

[a]I am not concerned here with the effectiveness of voting rights, about which much has been written. It certainly is true that at one point it could be said with some certainty that stockholders pretty much ignored their proxy cards, which allowed the board essentially to control elections. There is probably still some truth to this, although the rise of institutional stockholders, who now comprise over 50 percent of the public equities market (and who I'll discuss in chapter 7), may be helping to make exercise of the corporate franchise more effective. And it is also true that in recent years — even leaving aside the changes in corporate control brought about by hostile takeovers — stockholders have been increasingly willing to throw out underperforming boards, and boards have been more willing to fire underperforming managers. But regardless of these developments, the point is still crucially important because it creates a structure that forces a particular focus on the stockholders. Moreover, the inchoate power of stockholder voting, even if it remains largely unexercised, still gives directors a powerful incentive to look to stockholder interests.

So the fact that stockholders vote and have the power to oust the board of directors and corporate management is a very powerful incentive for directors and managers to focus their attention on stockholder happiness, which, for reasons I will discuss below, means stockholder wealth.

DERIVATIVE LITIGATION AND STOCKHOLDER SUITS

Another aspect of corporate structure that creates powerful incentives for directors to keep stockholders happy is the institution of the derivative suit. Simply put, directors and corporate officers owe two principal classes of duty to the corporation: the duty of care and the duty of loyalty. The first class of duty, the duty of care, goes to the issue of whether directors have done their job — in other words, whether they have bothered to make corporate decisions on the basis of real information about the corporation and whether those decisions are rational. While the duty of care is a loose one and has been increasingly diluted over the years by a number of factors (starting with director and officer liability insurance and continuing to widespread statutory provisions that allow corporations to hold directors harmless for breaches of the duty of care), it nonetheless exists as something more than a precatory message to corporate directors and officers as to how to go about discharging their duties. Every once in a while it results in successful lawsuits against directors who fail to do their job.

The duty of loyalty is a bit more complex. It holds that directors, officers, and employees with certain authority are obligated to act in the best interest of the corporation. Broadly understood, the duty of loyalty, also considerably diluted in recent years, is designed to prevent corporate actors from pursuing their own interests to the detriment of the corporation. The duty of loyalty, simply put, is a series of conflict of interest rules.

Now as I've described these duties, one thing should be clear: they are owed by corporate actors *to the corporation*. They are not, except in rare cases involving mergers and controlling stockholders, owed to the stockholders themselves. Yet the perceptive reader will note a problem. If the duties are owed to the corporation, and the corporation is run by the people who owe the duties, how can the corporation ever sue to enforce those duties when they're breached? What board of directors in its right mind would direct the corporation to sue itself for breaches of duty?

Well, the answer is probably none. And so corporate law developed the device of the derivative suit. Simplified as much as possible, the derivative suit is a two-step process in which a stockholder sues the corporation to bring action against the directors, and when that fails stands in place of the directors to bring the suit against them on its behalf. That is why it's called a derivative suit — the stockholder's right to sue is derived from that of the corporation.

Now the derivative suit has been an object of suspicion ever since it was developed by courts as a device to enforce managerial duties. The reason for the suspicion isn't hard to divine. You see, because the stockholder brings the suit on behalf of the corporation, any damages that the stockholder wins are paid to the corporation, not to the stockholder. So stockholders have little financial incentive to spend time and money bringing these derivative suits, and those that do are probably substantial enough to have some influence over the board in the first place.

So as a matter of financial incentive, it's hard to imagine terribly many derivative suits being brought against directors. But they are brought. So how do we ensure that the duties of care and loyalty are enforced? How do we ensure that derivative suits are brought? The answer is that the winning stockholder gets to collect legal fees from the losers. And so we've created a party with the interest to bring the litigation: lawyers. The stockholder plaintiff in derivative litigation is almost always a nominal plaintiff. The economic incentives are those of the lawyer.

Nobody likes lawyers very much, especially lawyers who have a strong financial incentive to win a case (or force the corporation into settling so they can collect legal fees). As a result, significant restrictions have been placed on stockholders' abilities to bring derivative suits, including the requirements that before filing suit they make what is called a demand on the board to take corrective actions, posting bonds to cover the expenses of litigation if the stockholder doesn't own a significant amount of the stock, and an entire series of complex rules that permit directors to dismiss the suit if certain conditions are met.[b]

Even within these restrictions, however, the simple fact remains that derivative litigation is a potent device for keeping corporate management in check. Perhaps its most powerful aspect, in light of the restrictions, is the threat advantage a plaintiff stockholder has in challenging the competence or integrity of a corporate board in a public forum like a court. In order to avoid the negative publicity that such suits can engender, corporate boards are prone to settle them prior to trial. And while the statutes I mentioned earlier can exculpate the board for breaches of the duty of care, they generally do not protect them in cases of breach of the duty of loyalty. In addition, typical director and officer liability insurance policies create exceptions for indemnification for willful acts like loyalty breaches. Finally, regardless of financial indemnification, derivative suits can result in embarrassing injunctions against directors to prevent them from violating their duties. So the derivative suit remains an important incentive for directors and officers to behave.

Behave with respect to whom? Why the stockholders of course. For one rule of derivative litigation is very clear: only stockholders

[b]There is also a significant sociological dimension to the restrictions on derivative litigation. Most of these restrictions were developed at a time when corporate defendants were represented by what are referred to as "white shoe" firms, that is, law firms primarily, if not exclusively, composed of white lawyers of Anglo-Saxon descent. These firms refused to hire Jews and other minorities, and the plaintiff's bar consisted largely of those lawyers whom the white shoe firms refused to hire, that is, Jews and other minorities. The language of some of the leading cases reflects a strong suspicion of the motivations of plaintiffs' lawyers, at the same time that it implicitly assumes only good faith of the defendants' bar and their corporate clients. I won't develop the argument here, but it is plausible, if not likely, that much of the motivation for restrictions on derivative litigation was grounded in anti-Semitic and anti-minority sentiment. Later restrictions, such as the ability of directors to dismiss derivative suits, were mostly put in place in the early 1980s and reflect a solicitousness of corporate management by business-friendly jurisdictions like Delaware and New York for the purpose of retaining their corporate franchises.

have the legal standing necessary to bring derivative suits.[c] Now there are other directorial duties besides care and loyalty. Beginning in the early 1980s, more than half of all American states adopted some form of what is called a stakeholder statute or constituency statute, usually as an amendment to that section of their corporate statute which lays out the directors' basic duty of care. These statutes typically were passed during a time of rampant corporate takeovers, when hostile bidders bought out the stockholders at premium prices, often by using large amounts of debt to pay them off. In order to reduce the takeover debt, these takeover artists would sell off substantial portions of the corporations they acquired, sometimes for good business reasons, or to reduce costs by laying off large numbers of employees or simply by closing down factories. The result was that not only many people in specific localities found themselves without work, but also entire towns that had grown up around the factories were deprived of their principal means of economic existence (remember the Willow Run case discussed in chapter 2).

In order to protect the economic health of their states, legislators added to directors' duties the rights to consider the interests of a variety of corporate constituencies that were not within the contemplation of corporate law, which, you will recall, acknowledges only directors, officers, and stockholders. Among these constituencies are employees, creditors, suppliers, customers, and even communities. So it might appear that the directors' incentives to look only to the stockholders, on which the entire thesis of this chapter is based, has been severely diminished, and so the problem I am addressing is more theoretical than real.

If that's your idea, you're wrong. The reason is that while these statutes may be on the books, they have very little effect. The reason they are ineffective is threefold. First, a significant number of the statutes apply only in the circumstances of a hostile takeover and so

[c]The American Law Institute in its Principles of Corporate Governance suggests that convertible bondholders, who have at least an expectancy interest in corporate stock, ought also to be allowed to bring derivative suits. This suggestion has not received wide acceptance.

do not address problems of corporate accountability in day-to-day operations. But there are other fatal flaws. Second is the fact that all but one of the statutes is permissive, not mandatory. While the directors *may* take the other interests into account, they are not required to. And given the facts of stockholder voting and stockholder selling (as I will soon discuss), there is very little incentive for directors to care about these groups. Third, and related to the permissive nature of the statutes, not one of them gives the other constituent groups the right to sue directors for failing to take their interests into account. Only stockholders have standing to sue the board. That remains the rule. And there is no reason stockholders would have any incentive to sue directors for failing to consider the interests of other groups that assert a claim on the corporation's assets, which claim, if satisfied, would diminish the wealth of the stockholders. So there you are; a right (sort of) without a remedy. Stockholders are the only group whose financial interests are affected by the corporation that can hold the directors accountable. So it's only natural that directors' incentives (at least directors who don't want to be sued) are to keep the stockholders—and only the stockholders—happy.

Now you might have two answers to this. The first is one that stems from corporate law. Remember the business judgment rule I described in chapter 3, the presumption that directors are acting in the best interests of the corporation and are thus protected from liability in the absence of a clear breach of their duties (which breaches are asserted in derivative suits)? Well, you could see stakeholder legislation as reinforcing what already exists by virtue of this rule—that is, that directors have wide discretion to run the corporation and therefore can take the interests of these groups into account. Maybe so. But recall that they can do so only against the background of a particular purpose: stockholder wealth maximization. And while some of the stakeholder statutes allow directors to consider the interests of other stakeholders on a par with stockholder interests, the fact remains that only stockholders can sue. So where's the incentive to care?

That brings me to the second possible answer. There is an incentive to care, you might say, provided by the various markets in which the corporation interacts with these other stakeholders. After all, corporations need employees, they need suppliers and customers, and often they need the support, at least in terms of services if not tax abatements, industrial revenue bonds, and the like, of the communities in which they operate. Don't they have a built-in incentive to keep such groups happy?

Well, yes, as a general matter. But general matters aren't especially interesting. The interesting questions occur at the margins, whether in terms of increasing marginal profit in the short term or the marginal benefits of externalizing costs on these groups to benefit stockholders in the long run. It seems clear that in order to maintain profitable corporations, directors have to make sure that each of these groups is kept happy. But the question is how happy? As the business scholar C. K. Prahalabad puts it, "Finance theory says, in effect, that corporations should devote resources to such stakeholders only to the point where the marginal dollar spent yields at least a dollar in return to the shareholders."[3] In other words, just happy enough to continue to do business with the corporation and no more. Just like the contingent morality we explored in chapter 3.

This last answer assumes of course that each of these groups has some choice in whether or not to deal with a particular corporation (leaving aside for the moment the question of bargaining power). Sometimes they do. As a customer, for example, I can select from a number of brands of breakfast cereal or automobiles or toothpaste. And I will be inclined to choose the one that not only satisfies my preferences but that I consider overall to be the best. But what if there are only a few products available? MS-DOS, for example, as my computer's operating system, made only by Microsoft. Or what if the corporations comprising an entire industry, in order to remain competitive with one another, give somewhat short shrift to consumer interests and as a result there is very little choice — as there was no choice of cars with airbags until the mid-1980s because the industry banded together to fight against the proposed regulation requiring them? My interests are taken into account only to the extent that the board thinks it's necessary to do so, remembering all the while that they owe their annual reelection to the stockholders, who are presumed to be watching the stock price.

Or what about employees? What if they have no choice at all, like the citizens of a one-industry town. I recall several years ago a student in my corporations seminar said of a hypothetical steelworker, "Well, why should the corporation's board care about him? After all, he chose to be a steelworker." After I rather less than gently pointed out that one doesn't choose to be a steelworker in the same way that one chooses to go to a prestigious law school and accept an obscenely paid position as an associate at a prestigious firm (now starting at around $160,000 a year, including bonuses), the student at least recognized that sometimes choices of career, like choices of employer, are limited. And when the corporate board knows that it has a relatively captive audience, it doesn't need to be quite as interested in its welfare as when it is facing reelection by a miraculously mobile capital market.[d] So the structure of directors' duties when coupled with the rules governing derivative litigation creates every incentive for a focus on stockholder wealth and very little reason to care about anything else.

SELLING THE FARM

The last aspect of corporate structure that gives directors and officers the incentive to focus their attention on maximizing stockholder wealth is the fact that as the nominal owners of the corporation — which in this context really means the voting constituency — stockholders have the right to sell the corporation out from under the management to the highest bidder. In light of the takeover

[d]Of course I recognize that workers can relocate or even retrain. But as to the first point, we need to at least question whether we want to create a society in which communities are even less stable than they are, with workers compelled to leave communities in which their families might have lived for generations, simply to maximize stockholder profit. As to the second, we need to consider the practicalities of worker retraining in an environment of great wealth disparity, especially if the corporation does not provide and has little incentive to provide that retraining.

activity over the past several decades, this right doesn't require a lot of explanation. While corporations have always been saleable either by merger or sales of their assets, transactions which require stockholder approval but also board approval, the device of the tender offer allows bidders to circumvent the board and go directly to the stockholders. For while mergers and asset sales are transactions directly involving the corporation and thus the board, tender offers are nothing more than public offers to the stockholders of the corporation to buy their stock. Thus the management can stand helpless while the stockholders sell control to a person or corporation that is likely to promptly issue a series of pink slips in the boardroom. This reality has the effect of focusing the directorial mind rather sharply on the issue of stockholder wealth.

The legally sophisticated reader knows that I've just overstated my case. In the first place, she will argue, there are a number of judicially approved defenses that, at least when exercised within proper legal limits, let the board gain control or at least influence the outcome of a takeover contest. Almost everyone has heard of poison pills and an assorted variety of other colorful takeover defenses. There are also statutes, developed since the mid-1980s, which can be used to impede and sometimes all but stop takeovers. So in fact the board has a role, and my argument about incentives goes too far.

Not true. The board can have a role — but it's a role within limits and a role that can be overcome. As to the limits, takeover defenses are measured by judicial tests that seek to determine whether the board is acting in the best interests of the stockholders — yes, the stockholders — or simply seeking to entrench itself in office. While these tests aren't perfect, they do provide a measure of scrutiny as to the board's motives in resisting a takeover, and some number of boards have been forced to remove these devices when the tests haven't been met. In addition, if the board *is* actively seeking to sell the company, it is constrained by a requirement that it do so at the best price available — that is, it cannot use defensive devices to keep out bidders who may fire them in favor of bidders who will treat them more kindly, at least so long as the latter are not offering the highest price. So while there's some truth to the assertion that directors are not powerless, their power is not without its limits.

The second argument is about the recently passed statutes that allow a board to block certain takeover offers. In the first place, these statutes have their own limits and never completely permit the board to prevent takeovers. In the second place, clever bidders have managed to evade the statutes, which either have to be opted into or opted out of by the corporation, by coupling their tender offers with proxy contests which enable them to obtain control of the board, lift the restrictions of the relevant statute (by opting out or revoking the opt-in), and proceeding with the tender offer. And as long as the price is right, that is, as long as the stockholders want to take the offer, they will cooperate and unceremoniously oust the board.

So while it may be true that boards have more protective options available to them than they did, say, in the early 1980s, it is nevertheless equally true that boards have every incentive to keep the stock price up and the stockholders happy.

SPEAKING OF OPTIONS

In 1994, Congress amended the Internal Revenue Code to provide that executive salaries in excess of $1 million were not deductible by the corporation unless they were linked to performance.[4] One result of this was the proliferation of stock options as the most significant component of executive compensation packages. Obviously this gives executives a sizable personal stake in their corporations' stock prices. One commentator referred to the 1990s as "the decade of executive stock options," noting that "enormous option grants have raised executive pay to staggering new heights, while intensifying its sensitivity to firm stock prices."[5] According to a study by the compensation consulting firm Pearl Mayer & Partners, stock reserved for option compensation represented 13.7 percent of outstanding shares in 1999, an amazing proportion of stock when you consider that institutional investors own just over a majority of the shares. A number of commentators saw options as a wonderful way to align managerial and stockholder interests. After all, if a manager's pay was principally dependent upon how high the stock price rose, he would have every incentive to do his best to get the price as high as possible. Well, if nothing else that I've said about the legal incentives for managers to focus on short-term stock prices has persuaded you that I'm right, surely this one is obvious.

As two compensation experts illustrated, "The typical chief executive officer . . . of a company under $500 million in revenues received $514,298 of cash compensation in 1995 compared with actual stock ownership valued at $3,084,275. . . . The situation is even more striking at the larger company level (over $10 billion in revenues), where current [1995] data reveals [sic] that the median CEO's actual stockholdings are over $7.9 million, almost four times the average cash compensation of $1,896,996."[6] They note that for the smaller company director, "the 'median' CEO is extremely sensitive to changes in the company's stock price. Considering only actual holdings, a 16.7% decrease in the stock price would reflect a loss of $515,000 to this CEO, effectively eroding all of the cash compensation received that year." And obviously the CEO of the larger corporation is also highly exposed to downward stock price movements.

Perhaps no executive has more successfully pursued this incentive than Charles Wang, chairman and CEO of Computer Associates International, Inc. (CA). In a plan proposed by the compensation committee of CA's board and approved by its stockholders in 1995, three executives were awarded stock options for which they were to qualify if they raised the price of CA's stock from $20 to $53.33. Only three years later they had succeeded. The result was that the three executives were granted more than $1 billion in stock options, $655 million of it going to Wang alone. The stockholders got what they wanted. But in order to cover the cost of the options, CA had to write off $675 million against earnings. Following the write-off, CA's stock price plummeted back into the $20s, although it later came back to the mid-$50s (probably at least partly as a result of litigation which resulted in an order that the three executives return 9.5 million of the 20.3 million shares they had been granted).[7,e]

---

[e]The judgment was followed by a settlement in which they agreed to return 4.5 million shares.

CA's stockholders were lucky that a Delaware court saved them from their own foolishness (although the complaint was notably based on the decreased stock price). But stockholders can't expect to be so lucky all of the time. Delaware, in which 60 percent of the Fortune 500 corporations and slightly fewer than half of the corporations listed on the New York Stock Exchange are incorporated,[8] is the undisputed leader in corporate law and has rather lax rules on executive compensation. The general idea is that unless managerial compensation rises to the level of outright obscenity, as it did in Wang's case, *and* that obscenity has no rational relationship to the corporation's (read stockholders') well-being, courts will not interfere with compensation decisions.[9]

In any event, the fact that managers increasingly find their compensation dependent upon stock price, as *Business Week*'s April 2000 report on executive compensation shows, clearly increases managerial incentive to worry about stock price every single year. While I can't prove the effect of this on long-term performance, it sure seems like there's every reason to think that this trend is creating serious risks.

The conclusion from our primer on corporate structure seems clear. Even in the absence of a norm that tells directors to maximize stock price, the structure of corporate law itself gives them every incentive to do just that. And despite the attempt by state legislatures to give the directors some greater independence, despite the attempt to allow them to think more broadly about the corporations' externalization of the costs of maximizing stockholder wealth, the simple fact remains: Corporations and the actors that motivate them maximize stockholder wealth with little or no regard for the consequences of such activity to other people. This is just another way of saying that, given the legal structure of the modern American corporation, we have every reason to expect it to behave irresponsibly. How do we fix the problem created by this structure?

LEAVE THE BOARD ALONE

My answer will be rather surprising, at least to those of you who have (correctly and unsurprisingly) perceived me to be a generally left-of-center sort of guy. The answer is to break the structures that tie corporate managements' actions to stock prices. The answer is to make the board more independent of stockholders. Now I know such an adjustment creates its own set of problems, and I shall be at pains to address them later in this chapter. But for now let me describe several possible solutions and the logic underlying them.

The first solution is my personal favorite. It's one I proposed several years ago in a law review article (it fell on deaf ears, although I can't imagine why the Business Roundtable didn't pick it up as their fight song). That solution was to eliminate the institution of stockholder voting entirely and make the board self-perpetuating. In other words, once the members of the board were put in place, either by a one-time stockholder vote or public appointment or something like it, the board itself was to fill the periodic vacancies resulting from death, resignation, and increases in board size by selecting the people to fill those vacancies. The mechanism already exists. Virtually every state corporate statute gives the board the power to fill vacancies that occur between annual elections. My idea is simply to extend that power by permitting the board to continue doing so ad infinitum, without stockholder participation at all. Note that this would also cut down on the threat of hostile takeovers if the bidder is not allowed to remove the board during its term.

Now this is a pretty radical idea. For that reason it isn't the one I'm ultimately going to recommend. Instead I'll make a more modest (and more flawed) proposal that I think has a greater possibility of enactment. But precisely because it is almost exactly the opposite approach to the one we now take, I will begin with my idea and work toward the middle, for the logic behind this proposal ultimately justifies the less extreme ideas I will support.

Here's the problem: the structure of corporate law focuses directors on stock prices. Now, leaving aside moral considerations, if stock markets were perfectly or even nearly perfectly efficient, this wouldn't be much of a problem, at least in theory, because even a short-term focus on stock price would equate with a long-term focus on stock price.[10] The reason this is true lies in the theories of efficient markets. In a strongly efficient market, everything that is known about a corporation is incorporated into its stock price. Of course everything that is known includes the anticipation of the corporation's future performance, and since a stock is worth only what you can get out of it, stock price in a perfectly efficient market would reflect the collective judgment of investors as to the discounted present value of the corporation's future returns—in other words, the long-term value of the corporation.

This would be great—still leaving aside moral considerations. Because in order to have the best current stock price possible, the corporation would have to aim for the best long-term stock price possible (at least within a sensible conception of the long-term so that discount rates weren't so high as to destroy present value), and that would mean making good products, having happy and loyal employees, having a steady source of supply, and the like. I've now twice said, "leaving aside moral considerations" because happy employees and loyal consumers are important in this way of arguing only up to the point at which the marginal cost of retaining them is less than the marginal benefit from doing something else. Financial logic might lead to maltreated employees and substandard products whereas moral theory might argue otherwise—but I'll take this up later.

The more relevant point for now is that nobody believes we have perfectly efficient markets, and nobody ever did. So instead we can consider whether we have somewhat efficient markets—markets that may not incorporate soft information like managers' judgments about future profitability but at least hard information as to the here and now. We'd still have the same moral problem, but we might be able to overcome a lot of the problems of financial incentives.

There used to be true believers in this kind of efficient market. Not any more. We don't really need sophisticated economics to confuse the issue: anyone who has followed stock price movements, individual and indexed, over the past couple of years intuitively knows that the stock market isn't anywhere near perfectly efficient. If it were, you wouldn't see the remarkable swings in stock prices that occur almost every day. After all, can we reasonably expect that corporate prospects change that much from day to day? Clearly not. And so even to the economically uninitiated, the idea that stock markets approach any meaningful efficiency seems like a fairy tale.

But we can also look at the economic sophisticates. For many of those very scholars who once sold us on the idea that equity markets were fairly efficient have emerged from their computer labs, seen the same things we have, and have either recanted their faith or struggled mightily to show why the market remains efficient despite all appearances.

More to the point, there is evidence that stock markets are highly inefficient. Perhaps the most damning bit of evidence, at least as to the market environment existing as I write, is given by the Yale economist Robert Shiller in his recent critique of the modern stock market, *Irrational Exuberance*. Efficient markets are supposed to discount the dividends a corporation ultimately will pay down to present value.[f] But Shiller shows that stock market performance from 1871 to 2000 doesn't correlate very well with the present value of dividends. It sometimes even diverges wildly. And it has never diverged more wildly than now, with the present value of dividends for the corporations comprising the Standard & Poor's (S&P) Composite Index in early 2000 standing at about 28 percent of S&P stock price index values. Or, to put it differently, from 1980 to 2000, dividend present value increased by about 50 percent. Stock prices increased during the same period by approximately 700 percent.[g] That suggests that the market expects a whole lot of dividends — far more relative to stock price than it ever has. And while dividends increased rather steadily, stock prices were relatively volatile, shoot-

[f]Present value is the amount of money that one needs to invest in order to realize a given sum later on. The converse, expected value, is what a given amount invested today can be expected to produce at a future point in time. The two variables that constitute the discount rate (or its converse, the expected rate of return) are the time value of money (i.e., inflation) and the risk that the anticipated profit won't materialize. At least as a matter of theory, the current price of a share of stock ought to be the future stream of dividends discounted to present value.

[g]Shiller doesn't give the actual numbers in his text. I have derived these percentages from my best reading of the graph on page 186.

ing up dramatically in that same period while dividends kept on a steady course. Shiller allows for the possibility of a significant disparity between price and dividends consistent with efficient markets, but he argues that there must be a much closer relationship between the volatility of the two factors to suggest meaningful market efficiency.[11]

There is one final point to be made, and that is that you manage what you measure. Even if the structure and rules of corporate law weren't such as to keep managements' eyes focused on the daily stock quotations, the simple fact is that the other set of performance measures available to them are the corporations' financial statements. Financially sophisticated people understand that the balance sheet is generally not a very good measure of the performance of a going concern, at least not in any given year. Balance sheets, to be meaningful, must be compared across time, and in order to get meaningful performance information from balance sheets you need to collect a bunch of them, which obviously takes time. Of course you could look at monthly balance sheets, but the net worth of most corporations doesn't change terribly much from month to month, no matter what's going on in the stock market. But income statements can tell you how you are doing, not just over time but every month, every quarter, and every year. And the bottom line number that accountants enter on income statements is earnings per share. So a manager who wants to know how her corporation is currently performing is most likely to look at that earnings-per-share figure — and she should, because that's what stock analysts and investors look at too. The stock price of Intel, a highly respected and very strong performer, dropped 20 percent on September 22, 2000, simply because earnings were not what they were expected to be.

Earnings per share is a measure, based on accounting conventions, of how much money each share earned during the period for which it is reported. And while earnings per share does not directly translate into stock price for a variety of reasons which are not important here, the important point is that it, like stock price, is a measure of *stockholder* value. So even if managers could ignore daily changes in stock price itself, they are still measuring performance by reference to what the corporation returns to its stockholders. And this is precisely the information the securities laws require public corporations to report quarterly and annually, so that it is readily available to stockholders for their evaluation and judgment. Everything that we have used to construct the modern American public corporation leads to a focus on stockholder wealth.

So where does all this leave us? With the conclusion that focusing on stock price as a measure of management (or protection of your job) is nothing more than focusing on stock price for the short term. This is not rational management. As Warren Buffett has famously said, "Our [Berkshire Hathaway's] owners and managers both have very long time horizons in regard to this business, and it is difficult to say anything new or meaningful each quarter about events of long-term significance." It doesn't take a financial genius to recognize that most corporations most of the time don't change all that much from quarter to quarter or even from year to year. You wouldn't know this from contemporary stock price volatility. But that has nothing to do with the long-term health of the corporation itself.

So what does this mean for managers? It means that long-term considerations give way to the desire to keep your job here and now—and that is rational, for who among us, including corporate managers, can know how long a term they'll be around for? Certainly what empirical evidence there is suggests that even those many managers who would prefer to think and act more broadly feel both a legal and practical imperative to focus on the short term. It means that even the financial incentives, leaving aside the moral ones, to treat employees well, avoid pollution, make safe and useful products, care about supplier relationships, and protect communities are no real incentives at all as long as our behavior gets us from today to tomorrow. And it means that expenses corporations incur today that will show benefits only in the long-run, for example, research and development (R&D), better worker training and care, and so on, will be skimped on. In the short term, such expenses reduce the bottom line and therefore current stock price, and the management that incurs them risks upsetting current stockholders and thus losing their jobs.[12] Richard Mahoney, the retired president of Monsanto, tells of his corporation's stock price being punished by analysts when Monsanto undertook an expensive, long-term R&D project, of analysts demanding reductions in the R&D budget and the use of cash that might otherwise be available to buy back stock to increase short-term stock price. One result of Monsanto's benighted efforts was Celebrex, an enormously successful product that not only has helped consumers but has enriched Monsanto.[13] Of course short-sightedness might not prevail if stockholders themselves took a long-term perspective: I'll explore this possibility in the next chapter.

Before going on, I should point out an anomaly that seems to contradict my argument. Some data indicate that since 1994, R&D expenditures as a percentage of GNP have been increasing, both when defense-related R&D and non-defense-related R&D are taken into account. These data indicate that the percentage of GNP devoted to R&D in the United States is exceeded only by that in Japan. Germany is fairly close behind the United States, France not far behind that, and then there is a significant decline to the United Kingdom, Canada, and Italy.[14]

So maybe I'm wrong, at least about managers' incentives to invest in the future, since the bare numbers seem to suggest that they are in fact doing so; yet there is also evidence that I am right.[15] Like all statistics, those in the previous paragraph don't tell the whole story. Michael Porter points out that there is at least anecdotal evidence suggesting that American corporations invest less than Japanese and German corporations in "non-traditional forms such as human resource development, relationships with suppliers, and start-up losses to enter foreign markets," and while there is other anecdotal evidence (some of which I've already mentioned) that at least some of these practices are changing, more troubling is harder evidence that the "R&D portfolios of American firms include a smaller share of long-term projects than those of European and Japanese firms."[16] And Robert Kuttner cites broad evidence to show that American corporations significantly underinvest in R&D.[17]

So the question is not a simple one of how much money is spent on R&D but what counts as R&D and where it is spent. It appears that while the evidence is somewhat conflicting, the kind of R&D expenditures that are showing up in the statistics are not the kind that increase future wealth and well-being. Consequently, I continue to conclude that managerial focus on R&D is blurry.[18]

If this is the case, if managers have every incentive to focus on short-term stock price in order to keep their jobs, what is the ideal solution? Free them of the pressures of the stock market. And how do you free them of the pressures of the stock market? Break the tie between their jobs and the stockholders.

LET MANAGERS MANAGE

As I noted, the first suggestion I have for breaking this tie is the most radical, and that is to eliminate stockholder voting entirely and establish self-perpetuating boards. Let me first outline the basic idea and then answer some objections and make some refinements.

Boards of directors need to be free to do what it is they do best, and that is manage (or provide for the management of) corporations for the long term. They need to do so responsibly, accountably, and in full recognition of the consequences of their decisions. As I have taken great pains to point out, the current structure and rules of corporate law make this difficult, while not impossible, and offer the possibility of at least a short-term competitive edge for those corporations whose boards choose to manage for the short term.

There is evidence that directors themselves feel this pressure. The business scholar Jay Lorsch surveyed more than nine hundred directors of Standard & Poor's index of four hundred companies. He concluded that directors generally were stymied in reaching consensus as to their corporate goals largely because of their perception that their legal duties are owed to their stockholders. At the same time, he found that most directors believed they owed moral and business duties to a much wider array of corporate constituents, including creditors, employees, suppliers, and customers as well as to the community at large. Lorsch also found that most directors felt a great deal of short-term performance pressure from institutional investors, an issue I will take up in chapter 7.

Everything I have said so far leads to one conclusion: Corporate management should be entirely separated from stockholder pressure. The easiest way to accomplish this is to break the annual cycle of stockholder elections of directors (unless you believe that one year is a long term). One way of accomplishing such a goal is to permit boards to be self-perpetuating and, through their own insulation from short-term pressure, insulate the managers under them from it too, to enable them to manage responsibly and for the long term.

This is practically easy to accomplish. Most corporations don't start out as public corporations, and so there is a board in place at the time the corporation goes public. No matter what, corporate statutes require those who form the corporation either to provide for an initial board or to hold a stockholders' meeting shortly after incorporation to elect a board. In any event, the boards are in existence, and the existing statutory mechanism I mentioned earlier can be used to keep them staffed.

Why haven't we done this so far? What would the principal objections be? It seems to me there are two: first, that stockholders own the corporation and so should be entitled to vote for the people who run it, and, second, that if left to their own devices, directors would engage in rampant self-dealing.

THE MYTH OF STOCKHOLDER OWNERSHIP

First, let's spend a minute on stockholder ownership, which I haven't mentioned yet because I consider it to be one of the greatest misunderstandings that exists in American corporate law. It is commonly said that stockholders own the corporation. This is a belief that my students universally bring to their first day of corporations class. It is a belief that is repeated endlessly in the financial and popular press. It is a belief that is articulated in a number of judicial opinions. And it is a belief that is loudly proclaimed whenever directors behave in a way the stockholders disapprove of, usually involving a drop in stock price.

Well, if all these people believe it, there must be something to it. So to get at the mythology of stockholder ownership, I will begin by asking what it means to say that stockholders own the corporation. And this will necessarily take us on a digression into the concept of ownership more generally.

Owning a corporation in the sense that stockholders do is not like owning your house or your car. Say you own shares of stock in Home Depot. What do you think would happen if you walked into your local Home Depot and helped yourself to what you wanted from the shelves and, when stopped by an employee, proclaimed that as a stockholder of Home Depot you owned what you were taking? Or if you tried to prevent your obnoxious neighbor from entering a Home Depot store on the grounds that you own it so you can decide who shops there? Or if you decided to go to headquarters and sit yourself down for lunch at the company cafeteria? Or if you felt like dropping in for a visit with the CEO or to attend a board meeting?

Clearly any of these things would get you an invitation to leave and maybe a night in jail. But each of the possible behaviors I've suggested reflects aspects of ownership. Your taking inventory reflects your right to use the thing you own; your attempt to keep your neighbor out reflects your right to prevent others from using what you own; your dropping in for lunch reflects your right of entry onto the property; and your visits to corporate officers reflects your right as the owner to control the behavior of your agents.

You can do all of these things with your house. You can take anything from inside it. You can go in anytime you like, keep anyone out that you like, except the police under certain carefully constrained conditions. If you have people fixing your plumbing or painting the house, you can tell them what to do and throw them out if you don't like what they're doing.

A stockholder's ownership of the corporation, however, is different. There is some degree of stockholder control, and I've already described what it is: stockholders vote, stockholders bring derivative suits, and stockholders can sell the corporation. But these are consequences of stockholder ownership, not definitional aspects of ownership. Stockholders can do these things because — and only because — we have decided that in some sense they own the corporation.

So what does it mean to say that stockholders own the corporation? It means they have the right to whatever wealth is left in the corporate till after everyone else who has a claim on the corporation has picked it over. It means they have the right to receive dividends if the directors feel like declaring them and if creditors haven't contracted with the corporation to prevent it from paying them. And it means that when the corporation meets its maker, when it dissolves and liquidates, they have the right to be paid whatever is left after all prior claimants.

Now we recognize that because ownership means that stockholders get only what's left, they are vulnerable to the forces of the markets, of business cycles, and even of bad management, and so we give them some limited control through voting and the right to bring derivative actions. And of course they can sell their stock if someone else wants to buy it. But notice that these possibilities that lead us to give some protection to the stockholders aren't very different from the position of other corporate claimants. Creditors, for example, while they get paid before stockholders, are also subject to the same financial risk that they won't get paid — the difference is one of degree, not of kind. Creditors, like stockholders, can also sell their debt to willing buyers, which is why we have a bond market. Employees are subject to losing their jobs and sometimes their pensions because of bad corporate performance — and they can sell their labor like stockholders sell their stock. And so on for suppliers who may sell on trade credit or have long-term supply commitments from the corporation, and customers who may have warranty claims or depend upon a steady supply of spare parts or other inputs.

It's probably the case that some of these other claimants can protect themselves through contracts a little better than the stockholders can. There's been a lot of academic debate about this, and it's a debate I don't need to engage in here. The salient point I want to make is that stockholder ownership isn't really that different from other forms of corporate claims; it's when you put the label "Ownership" on it that it takes on a mythical level of importance.

Something else about ownership makes appending this label to stockholders dangerous, and this ties back both to our earlier discussion of limited liability and to the idea of the single corporate purpose: We have structured this ownership in a way that we generally don't permit of any other property, and that is we allow it to be used without regard to the consequences to others. I suspect that even in the absence of traffic laws, most of us wouldn't drive the cars we own heedlessly, mowing down whatever or whomever might be in our way. And if you want to object and say that it's because we drive on public roads or that we're licensed to drive that we have restrictions on the use of our cars, it's clear that such an answer is nonsense; you have no greater right to run someone over on your private driveway just because you're in a hurry than you do on the public street. Yet we permit corporations, in the name of their stockholders, to mow down anyone they like in their pursuit of profit.

The point is that not only do we have laws that restrict the ways in which we may use the things we own: we also have moral responsibility for that use. And this moral responsibility is aided by the fact that when we use our property, we generally experience its effects on others; when we mow down our neighbor with our car, there's no denying what we did, that we did it, and the experience of doing it. The same can hardly be said for the owners of the corporation

So it's no answer to say that stockholders have to elect directors because they own the corporation. There are respectable arguments that say stockholder voting is the most efficient way of controlling the corporation. But this is just another way of saying that stockholder voting ensures that corporations make as much money as they can for the stockholders without a lot of regard to the consequences to others. In fact, according to the economic arguments, attention to the consequences to others would make the corporation and thus stockholder voting less efficient. This is exactly one of the principal questions I have put at issue. So there's no point in rehashing efficiency arguments here. The myth of stockholder ownership doesn't justify anything, including the right to vote for directors.

There is an alternative way of looking at stockholder ownership, and it's one that Buffett has described as the vision of Berkshire Hathaway: "Although our form is corporate, our attitude is partnership. . . . We do not view the company itself as the ultimate owner of our business assets but, instead, view the company as a conduit through which our shareholders own the assets." Now this flies in the face of every theory of the corporation on the books. And of course it's not the way Berkshire Hathaway really operates, except through its charitable giving program, which allows each stockholder to designate a charity to which the corporation makes a contribution. It couldn't actually operate this way, or all of the consequences of ownership that I described earlier would begin to assert themselves, and Berkshire couldn't operate in the centralized, efficient manner under Buffett's management that has led to its success. But the very expression of the attitude is significant and, if Buffett and his stockholders really believe it, has important consequences for the way we think about corporate responsibility.

Buffett's attitude at least has the potential to get stockholders to think about the corporate assets as their property. And, as I've already discussed, you can't legally use your property however you want, nor would you morally do so, especially because you have some identification with your property. You can see the consequences through the lens of the philosophy of David Hume. Because on some level you identify with your property, you are morally accountable for its use. Hume wrote, "Whenever any pleasure or pain arises from an object, connected with us by property, we may be certain that either pride or humility must arise from this conjunction of relations."

We care about the things we own — they may not exactly be extensions of us, but they are connected to us and identified with us in some ways, and so we take care of how we use them. Buffett's attitude, if taken seriously, has the potential to bring stockholders to thinking of the corporation as their property, and its use of those assets as their concern. Exploding cars and slave labor would come to be a personal embarrassment, much as during my college years embarrassed students attempted to persuade their colleges and universities to divest their portfolios of the stock of companies doing business in apartheid South Africa. Shame is an attitude that has strong implications for corporate governance as well as for accountability. But it's not an attitude that's widely held, at least not yet. So I return to my original conclusion: Stockholder ownership under the current model of the corporation justifies nothing.

THE SPECTER OF MANAGERIAL THEFT

The second principal argument against severing the management/shareholder connection is the fear that cutting directors loose from stockholders would be to let the foxes into the henhouse. Let's face it, American corporate law and theory are based on mistrust.[19] At least since Adolph Berle and Gardiner Means observed the substantial separation of "ownership" from control in the American corporation (and ignoring their cry for the reassertion of public control as the solution), corporate scholars, lawyers, financiers, and reformers have based their ideas about good corporate governance on the central premise of mistrust.

Mistrust is systemic. Not surprising, I suppose, in the radically autonomous society I described in chapter 1, where everyone is presumed to look out only for oneself. But nonetheless damaging for all that. The mistrust is evident in intercorporate relations (a subject beyond the scope of my argument and reflected at least in part in our antitrust laws), in intracorporate relations, that is, the relationship of stockholders to managers, which is at issue here, and in corporate managerial relations, that is, the hierarchy and monitoring of corporate employees, which I'll talk about in chapter 9. Taken together, these relations combine to form what I have elsewhere called the American monitocracy, the system of watchers watching watchers watching watchers that was described compellingly by David Gordon in his book *Fat and Mean* and that creates a pervasive atmosphere of mistrust and an attitude of self-protection.[20]

A system based on mistrust is bad. Mistrust has been blamed for hampering Italy's economic development and for stunting its community.[21] Mistrust leads to wasted social resources, what economists call agency costs and monitoring costs, which are a net social loss. And mistrust, as psychologists overwhelmingly tell us, leads those who are not trusted to be untrustworthy, whereas people who know they are trusted tend to behave in trustworthy ways.

So what's the mistrust about in corporate law? Money, of course, and the presumption that those who have control of it will try to grab as much for themselves as they can to the detriment of those who have parted with control over it. That's the central issue raised by the idea that stockholders invest their money in public corporations over which they have no real control and watch it increase or decrease in the hands of others. It is the central debate engendered by Berle and Means over how best to make management more accountable to stockholders and over which countless forests have been felled in the scholarly attempt to solve the problem. It is the fear that those in control of the money will take it, either by failing to do their jobs and thus being overcompensated for doing very little or by simply stealing it by paying themselves too much, by dealing with the corporation for their own advantage, or by taking opportunities that rightfully belong to the corporation and its stockholders. And as a consequence of this mistrust, we expend enormous amounts of intellectual energy trying to make sure these things don't happen.

This whole idea of monitoring based on mistrust is considerably overstated. The efforts that have gone into attempting to control corporate management have largely been for nought, the problem is one at the margins, and the atmosphere of mistrust created by excessive monitoring is worse than the problem it's intended to cure.

The first point is simply one of common sense. We know as an empirical matter that, despite its effect of focusing attention on stockholders, stockholder voting is not very effective. We also know, as I'll discuss in chapter 8, that the laws against managerial shirking and stealing are largely toothless. Yet people continue to part with their money in droves, often investing without knowledge of who the corporation's management is and certainly without having made their acquaintance. Why? Because they must assume, as I have assumed from the beginning, that most people, most of the time, act in good faith. They must assume that corporate managers aren't simply going to walk off with their money or play golf as the corporation trails off into bankruptcy. They must assume that, just like themselves, corporate managers generally feel some responsibility for doing their jobs. And they must assume this for several reasons.

In the first place, law can do only so much. If the principal constraints on which investors relied were those of the law, the number of lawsuits against corporate managers would be far greater than it is now and the degree of stockholder investigation into management practices would be far greater. The costs of such actions would diminish the money available for investment and the opportunity to generate real productive gains. Law may establish the rules of the game, it may set aspirational levels of conduct and baseline levels of behavior, but it cannot be the answer. Far more important are the social norms that drive people to do the right thing simply because it's the right thing to do. And there is no reason to think that corporate managers are any less affected by social norms than other people.

Of course there are abuses. Stories of managerial overcompensation, insider trading, and directorial entrenchment abound. But those are the stories you hear. And the bad publicity associated with these stories is one of the mechanisms that create the norms of behavior we expect from our corporate managers. Shame can be a powerful deterrent. In fact it's the very basis of the disclosure rules established by our federal securities laws.

But there are also the stories you don't hear. And that's most of them. Of course one reason you don't hear them might simply be that the press, the financial community, and individual investors don't have the resources to uncover all bad behavior. And that might be true to a limited extent. But if it were widely true, the productivity gains in recent years, the increases in corporate profitability, and the astonishingly low rate of unemployment would be impossible. The simple fact is that without some measure of integrity, the system wouldn't work at all. As all lawyers know, law can provide last-ditch solutions; it cannot be the principal governing tool of an entire society, even a corporate society.

But there's another reason law is not the answer. The laws we have designed to restrain managerial self-dealing are largely ineffective. Take managerial laziness, which corporate law deals with under the broad doctrinal heading of the duty of care. Every second-year law student can tell you that the only time the duty of care really makes a difference (and that only at the margins) is in takeover cases, and those are big enough, public enough, and transparent enough that we're pretty good at catching the cases of bad behavior.

More interesting is the law of stealing. It used to be a long, long time ago that corporate managers couldn't do business with their own corporations, couldn't take opportunities that might be desirable to the corporation, and had to be very careful about accounting for their compensation. No more. We've now evolved (?) to the point where we have procedural rules wide enough to drive a truck through that permit directors and managers to do practically anything they want. Of course most of the time they don't. They don't because it's wrong, they know it's wrong, they know their reputations will suffer if they're caught and their careers might be destroyed. Besides, for the most part, the amounts of money they could take without getting caught are penny ante.

The one area in which the stakes are higher is management compensation. The name Michael Eisner alone conjures up images of executives paid well above what any human being is worth, well more than any value they could possibly add to the corporation. I'll talk about this later, but the major way compensation is kept in check is not by law — it's by public disclosure and embarrassment, by outrage in the investing community. The impotence of law is clear; very little stops managers from paying themselves whatever they want.

A recent case from Delaware illustrates the point.[22] A board of directors developed an option plan for themselves. The result was that they stood to make a whole lot of money. In fact they did. Lots of it. Some stockholders sued, claiming that the directors hadn't disclosed how much money they would actually make from their options when they asked for stockholder approval. The chancellor told the stockholders to go away: options are too hard to value, especially the particular kind of options the directors had given themselves here. So the directors kept their options and their money.

The opinion is ridiculous. For what the directors must have known — what the chancellor must have known the directors must have known in creating the option plan — is what *they* thought the options were worth. They might not have been certain of course. But nobody accepts an offer of compensation without some idea of what they're getting. What's more, if they didn't have some idea of what the options were worth the directors would not have enough information to fulfill their legal duty of care in approving the options in the first place. The opinion and its outcome are fantasy. But they show what happens when, as a matter of legal policy, we decide we don't care that much about self-dealing.

A reading of countless cases on the subject supports my conclusion: we really don't care that much about self-dealing. We permit it, and we set up rules to show managers how to do it. Once we've gone this far, to say that boards need to be elected by stockholders in order to ensure they're monitored and controlled is silly.

So if we don't really need to worry about managers stealing except at the margins, and we don't care enough to have strong legal rules preventing it, then the two principal reasons for putting directors under stockholder control go away.

We could take a different theoretical approach. We could say that because the corporation is a creation of the state, a creation that is given its existence for public purposes, and because the board is, as a legal matter, empowered by the state and not the stockholders, managers must be answerable to the state for their misbehavior. We could, if we cared, tighten up the rules against managerial theft and let anybody who wanted to sue. Don't worry, we could create some limits and restrictions to prevent an explosion of opportunistic litigation. And we could also be certain that only those people who had a real stake in the corporation would have an incentive to sue. But this would be a far more rational way of addressing the problem than a system that insists on tying managers to stockholder monitoring.

So the main excuses fail, and there's no reason not to free managers to behave professionally, to manage for the long term, to do what they do best. Would they forego profitability? Clearly not. Without profits, the corporation wouldn't survive and they'd be out of a job. Would they steal? Not unless we assume that they're any worse than the rest of us. We might even develop strong enough rules so that when they did steal the law would at least be effective at catching them. The rules themselves would set an aspirational level at which we expected them to act well, in sharp contrast to the current monitocracy combined with loose legal rules that tell them we expect them to act badly. And so it is hard to imagine a serious disadvantage to freeing up boards and relatively easy to imagine an improvement in the current state of affairs.

Now perhaps my proposal makes you nervous. Maybe it looks too much like unchecked power, and in American political theory unchecked power is a very bad thing. Well, in the first place it's not really unchecked power — as I noted earlier, the corporation would have to be profitable to survive and enable the managers to keep their jobs. It would also have to do well enough to attract investors. And it wouldn't be unchecked if we had some real serious rules against self-dealing and left enforcement power to the state, either directly or through private attorneys general.

But I'll accept the possibility that the idea of apparently unchecked power makes you uncomfortable. So here's a middle ground. Like most compromises, it's not as good an idea as the original — as that of self-perpetuating boards — because it retains some of the problems of the current system. But it does reduce their effect. It's an idea that was floated some years ago in the *University of Chicago Law Review* by the famous takeover lawyer Marty Lipton.[23] The idea is that boards should stand for election every five years rather than every year.

Now I don't question Lipton's motivations, but I bet a lot of his corporate clients liked the idea. That doesn't matter. It's a good idea, for the same reasons that my suggestion that we separate management from stockholder influence is a good idea. It's just a little less scary to contemplate. So let me spend a few minutes on Lipton's logic before I go on to my last suggestion of reforms for financial and corporate reporting.

QUINQUENNIAL ELECTIONS

Lipton recognizes the same problems I have described, from an overemphasis on stock prices to an irrational concern with managerial theft to a variety of pressures that lead American corporate management to focus excessively, if not exclusively, on the short term. This, as I have argued, is bad for the long-term welfare of the corporation, leading to inadequate investment in R&D, employee training, and the like, and is also to the unfair disadvantage of the constellation of constituents with whom the corporation does business. So his proposal, like mine, is geared toward ameliorating these problems and letting corporate management work for the long term in a responsible, accountable way.

Lipton suggests a solution similar to mine, but does so in a way that accounts for the American fear of unchecked power that ultimately leaves the stockholders in charge. More or less arbitrarily adopting five years as an adequately long-term management horizon (with subconscious echoes perhaps of Soviet five-year plans), he creates the idea of a board election by the stockholders only once every five years, with a moratorium on hostile takeovers in the interim and strengthened legal rules to make it easier to remove misbehaving directors. The election is to be accompanied by a five-year report on the performance of the company and a five-year plan, both evaluated by independent auditors. While his idea allows for the possibility of boards being thrown out for underperforming during the five-year period, his expectation is that directors and stockholders will develop working relationships that lead to greater trust and understanding such that we would expect boards to remain largely the same from one quinquennial election to the next —and so the end result is not too different from my self-perpetuating board. This is also its disadvantage relative to my proposal: stockholders remain in control, and it is likely (and indeed Lipton contemplates this) that stock price performance will be an important factor in whether or not directors are reelected.

But that's really sort of quibbling. It's probably not unreasonable to care about the five-year performance of a corporation's stock. The basic idea is the same, although what I have written thus far suggests that if there is to be a check on directorial power by means of periodic elections it is not obviously the stockholders who should do the voting. While I don't want to thoroughly develop the proposal here, largely for reasons of space and because the parameters of the issue and its resolution are clear enough to facilitate intelligent public debate, the corporate franchise could rather easily be extended to a broader variety of constituencies. There is no reason, for example, that a corporation's employees and creditors couldn't vote along with the stockholders. Certainly the employees have a kind of knowledge about the corporation and its business that the stockholders lack, and creditors, like stockholders, have interests in the long-term well-being of the corporation. I admit that extending the net more broadly creates practical problems and also makes the directors' election begin to resemble a legislative election (which begs the question of why we don't have the government appoint directors—and there are a lot of reasons that keep me from suggesting that). But there's no reason to think, unless you view stock price maximization as the corporation's only legitimate goal, that allowing employees and creditors to vote too would damage the corporation.[h]

I am not suggesting, as some reformers have, that workers and creditors be allowed to elect their own representatives to the board. That idea seems to me contrary to the spirit of my entire critique. The general American rule, which if it were followed and backed up by the right structures and incentives would be a good one, is that every director is responsible to the entire corporation. My proposal retains that spirit—it just makes it more likely to work.

Now I know that a lot depends on voting power; there are more shares of stock than workers in most public companies, so it's probable employees could be outvoted. But if elections were to become real horse races (and Lipton suggests some reforms of proxy voting

[h]The principal argument that has been made against employee and creditor participation in voting is that their interests are different from those of stockholders: employees and creditors would be more interested in the stability of the corporation over the long term, while stockholders benefit from greater risk taking with the related potential for greater financial rewards. There is, of course, some soundness to this view. But if I'm right about the short-term pressures created by stockholder voting, it seems reasonable to include within the corporate franchise constituent groups whose interests would tend toward the longer term.

rules that might make them just that), there is no reason a priori to assume that stockholders as a group would choose different directors than employees as a group. It all depends on how things are going and the individual investors' time horizon. The flaw in my modification of Lipton's suggestion is the flaw embedded in that suggestion itself: Making directors accountable to constituencies with specific interests will lead them to favor those interests unless the incentive structures to do so are broken. That's why I prefer the self-perpetuating board, along with the elimination of the stock price maximization rule.

INFORMATION

Another piece of the puzzle needs a bit of fleshing out. Central to Lipton's proposal is that the board provide extensive audited and *evaluated* information, looking five years back and five years forward. That makes a lot of sense and seems essential if his idea is to work. But whether you reject his proposal, my proposal, or any other proposal and think that for some reason annual board elections are a good idea, there is yet another more moderate suggestion which can help break managements' incentives to focus on the short term: lengthen the periods between financial reports.

Under current federal securities laws, every registered corporation has to file quarterly and annual financial reports with the Securities and Exchange Commission, parts of which go to the stockholders.

Now someone who takes long-term investing seriously (I hate to keep using Warren Buffett as the example, but he really is the prime role model, at least for this) recognizes that quarterly changes in performance are close to meaningless and even annual changes, though somewhat more revealing, are not of earth-shattering importance. This is especially true if you pick your investments carefully in the first place and understand that your corporations, like any corporation, will suffer temporary ups and downs.

If our goal were to try to stabilize our capital markets and free management from short-term pressures so that they felt empowered to manage for the long term, we might all get together and agree that we wouldn't make buy and sell decisions on the basis of quarterly reports, and that we might not make them even on the basis of annual reports. The problem is, even if each of us individually thinks this is a good idea, we don't have a mechanism to call a group meeting on the subject, no way to draw up some norms of restraint. We don't really individually have a way of signaling to other investors that if they behave the way we all agree is right, so will we. As a result, we live in a market environment in which we are at a competitive disadvantage if we don't account for price movement and volatility in making our investment decisions.

So what do you do in a situation like this? You do what Ulysses did when faced with the Sirens' song and with his lack of confidence in his self-restraint: you tie yourself to the mast. In financial terms, this would mean changing the securities laws to lengthen the periods between financial reports. We'd certainly want to eliminate quarterly reporting. And we might also get rid of annual reports. Maybe we'd require them every two years or every three years or every five years, as Lipton suggests (although he nowhere advocates eliminating the current system of reporting — just enhancing it).

Nothing would stop companies from voluntarily reporting more frequently. In fact there may be entire industries, like those involved in high technology, for which more frequent reporting reflects business realities better than longer reporting periods. These industries could be treated as exceptions in any new regulated reporting regime. But in the new environment, frequent reporting would be a risky business: live by the short term, die by the short term. The entire reform would be aimed at giving managers greater freedom to let their long-term plans mature, to free them from the fear of stockholder wrath, and to let them make investments that might not pay off for several years and that might reduce earnings per share. If they really want to risk short-term pressures, nothing would stop them.

And nothing would stop shorter-term speculators either. In the first place, speculation by definition means guessing, and nothing would prohibit their guessing between financial reporting periods. In addition, I've said only that we should extend the interval between financial statements, not deprive the investment community of information altogether — managers could prepare all the quarterly and annual narrative reports they like, talk about their plans, successes, and failures, all ultimately subject of course to existing antifraud laws. The goal is not to keep everyone in the dark, but merely to remove the perverse incentive that prevents long-term management.

Chapter 6

**TRADITIONAL
STOCKHOLDERS:
THE NIGHT OF THE
LIVING DEAD**

How many times a day do you log on to the Internet to check your
stock prices? How much do you know or care about the corporations in which you invest — how they treat their employees, where
they do business, what their environmental record is? How much do
you treat stocks like the day trader quoted in the *Washington Post:*
"Who cares whether it's a car company or a chemical company?
Who cares what they're going to be doing in 2000?" One study
reports that there are approximately fifty thousand people engaged
in day trading every single day. These investors have a profound
effect on stock prices and market volatility, trade solely on rumor
and volume, and care nothing of and know nothing about the corporations in which they invest.

And remember the data I discussed in the introduction that show
that stock market volatility has increased dramatically. On Wednes-
day, March 8, 2000, as I was writing this chapter, total trading volume on the New York Stock Exchange was slightly over one billion
shares, and total trading on the NASDAQ was just under two billion
shares. That's a lot of shares of stock changing hands every day.

Modern finance theory supports the thinking of day traders, at
least to some degree. It tells them that corporate stock is nothing
other than a measure of its risk in relationship to that of other stock.
And the way to handle this risk is to develop a diversified portfolio
of securities. As the popularity of index funds demonstrates, once

you've done this, the particular corporation doesn't matter at all. All that matters is the risk and return it represents in your portfolio. Long-term, responsible corporate management will not become the norm until we change our attitude as stockholders, until we see that the individual corporation *is* what matters.

If American corporate directors are encouraged to be Mr. Hyde, traditional corporate stockholders, by which I mean individuals who invest their money in the stock market, are encouraged to behave as if they were among the living dead. They are encouraged to act as if they had no conscience, no soul, no responsibility for their ownership. They are encouraged to care only for themselves. Who reads a proxy statement? Who bothers to return proxy cards and vote for directors? Who thinks or cares about the long-term direction of the business? But who cares about daily stock prices? Individual stockholders are encouraged to behave as if their single goal were the consumption of corporate wealth. Former Securities and Exchange Commission Chairman Arthur Levitt recently criticized on-line brokers' get-rich-quick advertising as "trivial[izing] a process that is so crucial and so important."

The question is why U.S. stock markets have become even more casinolike than ever before. Why have stockholders become completely detached from the corporations in which they invest? There are several answers, all boiling down to the central theme of this book: stock price maximization.

ALLOCATING CAPITAL AND PROVIDING LIQUIDITY— THE ROLE OF THE EQUITY MARKETS

Forgive me for going over some basic material, but I think it's important to reflect on the question of why we have stock markets in the first place before engaging in a specific discussion of the problems of the American stockholder. There are two components to the American equity markets, which I am defining broadly to include all of the national and regional exchanges as well as the NASDAQ.[a] The primary market is the market for new issues: initial

[a]There is another important capital market which is beyond the scope of

public offerings and subsequent offerings by public corporations which are designed to raise capital for the issuer. These are usually underwritten by investment banking firms, which purchase all of the securities to be sold directly from the issuer at a discount from the issuance price and then resell them to the public. The difference is referred to as the underwriting commission or spread. This is how underwriters make their money, and it's how corporations obtain the capital they need to finance their businesses. Of course they can also obtain capital by borrowing money, that is, issuing debt, but that presents a different set of problems from the ones I want to talk about here. In 1997, some $82.4 billion of new common stock was issued in the United States. The market value of sales of stock on all registered exchanges was $6.879 trillion, with an additional $4.482 trillion traded on NASDAQ.[1] So only $82 billion of a total of more than $11 trillion in stock transactions, about .74 percent, consisted of issuances of new stock.

Obviously the secondary market is where most of the action occurs (over 99 percent, to be precise) and where most of the problems come from. Now don't get me wrong, the secondary market is very important. That is the market in which people who decide they no longer want to own their shares of Intel or General Electric or AT&T find, usually through brokers, people who want to buy those shares. It's just like the market for used cars, although ideally a lot more profitable. The secondary market simply is the aggregate of all of the individual transactions between buyers and sellers of stock that has already been issued. The buyers get the stock; the sellers get the money; the corporation gets nothing.

The importance of the secondary market is fairly obvious. There are only two ways you can get your money out of a corporation: first,

---

my discussion here, and that is the *internal* market through which individual corporations make capital allocation decisions as to the projects they will invest in. Clearly this market is related to the capital markets which are external to the corporation, but what I have to say about the latter should be sufficient to suggest their effect on the former. Greater discussion of the internal markets and their relationship to external markets may be found in Michael Porter, *Capital Choices.*

when the directors declare dividends, usually a return *on* your capital, that is, the corporation's earnings, rather than *of* your capital, the money you invested; and, second, when the corporation liquidates and dissolves, in which case you get your investment or whatever is left of it back. Now the latter is a relatively rare occurrence, and in fact the former is becoming increasingly rare as well. And you want these to be rare occurrences because a company's liquidation is usually a sign that it hasn't done very well, and excessive dividends suggest that your corporation's directors don't know how to invest its cash. But look at the problem: once you've invested your money in the corporation you have no way of getting it back, and you might as well assume that you're locked in forever. I suspect that not terribly many people would be enthusiastic about investing money if they thought they'd never see it again.

This is the importance of the secondary market. One of the characteristics of stock ownership is the right, within some federal restrictions, to sell that stock generally whenever you want and to whomever you want. This is the principal way most people realize a return of their capital. And for corporations that don't pay dividends, it's also the principal way most people realize a return on their capital, as the money that would otherwise have been paid out in dividends gets reinvested in the company to generate greater profits and higher share prices.

That's the way it's supposed to work. And, to a large extent, that's the way it does work. The primary market provides investment capital; the secondary market provides liquidity. The secondary market serves another function as well. To the extent that stock trades are based on investors' assessments of the future economic well-being of their corporations, they provide information through the simple law of supply and demand. If more people are selling Coke stock than buying it because more people think its prospects are less than rosy, the price will go down. Conversely, if more people are buying Cisco stock than are selling it because they perceive Cisco to be one of the driving forces of the new technology economy, the price goes up. Such information is useful in the primary market because when these companies want to issue new stock it allows them to "correctly" price the issue, that is, set a price at which it will sell. The main social function this serves is to ensure that capital in the primary markets is allocated correctly, that is, to those issuers who appear most likely to make the best use of it.

There have always been people who choose companies carefully, invest in them, and hold the stock until they need to sell it to buy a house or send a child to college or to have funds available for retirement. And there have always been people who have speculated in stock by taking advantage of price movements or anticipated price movements based either on information from the company or market psychology. One of the market psychologists was the great English economist John Maynard Keynes, who spent an hour trading from his bed each morning and wound up making quite a pile of money. He described the market as something like the beauty contests English newspapers used to run. They would publish the pictures of a number of women, and the winner was the person who correctly identified the most attractive of them. Of course the way to win was not to pick the woman *you* thought was most attractive, but rather the one you thought the greatest number of *other* people would identify as most attractive. That's the psychology of secondary market speculation.

But while speculators may play an important market role — for example, in ferreting out information and helping to move stock prices to their correct levels, which affects the primary market and thus the allocation of capital — the principal purpose of the secondary markets, at least historically, was to provide liquidity.

Is this still the primary purpose of the secondary markets? If not, are the secondary markets only about speculation? If they are, is that a good and healthy thing for corporate governance, resource allocation, and the well-being and sustainability of our economy?

The trading volume by number of shares in 1970 was 4.23 billion. This compares with 21.11 billion in 1980, 82.59 billion in 1990, and 508.6 billion in 1999.[2] In 1970, about 30.5 million Americans owned some kind of stock, directly or indirectly.[3] In 1999, that number had risen by over two and a half times to 78.7 million.[4] *But the volume of shares traded increased over 120 times,* and the value of the shares traded increased more than 173 times. Now maybe a lot more people were buying houses or sending kids to college in 1999. But it sure looks like something has changed.[b]

As the stories with which I began this chapter indicate, the changes have not escaped public attention. It seems unquestionable that secondary market speculation isn't just for professionals anymore — that in fact it is the driving force of the dramatic increases in our capital markets. There are, undoubtedly, lots of reasons this may have happened.

OF EFFICIENT MARKETS, PORTFOLIO THEORY, AND RATIONAL APATHY

Modern finance theory offers a stunning array of justifications for contemporary market behavior and even some plausible empirical and theoretical explanations. It does not, however, offer any sort of normative excuses for the behavior we've seen, and so I'd like to take the economists on their own terms and describe what follows as purely positive, that is, as an observation of what is rather than what should be.

When it comes to investing, finance theory is intertwined. So I'll start with a little deep background and then go on to explain the way modern financial economists have defined the world.

There are, as far as the history of twentieth-century financial thought goes, a few ideas that transcend Keynes's bedroom trading.[5] The first comes from John Burr Williams, whose ideas more or less gave birth to the dividend discount model of valuing stock.[6] Earnings had been, as they still often are, taken as a central measure of a company's and therefore a stock's performance. But earnings are the product of accounting conventions, and while they may give some indication of a corporation's profitability they do not reveal the amount of cash it generates.[c] Viewing the world from the per-

[b]The *2000 Securities Industry Fact Book* reports that the supply of equities diminished over the five-year period ended 1999 while demand significantly increased.

[c]Earnings are determined by a complex set of rules that involve timing,

spective of an investor whose major interest is the cash he can reap from the stock, Williams suggested that looking at the dividends a company would pay—that is, the cash that would come out of it—was a far more potent indicator of value than earnings. The way to value stock, then, was to project the amount of cash the company would produce for the foreseeable future, make some reasonable predictions as to future growth beyond that point, and discount the total amount down to present value. The discount rate you used would combine an element for the time value of money and an element for the risk that you anticipated taking with the particular company. Then you would know what the stock would be worth—not without some guesswork and judgment mind you but in the ballpark.

Now that's one way of doing it. Investors still use it, just as they still use earnings, net assets, and other aspects of the corporation's individual characteristics to come up with estimates of value. But all of these methodologies have one thing in common: they focus on fundamental aspects of the company, the characteristics that make it special and unique, and that includes not only numbers but the nature of its business, its management, and everything else you could find out about it. This style of investing, called fundamental analysis, was championed by the finance professors David Dodd and Benjamin Graham in their famous book *Security Analysis* (1934). It is the method still used today by their disciple, Warren Buffett, and by a number of investors known commonly as value investors. It is a method that, curiously, remains out of favor.

Things began to change, starting with real breakthroughs in the academy in the early 1950s and on Wall Street in the 1970s, in ways that are intertwined and complex. I'll try to lay out the various strands in a way that shows how they all come together and create the modern legal model of the stockholder.

Let's begin with a basic truth developed by the economist Harry Markowitz, a truth known to economists as portfolio theory. The

---

inventory, depreciation of assets, tax matters, and the like. Some of these involve noncash adjustments to earnings. Thus earnings, as far as the corporation's cash goes, can be a misleading number. Cash, on the other hand, is cash.

idea is very simple, so simple that it's embodied in a folk saying: "Don't put all your eggs in one basket." (I don't mean to poke too much fun at economists for proving the obvious. After all, it's nice to know that what we know to be true is in fact true. I'm just not sure why they give Nobel Prizes for it—maybe it's because the economists use nifty mathematical models that the rest of us don't really understand but are comforted by because they look so much more authoritative than our intuitions.) Anyway, Markowitz showed that if you bought a group of stocks rather than a single stock and paid a little bit of attention to what the companies did so that there was some balance to what you bought (though it didn't have to be a lot), you could cancel out a lot of the specific risks of owning stock in a particular company and still make a pretty good return.

An example will make the obvious even more so. Assume you buy stock in a company that makes sunscreen. If that's all you own, and the weather is rainy one summer, you're likely to lose money. But now let's say you also buy stock in a company that makes umbrellas. Voila! You profit from the rainy season, and that offsets your losses in the sunscreen company. As my fourteen-year-old son would say, "Duh!" (Of course he doesn't have a Nobel Prize—yet.)

Anyway, the important thing for our purpose is the implication of portfolio theory (which by the way is an implication that is part of the force behind the development of mutual funds). If you own a reasonably diversified portfolio of stock, you don't have to worry about or really pay attention to any specific corporation because the return you are looking for is a return on your portfolio as a whole, not on any individual stock. And the risks of owning any individual stock are balanced out by diversification. You can do it yourself or you can buy a mutual fund and let somebody else do it—either way, once you're invested the uniqueness of any individual corporation becomes entirely irrelevant to you.

Now there's a greater advance on this theory, one that became all the rage in the 1980s and early 1990s, although it has lost some of its charm by now: that is an investment theory known by the impressive name of the capital assets pricing model (CAPM). A logical, if more mathematically sophisticated, advance on basic portfolio theory, CAPM skips the corporation entirely—we don't even have to look at what the company makes anymore — and goes directly to what we are presumed to care about, stock price movement. Simply put, CAPM theorizes that the price of a stock moves in some proportion to the rest of the market, and that proportion is determinable for any given corporation's stock. All you do is perform a regression analysis, evaluating the way the stock has moved in relation to the market as a whole in the past. This gives you a number, called beta, which tells you the relative risk of your stock to the market as a whole. For example, according to the beta book compiled by PaineWebber for April 2000, Lexmark International Group had a beta of 1 (a beta of exactly 1 is rare). This means that if the market as a whole goes up one point, so does a share of Lexmark. Likewise if it goes down.

The implications of CAPM are striking, especially when you combine it with portfolio theory. Because now you don't need to look at whether the corporation makes sunscreen or umbrellas — all you need to look at is its beta. And you decide the level of risk with which you're comfortable and then put together a portfolio of stocks using their betas. That's it.

Both of these theories do make an underlying assumption, one that ties together all of modern finance theory. The assumption is that the stock market is efficient. Not to worry — it's an assumption that, at least for a while, had some empirical proof behind it. In 1970, the economist Eugene Fama published a paper reviewing the literature on market efficiency and concluding that the stock markets were at least semistrong efficient.[7] What this means is that there is enough information and enough traders (and that transaction costs are low enough) so that at any given time the price of a share of a corporation's stock reflects all of the company's past information (no big deal) and all of its publicly available current information as well (a much bigger deal). The implication of this is fairly important: at any given time and for any given stock, the market knows all, which means that each company's stock trades at the supposed right price. You can beat the market only if you have inside information.

Maybe it's not surprising that Fama's article was followed by a widely publicized spate of insider trading in the early to middle

1980s. But for the average person who had no access to inside information or wouldn't use it if he did, the implication is clear: don't bother trying to beat the market because you can't. Just assemble your diversified portfolio and sit back and collect reasonable, but not extraordinary, returns.

The late 1990s showed that ideas about market efficiency were at least questionable and have gone from near-gospel to real controversy. The stock market volatility and trading volumes I've described seem like good enough evidence of this.[8] (Just as a reminder, daily trading in 1998 on all exchanges reached 1.6 billion shares, an increase of 1,300 percent from 1982, when 113 million shares were traded daily.)[9] Controversy over the theory didn't stop the Supreme Court from basing an entire jurisprudence on it, nor did it stop lots of investors from putting their money into index funds and other widely diversified mutual funds, contributing enormously to the growth of institutional investors (the subject of the next chapter). My point for the moment is what happened when people believed that the efficient market theory was right. When you embellish it with portfolio theory and CAPM, you have a logic that denies the importance of any single company to the capital markets or your portfolio, a logic that denies the uniqueness of any single company, and instead argues for understanding such companies as nothing more than the risks and returns associated with their stock. It is a logic far removed from that of the individual businessman who runs his own small company, or the family corporation, or even the investment technique of Graham and Dodd and Buffett. It is the logic of the day trader whose statement began this chapter: who cares what the company does, what the company makes, what the company's long-term prospects are — or for that matter, how it behaves? How is its stock doing and how does it fit into my portfolio?

This is not an attitude that produces caring stockholders. It is certainly not an attitude that would lead a stockholder to read an annual report or proxy statement, much less to fill out and return a proxy card and vote for directors. It is not an attitude that would lead a stockholder to pay any attention to whether the corporation was closing factories and destroying towns, making exploding cars, or employing slave labor in Burma; that would lead a stockholder to feel any loyalty to or concern with the corporation at all. It is an attitude that would lead a stockholder to focus solely upon the price of the corporation's stock.

The point is that finance theory, no matter how descriptive it may claim to be, has significant normative implications. And finance theory can be wrong. Right or wrong, however, it is important that we understand these normative implications, that we see the kinds of behavior that finance theory, trickled down through the business schools to the analysts and traders and portfolio managers to the masses, produces. And it is especially important and interesting to see the ways in which finance theory and legal theory intersect.

THE LEGAL MODEL OF THE STOCKHOLDER

How does this financial model of investing (or stockholder perspective or whatever you'd like to call it) relate to the model of the stockholder constructed by law? The answer turns out to be that it relates very well, with the longer-standing legal model reinforced by the more modern financial model. The result is to produce legally constructed actors who predictably behave more like automatons than the corporation or its managers and wreak havoc on corporate accountability and responsibility in the process.

You already know something about the stockholder model. As I discussed in chapter 5, stockholders have the power to vote on certain limited matters, including the election of directors, bring derivative litigation, and sell their shares. It was long believed, at least before the takeover wars of the mid-1980s, that these powers were relatively meaningless, that stockholders were impotent to effect a change in directors, that (as I've described the rules governing derivative litigation) stockholder suits were hard to bring and generally ineffective, and that the principal mode of selling a corporation was a merger, which required board of director approval and sometimes wound up preceded by a proxy fight that the directors controlled.

The 1980s challenged some of these ideas about stockholder

power. But at the same time that the events of the eighties and the decade following resulted in some very real stockholder empowerment through the device of the hostile takeover, they also exacerbated the short-term profit mentality prevalent in the market today.[d]

The change didn't occur in the more traditional legal mechanisms of voting and suing, although there was and still is hope within the institutional investor community that the extraordinary rise in institutional holdings will result in a more effective franchise. Rather the change came about as hostile takeovers showed stockholders they had the power as a group to sell the company out from under management. Of course they couldn't and didn't act as a group. Stockholders generally are too widely dispersed to be able to coordinate their actions, again excepting institutional stockholders. In fact the recognition of this prompted state courts and then legislatures to create ways for the incumbent board to act as a central negotiating mechanism for the stockholders.

It might appear at first that if the board were put in a position to negotiate for stockholders they could serve their own interests at the same time and so the stockholders aren't really empowered in a meaningful way. But courts developed fairly finely tuned rules to determine whether the board was acting in the best interests of the stockholders or for its own benefit. And Delaware went so far as to say that, while the board didn't have to permit the company to be sold at all (and it could prevent the sale through defense measures like poison pills and later by statutory mechanisms), as soon as it decided to take measures that would result in a change of control it was obligated to seek the highest price reasonably available for the stockholders. Clearly a rule about short-term profit maximization. Clearly a rule about stockholder interests.

[d]Some of the stockholder-empowering effects of hostile takeovers were blunted by the rush of states in the 1980s and 1990s to pass management-protective antitakeover legislation. But creative would-be raiders have evaded many of the blocks through the revival of older devices like proxy contests and the use of newer techniques like consent solicitations, through which they replace the board and lift the protections (or satisfy their requirements).

Who is the stockholder and what motivates her? On one level, the answer is simple: the stockholder is you and me. While we have scarcely reached the point of Peter Drucker's neosocialist world of universal stock-ownership,[e] it is the case that as of 1999, some 28.6 percent of the American population in 48.2 percent of all households owned stock in some form.[10] Fifty-three percent of households that owned equities did so in the form of both individual stocks and mutual funds, with 15 percent owning individual stocks only and 47 percent owning only mutual funds.[11] Eighty-five percent of households that owned equities owned at least some of them in a form that placed an intermediary between the shares (and the corporation that issued them) and their owners. But the number of Americans owning equity in some form has dramatically increased, from 19 percent of households (42.4 million individuals) in 1983 to 48.2 percent of households (78.7 million individuals) in 1999.

So things are looking up, as far as the distribution of corporate wealth is concerned, and we have looked at the stockholder and he is us. But is he really us? The answer is far more complex, but ultimately I think it is fair to conclude that stockholders, at least as the law conceives of them, look nothing at all like us. And therein lies a problem, a problem similar to the one I described in the preceding chapter.

I started with the proposition that stockholders are the owners of the corporation and then deconstructed that popular misconception to show that stockholders are not in fact owners in any way we would sensibly recognize as such. The conclusion is compounded when we look at patterns of stock ownership. In the first place, as we

---

[e]I call it neosocialist because, while Drucker envisions a world of virtually universal stockholding, the manner in which he envisions such wealth sharing coming about, through what he calls "pension fund capitalism," seems poorly poised to reduce or eliminate significantly the serious conditions of poverty in which so many Americans (not to mention other humans) live, nor to redress problems of income distribution. While it might go some way toward ameliorating problems of *wealth* distribution, that hardly amounts to the same thing, for reasons I will discuss in chapter 9.

have seen, by far the lion's share of stock owned in the United States is owned through institutions. Sometimes, as in a single-asset ownership vehicle like an employee stock ownership plan, the ultimate beneficial stockholder, in this case the employee, knows what stock he owns, although the way the plan operates requires him to cede his traditional rights of voting, suing, and selling to the plan trustees. He therefore has no control whatsoever over the corporation (or even the choice of investment itself, although he has chosen to work for the particular corporation), and so looks even less like an owner than most stockholders. On the other hand, his choice to work for the corporation sponsoring the plan as well as his ability to contribute to the operations, conduct, and success of the corporation gives him more of a real ownership identity and provides him with potentially greater ownership behavior than other forms of stock ownership. I'll talk about this more in the discussion of employees.

Other forms of indirect ownership are far more removed than this. One suspects that if you polled most owners of mutual funds about what stocks their funds held, they couldn't answer. They certainly would be likely to identify the industry sector as well perhaps as the general investment goals of the fund. And they might be able to name a stock or two. But more than that? Doubtful. It's even more unlikely that they would follow the corporations or even the stock prices of the corporations of that stock which they knew their funds owned because their concern on any given day would be with the fund price, not the individual stock price.

Now notice where we've been going — further and further away from the corporation as a thing in itself and more toward the idea that it is nothing more than one of a number of diversified streams of risk and return. That's the stockholder worldview to which, I suggested, modern portfolio theory leads. And it's no surprise to see this with institutional investment vehicles. After all, a mutual fund is nothing other than a means of diversifying your investments. People who own stock through institutional mechanisms, which is most of us, are unlikely to pay any attention at all to individual corporations. We have, in a very real way, ceded not only our investment decisions but our right to corporate citizenship to the fund managers.

Well, what about individual stockholders? While we still comprise a small percentage of the market, it's not an insignificant amount. In considering what the individual stockholder looks like, let's start with day traders, those spawn of the Internet age who now, according to one study, make up some 17 to 18 percent of the daily trading volume on the New York Stock Exchange and the NASDAQ and 75 to 80 percent of all on-line trades.[12] Unlike stockholders who have relinquished their citizenship by choosing to invest through institutions, day traders are the mercenaries of the corporate world, claiming allegiance to no corporation at all and moving in for the kill to take advantage of price movements with speed and stealth, grab their gains, and get back out before being caught with (heaven forbid) an "investment" that might go down.

That's an unflattering portrait, I know. And I don't mean to suggest that day traders are evil people. But the metaphor is apt, of renegades serving themselves regardless of the consequences. It is apt, that is, unless we can find a socially advantageous justification for their behavior.

Let's step back and try to do that. Day traders are, after all, nothing but speculators. And speculators have always existed in the market, will always exist in the market, and in fact have an economically and socially justifiable role in the market. Even educated investment banks engage in speculation and always have — but they call it market making or specializing. What is the function of speculation and are day traders filling it?

Well, as traditionally practiced, speculation in the form of market making is designed to do something very important for the market: stabilize stock prices. The idea is that, for any number of reasons, the stock price of a given corporation can on any given day suffer a short-term drop or experience a short-term gain because of mismatched supply and demand, for good reason, for no apparent reason, or for reasons that have little if any relationship to the long-term performance of the corporation. If these fluctuations were able to occur unchecked, the liquidity of the corporation's stock in the market, the corporation's ability to raise capital, and the managers' ability to maintain a stable investor base would be threatened, and managers would be facing all of the short-term pressures that they currently do and more. So specialists are obligated to buy and sell stock of the corporations in which they specialize to maintain an orderly market—a reasonable equilibrium of supply and demand. Sometimes they win, sometimes they lose, but that's their job, and they get paid quite well for it.

Speculators serve another function as well. Through research, speculators seek to exploit variances in stock price by using their superior information either to buy securities they think, based on their information gathering, are undervalued, or to sell (or sell short) securities they think, based on that information, are overvalued. If they're good, they make quite a lot of money at this. And they deserve to be well compensated because in taking significant risks they serve an important social function, namely, they help to move stock to its correct price. That is to say, if anything ever said about market efficiency ever were true (and it was and to some extent may still be) — they buy and sell in quantities, or by being watched by other investors who then jump on the bandwagon stimulate buying and selling in quantities sufficient to move the stock price of a given corporation to what it would be if the information that they've worked to acquire (hopefully legally and not in violation of the insider trading rules) were known to the market as a whole. That's a good thing because it helps to serve the principal market function of allocating capital to its highest-value uses. The corporation whose stock is correctly priced will raise equity at the right price and will borrow money at the right interest rate.[f] Any of us could do this job if we had the time, inclination, talent, and taste for risk to do so. But we don't. So speculators serve an important function, and we should be grateful.

Do day traders stabilize the market? Do they help to move stock

[f]The relationship between stock pricing and debt pricing is beyond the scope of my inquiry here. It should be enough to recognize that both are based on the (relatively invariant) time value of money and the risk of investing in the particular corporation.

to its correct price? Do they do anything for us at all? Nope. In fact day traders destabilize the market by their excessive in and out trading to take advantage of stock price fluctuations without regard to the reasons the price is moving; and they do nothing to move the price in the correct direction because they typically know nothing about the corporations in whose stock they trade. Their trading is largely random, based on price movement alone, and so their activities create what is generally referred to as noise — which interferes with market efficiency rather than advances it — and an awful lot of noise at that. So forget about looking to day traders for responsible corporate ownership — we can't expect them even to trade responsibly.

THE REST OF US

So what about the rest of us? What about the 53 percent of the American stockholding population that directly chooses at least some of the corporations in which they will invest, that directly invest in those corporations and receive annual reports and proxy statements? How optimistic can we be about responsible corporate ownership from ourselves?

Well, again the answer doesn't look very good. While data are unavailable (or at least I haven't been able to find any), it is common knowledge that few individual stockholders ever bother to return their proxy cards — or if they do, they simply vote for management's slate — or attend an annual meeting for the election of directors. One would expect that if any stockholders anywhere would make their influence felt it would be in this arena. But one would be wrong. In the first place, as I suggested earlier when I described the implications of modern finance theory, most of these stockholders hold diversified portfolios of stock and have no special concern with the welfare of any given corporation. The logic of diversification is the logic of apathy. And one can hardly blame people for behaving logically.

Even if stockholders wanted to have a direct influence on their corporation's behavior, it would be difficult. Securities laws make it relatively difficult for individual stockholders to have any influence at all, and least so when it comes to issues that deal with responsible corporate behavior. So you wouldn't expect stockholders to push much of a social agenda — they can't. Or rather they can, but only by choosing to invest in corporations of whose behavior they approve, and the barriers to obtaining adequate information on corporate behavior are high.[g] Moreover, as I have previously discussed, limited liability and the norm of stock price maximization are powerful competitive disadvantages to corporations who try to behave well and publicize their practices, unless they also happen to be outperforming the market.

So what's a stockholder to do? Nothing really, but what the combination of law, structure, markets, and accounting rules leads us to do: sit back and watch our gains and losses. The rational stockholder is the apathetic stockholder. The law exacerbates such an attitude by depriving the stockholder of any real power or influence and thus of any real reason to try to influence or even care much about the corporation's conduct. The law provides a maxim of stockholder profit maximization to the corporation and its directors, and so the management is told, in effect, not to look at stockholders as individuated people, not even for purposes of caring about such financial consequences as the diverse tax effects on stockholders of distinct corporate transactions like takeovers. Stockholders are all alike — and what they are is receptacles. You can't expect much input from a receptacle.

LEAD, FOLLOW, OR GET OUT OF THE WAY

So what's the solution? One answer is simply to do nothing: continue on our current course and let the faceless, soulless market push corporations as they will through the combined and often

[g]I've already discussed the limitations of modern accounting practices. There is a nascent move to require forms of social accounting and social auditing, both in the accounting profession and as a form of disclosure under the federal securities laws, but these movements have their own difficulties and have yet to bear much fruit. I'll discuss some of these problems in the concluding portion of this chapter.

disparate forces of institutions, day traders, professional speculators, and long-term investors. As I've already argued at some length, though, if this is the course we choose it is unlikely to be sustainable in the long run. Our economy may run on steam for a while. But the short-term pressures that the modern construct of the stockholder puts on corporate management are designed to lead to long-term disaster.

We have two options. Either we ignore stockholders entirely, which doesn't seem like a plausible or even very desirable solution in a world in which stockholders ultimately supply the principal capital on which our businesses are built (although when we look at the German system in chapter 11 we will see a successful alternative to a system based principally on equity capital, even as it is one that the Germans appear to be, for reasons I shall discuss, abandoning). Or we can change the incentives that shape stockholder behavior. I won't pretend that the circumstances are ripe for a wholesale transformation from stockholder apathy to stockholder activism — nor do I think, for the reasons I've already given, that this outcome would be highly desirable. But we can create incentives for stockholders to behave more like long-term investors, thereby giving management the space and room it needs to manage for the long term in a responsible and accountable manner and without the pressure of having to respond to the modern construct of the apathetic stockholder demanding instant gratification.

LOYAL CAPITAL IS HAPPY CAPITAL

Why should we as a society care about stockholder loyalty to any particular corporation? Why should managers care? What difference does it make to the profitability and responsibility of our corporations? What difference does it make to the well-being of our society?

A lot. Let's start with the words of Warren Buffett, the acknowledged guru of long-term investing. Several years ago I wrote about Buffett's approach to cultivating stockholder loyalty and suggested that one reason for his success might be nothing more than the extraordinary performance of Berkshire Hathaway stock, coupled with the fact that the Buffett family group held 46 percent of Berkshire Hathaway's common shares; I speculated that a substantial downturn in the price of Berkshire Hathaway might one day lead to dilution of that loyalty.[13] Well, that day is upon us. Berkshire Hathaway's Class A common stock dropped from a high of $78,600 per share in 1999 to $40,800 and had rebounded to $59,300 at the time of this writing. Yet the trading volume of Berkshire Class A stock during the months of decline was an astonishingly low average of three hundred shares.[h]

Why the loyalty? As Buffett writes, "In large part, companies obtain the shareholder constituency that they seek and deserve. If they focus their thinking and communications on short-term results or short-term stock market consequences they will, in large part, attract shareholders who focus on the same factors. And if they are cynical in their treatment of investors, eventually that cynicism is highly likely to be returned in the investment community." I'll have more to say about Buffett later. But what he says is quite consistent with what I've written so far and, perhaps far more important, is simply common sense. This idea is echoed by the management consultant Frederick Reicheld, who writes, "Many managers find it nearly impossible to pursue long-term, value-creating strategies without the support of loyal, knowledgeable investors." Reicheld advocates corporate programs to educate investors as to the benefits to themselves of loyal, patient capital and attempts to teach management the substantial benefits they will derive from such an approach.

[h]I recognize that it may well be that the relative stability of Berkshire's stockholder base may be owing at least in part to investors' unwillingness to realize significant losses when the potential for price appreciation continues to exist. But the fact that 97 percent of Class A Berkshire stockholders who start every year with the company continue to own the stock at the end of each year implies long-term ownership and suggests that most could still get out with substantial gains despite the drop in price and despite Buffett's prediction, in his letter to shareholders in Berkshire's 1999 annual report, of substantially lower returns. See Berkshire Hathaway, Inc., 1999 and 1997 Annual Reports.

So forget about responsibility. Loyal and patient capital is good for business. But it's also necessary to permit management to demonstrate the kinds of accountability that not only contribute to the long-term bottom line but are also simply good and right behavior. Reicheld tells, for example, of John Deere's policy of limiting its profit margins on replacement parts specifically to prevent customers from feeling gouged and building loyalty for business purposes. But taking advantage of a captive market is also simply wrong. He describes State Farm's behavior in the wake of Florida's devastating Hurricane Andrew in 1993. Unlike other insurance companies, which paid claims and refused to renew customers' policies, State Farm actually overpaid claims to enable its customers to replace substandard roofs with roofs that met liability codes. Good behavior, good business. But the results of such good behavior won't be apparent to stockholders in the short term; in order to make them understand the business benefits, they need to be in it for the long haul. In order for managers to behave so responsibly, they have to educate their stockholders as to the benefits. For we cannot assume, at least in the short run, an overwhelming wave of stockholder concern with corporate behavior for its own sake. So we have to work toward that goal first by disseminating an understanding of these benefits in business terms.

When I put the matter in business terms — at least in terms of profit — I am by no means abandoning my argument for responsible, accountable behavior for its own sake. I am not sacrificing the language of moral responsibility for the more pragmatic approach of business benefit. That would undercut my argument substantially, for reasons I've already discussed: Good behavior justified in business terms extends only as far as the marginal benefits exceed the marginal costs. And that might extend far or it might not. As Buffett, whose record on moral business behavior is spotty, put it, "I won't close down businesses of sub-normal profitability merely to add a fraction of a point to our corporate rate of return. However, I also feel it inappropriate for even an exceptionally profitable company to fund an operation once it appears to have unending losses in prospect." Moral corporate behavior recognizes the need for profitability earned in a manner responsible to all those whose lives the corporation touches. A pure profit-maximizing argument gives a moral out.

But, having made the moral argument at some great length, I will base my reform suggestions in this chapter on business justifications. The reason is simple and as old as Aristotle's argument for compelling people to behave as if they were virtuous even if they failed to understand the reasons for virtuous behavior. It's an argument that is popularly summarized today as "fake it 'till you make it." The argument is that if you behave as if you were responsible, as if you accepted and understood the reasons for your behavior, eventually you would come to understand the reasons for your behavior and internalize the moral principles which underlie it. It's not too far off from the way Piaget observed kids develop their moral consciences.

Okay. I know that sounded arrogant, paternalistic, and elitist. Nobody ever accused Aristotle of being a populist. But it's not an arrogant argument at all. In fact if you've followed me to this point you probably agree that something in our current corporate system is terribly wrong. But you may not know quite what (although I'm trying to explain it), and even if you do know what's wrong you're almost certainly unable to act by yourself. Moreover, not one of us, including me, is exempt from the temptations of greed, and to sacrifice big returns today for a sustainable future is indeed an act of sacrifice, especially when done alone. And there are undoubtedly a number of people who are sufficiently unreflective or sufficiently greedy that they don't care. Well, they need to be brought along for the greater good. So my suggestions are aimed at overcoming collective action problems and at giving us a chance to stop, breathe, see what we've done, and come to understand the collective responsibilities of stockholders — not the legal construct of stockholders, not the anonymous market, but the flesh and blood stockholders that we are — for the future health and well-being of our corporations, of our economy, and of our children. That's not arrogant or elitist — it's our responsibility.

Creating incentives for long-term management and patient capital isn't easy. People buy and sell stock for a lot of reasons, even within fairly short periods of time, and it would be a serious mistake to prohibit or interfere with legitimate activity while attempting to curb abuses. Some forms of restraint are more appropriately reserved for the discussion of institutional investors in the next chapter. But the argument so far has pointed to a number of possible solutions that I will set forth here simply as suggestions for thinking about reform. It may be that some of them are worth adopting, but the main point is to stimulate thinking about ways to solve problems.

LENGTHEN FINANCIAL REPORTING PERIODS
AND CHANGE ACCOUNTING RULES

The first suggestion, or set of suggestions, begins with an idea I discussed in chapter 5, so I will not belabor the point. It is to lengthen corporate reporting periods in order to eliminate pressure on management to produce good short-term numbers and to allow them to focus on the long term, as well as to eliminate the spectacle of speculative reactions by the stock market and its concurrent destabilizing effect based on short-term numbers. Allowing managers to focus on the long term will make stockholders behave more as if they were real owners of the corporation and will lead management to act on that ownership function more responsibly, both for the long-term financial health of the corporation and for the greater welfare of society as a whole.

But the answer depends on far more than the less frequent reporting of numbers. I have already noted several times that *what* you measure and the way in which you measure it are as critically important to the ultimate direction and behavior of the enterprise as anything else. There has been a great deal of recent work on revising accounting inputs and procedures to rethink the way we treat costs, expenses, investments, and the like. It is odd that short-term corporate wealth decreases when management spends money on things like R&D and employee training that are treated as current expenses but are designed to increase corporate profitability in the long run.

These observations lead to one possible conclusion, and that is to revise the way we think about costs and expenses. Maybe some employment costs are really investments in long-term increased productivity. Investment in workers and in R&D clearly can be seen as a down payment on future profits, much like building a new factory. So capitalizing at least some of these expenses rather than taking them as current hits to the bottom line would create a powerful incentive to increase them for a collective long-term benefit. A corporation that forgoes the opportunity to squeeze its last profits for the sake of improving customer relations to develop a loyal consumer base is one that may well enjoy the best results in the end, although it may do less well than its competitors in the short term. And a corporation that does all of these things is, at least implicitly, recognizing its responsibility to those whose lives are impacted by its behavior, as well perhaps to the broader community of which it is a part. So at least as a first step, revising accounting rules so that these long-term investments are not treated as short-term costs is a good idea.

But it may not be enough to take the current accounting structure and alter the inputs. The sociologist Fred Block, in his account of modern economic policy, suggests that the problem lies not only with the inputs but with the entire way we think about economic enterprises.[14] Block presents a way of looking at the economic world from the perspective of what he describes as economic sociology. The principal difference between traditional economics and Block's approach is that while the former assumes self-interested actors seeking to maximize their wealth in relatively free and efficient markets, the sociological approach taken by Block recognizes that economic systems and thus economic behavior are both socially constructed and necessarily embedded in historical, social, and political structures (much in the way I have argued that we should see the modern corporation).

This insight, which seems fairly obvious to anyone who looks out the window of the ivory tower, is important in the implicit critique, made explicit by Block, that it levels at our entire financial reporting system — and indeed our entire financial understanding of the corporation. Corporate profitability depends on measurable inputs and outputs. But it depends at least as heavily upon the organizational structure in which collective behavior takes place, the interactions among managers and employees, and the effects on all personnel of new technologies and new ways of organizing business. The point is that form, behavior, culture, incentives, human synergies, technologies, job descriptions, and the like have impacts on corporate value: they are part of the inputs that create or reduce value, and they are inherently difficult to measure precisely.

These dilemmas are more than theoretical — the inability or unwillingness to account for social factors in evaluating corporate performance can create incentives for managers to avoid making changes and investments and to avoid taking risks. They can create incentives for employees to shun participation, avoid responsibility, work at minimal levels. If you truly manage what you measure, then perhaps it is time to start measuring or at least finding ways of accounting for these factors, which every manager and employee intuitively knows are important but is afraid to base decisions upon because of the challenges in making quantitative justifications and the difficulty of defending mistakes.

Understanding the need to reconceptualize the inputs and outputs of the corporation is important. Peter Drucker has recently described in detail the shift he claims we largely have undergone from a society in which cash is capital to one in which knowledge is capital. Block too calls the cash society into question. Drucker's view strongly suggests that in a knowledge-based economy the workers are the owners of capital, not in the sense of pension fund ownership and thus indirect ownership of capital stock, but through ownership of the actual means of production, which consists of the knowledge and ability to do things. While I will take this idea up in more detail in chapter 9, the point meshes well with Block's, namely, that our current systems of measurement of corporate performance measure either the wrong thing or only part of the right thing and must be rethought.

Block suggests some alternatives, although he doesn't see a quick solution. As he puts the issue of imaging alternatives, "The problem is circular, since people experience reality through the lenses of the earlier set of categories. In some historical transitions, an extended period of social learning is necessary before an alternative set of concepts begins to appear concrete and practical."[15] Nonetheless, if we fail to take the time to step back, understand our social world and its various aspects as humanly constructed, and consider alternative possibilities, we wind up as prisoners of our own constructions, headed on a course that may or may not lead where we want to go.

Block's alternatives all stem from a reconceptualization of economic growth in a manner that is qualitative rather than quantitative. He suggests that we frankly accept the fact that we cannot measure all of the inputs and relations that in reality (in contrast to a highly constrained and stylized neoclassical economic model) go into economic production. In so doing, we can begin to look at all of the relevant inputs and factors, including organizational and structural factors, and evaluate their effects on growth, productivity, and accountability.

Block is necessarily general about how to make this new approach operational. The most important point he makes is that we should look beyond the amount of growth to the quality of growth, including the effects of growth on the environment and on the creation of meaningful and rewarding work, as well as the effects of increased leisure and education not just on growth but on worker participation and satisfaction, and the like. It sounds like a different way of looking at corporate accountability as we have been discussing it, and of course it is. What is novel about Block's approach is his attempt to demonstrate that there is a qualitative difference — one that affects our happiness — in conceiving of economic growth in terms of numbers and in terms of social inputs.

Now there are clear problems with this approach, problems that disappear when we consider changing some of the employee costs we now consider accounting expenses to assets (as capital acquisitions are treated). The main problem is that it's much more difficult to incorporate this view of the world into the current model of SEC reporting. It doesn't appear on a balance sheet or income statement; it's not quantifiable in the Management Discussion & Analysis section of a corporation's Annual Report on Form 10-K (the MD&A). But that doesn't mean that it's unreportable.

Take, for example, that very MD&A. As currently implemented, it is designed to give management an opportunity to evaluate the changes that have occurred in the corporation's financial performance as well as other material changes. The discussion takes place against the background of the Form 10-K, the corporation's financial statements prepared in accordance with generally accepted accounting principles consistently applied and certified by the corporation's accountants. One could imagine, instead, revising the regulations in order to include analysis based on an annual certification performed by a management consulting firm or a certified business sociologist or organizational theorist that evaluates in a qualitative way the effect of organizational changes, compensation changes, shop-floor changes, changes in technology and production methods, and the like that have taken place over the preceding year. One might even consider including a discussion of community activities, environmental activities, even an ethical section which enables management to discuss decisions it has made or activities it has undertaken that might not necessarily result in short-term profit maximization but that management believed were ethically right or in the corporation's long-term financial interest.

The inclusion of such a report would serve an important symbolic purpose. It would, at a minimum, help to convey to stockholders the belief that the ownership of corporate stock is not ownership as traditionally conceived and is burdened by the same kind of public obligations we expect people to have in the conduct of their individual lives — perhaps even more so given the public privilege that incorporation is. It would also, ultimately, serve to educate stockholders, as well as managers through the process of creating such reports, in a new way of thinking about corporate behavior that is likely to lead not only to greater accountability and responsibility but also perhaps to greater sustained growth and ultimately profitability (although I confess that this last aspect is of less importance to my argument as long as some sufficient degree of profitability is maintained — wealth is *not* a value). Qualitative reporting may not work. But it's a good idea, and it's worth trying. It's also a lot less radical than some of the proposals I have made so far and will continue to make, and so can serve as a first attempt at creating greater corporate accountability before we decide that we need to take more drastic measures.

THE LAST-DITCH ALTERNATIVE—
TAXES, TAXES, TAXES

If all else fails, there is a last-ditch alternative to which we could turn to create incentives for long-term stockholding. Increasing taxes is not a very popular concept these days. But before you completely dismiss the idea (which, remember, I am suggesting only as a final alternative), there is a justification.[16]

Remember the purposes we ascribed to the capital markets, the justifications for their existence? And remember that we discussed the role of speculation in the markets, good forms of speculation as well as bad? Well, if traders are misusing the market, as I suggested most day traders are, then it is our right and duty to restore our capital markets to their proper functioning and purposes. If excessive speculation distorts the market, makes it *less* efficient, and winds up misallocating capital, then excess speculation needs to be stopped. Law enforcement resources are sufficiently scarce (and would be so in this context) that attempting to levy penalties for undesirable speculation probably would fail. But levying penalties by imposing heavy tax burdens on those who misuse the market would not only discourage irrational and damaging speculation but would at the same time enhance federal revenues. The problem is, as we have seen, some forms of speculation stabilize the market. Any taxation solution would have to account for and exempt such beneficial speculation.

There are a number of ways of crafting such taxation programs, although it is beyond my scope here (and my ability) to detail all of them and their potential consequences. As a relatively crude first-ditch effort, we might impose a sliding-scale tax on trading that occurs within an irrationally short period — say, a punitive tax of 75 percent of the profits for trades that take place within a twenty-four-hour period. (I know this is arbitrary, but I am suggesting it only for purposes of stimulating thought.) The amount of tax could go down by, say, several percentage points for each twenty-four- or forty-eight-hour additional holding period, until it levels out after several weeks or a month. Specialists and those who can demonstrate that their principal occupation is speculation, for example, by at least being registered broker/dealers, would be exempted.

This proposal would not radically alter what we already do. We currently distinguish between long-term and short-term capital gains for tax purposes, with advantageous treatment for long-term holdings. And while there has been controversy from time to time over the appropriate tax rates as well as the appropriate holding periods for particular types of assets, the logic underlying this distinction is much the same as the logic underlying my proposal. But the long-term/short-term distinction, introduced in 1921, is now seriously outmoded given the radical changes in the nature of trading in equity markets that I have previously discussed.[i] It seems appropriate to change the tax laws to account for these changes.

If you didn't want to penalize trading in individual accounts in this way, there is another alternative. Pensions, 401(K) plans, and other retirement vehicles receive advantageous tax treatment for the purpose of allowing individuals to build up their wealth over the long term for retirement. If one begins to invest in such a plan relatively early in her employment history and expects to live a normal life span (and indeed has to live to be fifty-nine and a half to begin making withdrawals), then such a plan by definition is a long-term investment vehicle. There is no justification for frequent trading in these plans; if one chooses one's investments carefully and treats them as investments, then there should be no reason, absent extraordinary circumstances, not to stay in a particular stock for the long haul. We could, therefore, pass laws that lift the tax advantages of retirement vehicles by penalizing trades at a given level of frequency or in defined short-term periods.[17]

There is a risk to these schemes. We might not get it exactly right and thus might create unintended consequences like excessive chilling of trading activity and consequential damage to our ability to raise corporate capital efficiently. But I think we're a long way off

[i]Congress has periodically adjusted the holding period for stocks to deal with the market efficiency implications of locking investors into given holding periods in order to gain the tax advantage.

from that stage, and economics as a predictive discipline, aided by the power of modern computers, is probably adequate to the task of anticipating probable financial effects. In any event, the logic is sound, and the solution is one well worth pursuing. Even some short-term harm may well be a cost worth incurring, if the long-term benefits of more accountable and sustainable corporate management are great enough. The point is we don't know. But we should think about it, and my hope is that readers will take the suggestion seriously and that those with economic training will pursue the solution to enable us to understand both its costs and its benefits.

THE NEW
STOCKHOLDER:
KING KONG WITH
A QUOTRON

The traditional stockholder still exists.[1] As frightening as I've made her appear, she's at worst negligent, not, except for day traders, destructive. In this respect, as I've noted, she resembles the aggressively individualistic automaton that has come to caricature American social norms and behavior. As bad as this may be, however, there is worse. For the traditional stockholder has been substantially displaced by institutional stockholders, the massive growth of whom has occurred mostly over the past two decades. Mushrooming through the 1980s and 1990s, institutional stock ownership now accounts for some 58 percent of all equity of the top 1,000 American corporations. And some corporations have most of their stock held by institutions — 85 percent in the case of Coca-Cola. Institutional ownership in the largest 50 companies was 58.2 percent in the third quarter of 1999, with 62.7 percent of Home Depot, 64.4 percent of MCI Worldcom, 61.5 percent of Cisco Systems, and 63 percent of Citigroup controlled by institutional investors.[2] Institutional ownership was as high as 62.5 percent for the top 101–250 companies.[3]

Finally, the number of institutional investors compared with individual stockholders is relatively small, with the 25 largest institutional investors controlling 22.7 percent "of total outstanding equities in 1998, up from 19.7 percent in 1997 and 15.4 percent in

1995,"[4] compared with 49 million households owning 42.4 percent of all outstanding equities in 1999.[a]

Even more startling perhaps, at least to those who have an instinctive fear of great concentrations of wealth, these 25 institutions accounted for 47.9 percent of all institutional equity in the United States. Such figures suggest that this new breed of stockholder is highly concentrated and has enormous potential power. Is that power used? is it used well? That depends on what you mean by "used" and "well." The influence of institutional stockholders over their portfolio companies has been increasing. But it has been increasing for the purpose of maximizing stockholder value. As we shall see in chapter 11, this is a theme that is increasingly heard 'round the world—at least the industrialized world.

Legal scholars in the early to mid-1990s embraced the hegemony of the institutional stockholder with almost messianic fervor. Here, they argued, was the solution to the long-standing problem of the separation of ownership and control, the way to unite stockholding with real managerial oversight in order to better align managerial behavior with stockholder interests, cut down on the costs of monitoring management, and bring in a new age of responsible ownership. Some people still believe this. But the bloom is off the rose.

In the first place, as I will shortly discuss, the promise of institutional stockholder activism has been distinctly less significant than was originally hoped. For the most part, these institutions tend to remain passive and have every incentive to do so. Second, when they do motivate themselves to act, through stockholder proposals at corporate annual meetings or by putting informal pressure on boards of directors, they almost always do so in the name of increasing stockholder profit—and specifically of increasing short-term stock prices.[5] So their activism, to the extent it exists, is based on precisely the problem of corporate governance that I have tried to isolate. Some institutional investors whose purpose is to create and

[a]The 1998 and 1999 data are the best numbers I can find. In 1998, the year given in the text for institutional holdings, households held 41.1 percent of all outstanding equities.

manage funds of "socially responsible" companies have arisen, but they remain relatively few in number. For example, only 175 of a total of 7,500 mutual funds (3,952 equity funds) engaged in some form of "social screening" in 1999. One study, however, by the presumably biased Social Investment Forum, reports that 13 percent of all professionally managed money in 1999 was "part of a socially responsible portfolio."[6]

And there is a great deal of debate as to what it means to be a socially responsible corporation to qualify for such investment. The Social Investment Forum includes within its group of socially responsible investors any institution that employed one or more social screens in determining its investments, sponsored or cosponsored a shareholder resolution on social responsibility issues during the preceding three years, or was what the report calls a "community investment institution." By far, the overwhelming socially responsible activity of choice was social screening, which means that an institution would be counted if, for example, it simply refused to invest in tobacco stocks (as 96 percent of the included institutions do). To be fair, the vast majority also decline to invest in gambling, alcohol, and weapons stocks, but the bulk of the screening activity seems to end there. Although the Social Investment Forum reports, for example, that 79 percent of "screened assets also address environmental concerns," this is a weak criterion as the report defines this screen *either* as avoiding companies with bad environmental records or including companies with good records, the latter being presumably a less rigorous criterion. Moreover, socially responsible investing seems flabby in concept, by which I mean that it doesn't take much — or much of your investment portfolio — to qualify. For example, the Domini Social Equity Fund, the largest of the social investment funds with more than $1.8 billion in assets in March 2000, held substantial portions of its portfolio in the convicted monopolist Microsoft (7.72 percent), Cisco (7.38 percent), and market-dominator Intel (6.15 percent), among others. It looks like the fund's criteria are relatively loose, and its portfolio looks very much like that of any other fund. No wonder the Social Investment Forum proudly proclaims the success of social investing, noting that both the Domini 400 Social Index and the Citizens Index have consistently outperformed the S&P 500. Under these criteria, it's easy to be socially responsible and highly profitable at the same time simply by avoiding Philip Morris.[7] So even if a new day is at hand, it is a new day grounded in the old model.[b]

Here is where the power of institutional investors becomes somewhat frightening. If their principal motivation is to increase stockholder profit (and they have every incentive to do so), and they unite to make their presence felt, then all of the problems we have so far seen to stem from the stockholder profit motive become exacerbated. We should breathe a sigh of relief that they haven't been more effective. But the jury is still out.

To talk of institutional investors is, to be sure, to talk of a somewhat varied group.[8] Generally speaking, they consist of corporate pension funds, public pension funds, mutual funds, money managers, insurance companies, and banks. And they not only have differing investment goals, they are also subject to varying regulatory regimes.[9] The largest group of institutions consists of pension funds, which control 48 percent of institutional holdings, with investment companies controlling 24 percent, banks 12.8 percent, and insurance companies 18 percent.[10] By far the fastest growing group among these is open-end mutual funds, which experienced a 27 percent growth in 1997, outpacing total institutional growth of 18 percent; such expansion reflects at least in part a substantial historical shift in retirement accounts from defined benefit pension plans to defined contribution plans, most of which are invested in diversified funds.

Each of these types of institutions has a characteristic investing agenda. As the Conference Board reported in 2000, they are "not monolithic — instead they pursue a variety of investment strategies that, in turn, produce very different turnover and trading patterns."[11] But the point is that whatever their particular trading strat-

[b]Even as a purely economic matter, giving institutional investors increased power over corporate governance might be counterproductive. As Michael Porter notes, "Giving institutional investors more power over management without changing their goals . . . may heighten pressures toward underinvestment." *Capital Choices.*

egy, they remain sharply focused on stock price as the ultimate measure of corporate achievement.[12] Not only is this how they make money for their investors — it's how the institutional managers usually (but not always, as in the case of public pension funds) are compensated.

If nothing else, you would think that all of this institutional concentration would bring some measure of stability to the market. And it does: institutions trade at a slower rate than individuals. But their rates of turnover are hardly slow. Recall that I earlier noted the dramatically increased rate of turnover on the New York Stock Exchange: in 1930, the turnover rate was, not surprisingly, 67 percent. It was 12 percent in 1960, 19 percent in 1970, 36 percent in 1980, and a whopping 76 percent in 1998.[13] While there is significant variance in the rate of turnover of the different types of institutional investors, they range from a low (although historically rather high) of 33.7 percent for banks to a high of 59.7 percent for money managers, the fastest growing segment, with a weighted average turnover of a still significant 44.3 percent.[14] As Michael Useem more generally put it, "Institutional investors continually trade, increasing or decreasing their holdings by as much as 25 percent or even 50 percent per quarter."[15] Equity markets certainly seem more stable with institutional investors than without them, although based on what we've discussed about individual stockholders that's not saying a whole lot. But it seems pretty clear that institutional investors are significant and active traders.

Who runs the institutions? The power behind each of these stockholders is like the Wizard of Oz behind the curtain — an ordinary person. Consider Peter, a twenty-five-year-old graduate of an Ivy League college. He manages a portfolio for a billion-dollar pension fund. He's a moral person and generally cares about others. But put him in front of his Quotron and he becomes King Kong, pursuing short-term profit with a fervor that makes the search for Ann Darrow, aka Fay Wray, look like a walk in the park.

On the one hand, the growth and concentration of institutional stockholding presents the real possibility of replacing the living dead with real live human beings like Peter. For example, there were only 228 stock mutual funds in 1980 with 5.8 million accounts. By 1999, that had grown to 3,952 with 149 million ac-counts.[16] So there are an awful lot of Americans involved in the stock market, even without regard to pension accounts, who might take an interest in long-term corporate welfare (although for the same reasons I discussed in the last chapter, they generally don't). And, given the size of the institutions through which this stock is held and the large and illiquid positions they hold in various corpo-rations, the institutional managers are human beings with incen-tives to invest for the long term and the potential power to compel responsible corporate behavior.

But who are the people behind these institutions? The example of Peter is drawn from real life, a person with little life experience or exposure to the world who, most importantly, is given the job of maximizing the profits of the institution's investors, just as the cor-porate director is given the job of maximizing stockholder profit. Money managers are young. One report gives their average age as thirty-six, another as twenty-eight, and a third as forty-four, still fairly young considering the vagaries of statistics.[17] (One analyst, com-menting on the reported average age of forty-four, notes that younger managers work longer hours and have more energy, so it's possible that their effect on the market is disproportional to that of their older colleagues). And, worse, his pay depends upon profit maximization. Like most money managers, he is paid on the basis of how much money he makes for the fund in the short run, a fact which focuses his attention on the short-term performance of his portfolio corporations.[18] Instead of using his power as a responsible owner, he is encouraged to use it to increase the short-term focus that managers already have. As one critic notes, "Most money man-agers focus on quarterly profit statements and early cash dividends." This hardly encourages long-term, responsible management.

Before we go further, then, let's look at the current state of institutional investor attitudes and activism.

CORPORATE GOVERNANCE FOR THE BOTTOM LINE

It shouldn't come as a surprise that institutional investors are centrally concerned with portfolio value. A survey in 1999 by the executive and director search firm Russell Reynolds Associates reports that corporate governance has become an increasing focus of institutional investors throughout the industrialized world. So while investor activism may have been relatively insipid in the 1980s and 1990s, the late nineties showed a sharp increase in institutional concern with governance activities. And why? As the survey reports, "The interest of institutional investors in boardroom practice is rooted in a very real concern over the value of their portfolios. . . . Less free than others to 'vote with their feet,' institutional investors have turned to corporate governance activism as one way to pressure boards and senior management to improve corporate performance."[19] Moreover, corporate governance factors into investment decisions, bringing market pressure to bear on managements, just as I have thus far argued the structure of corporate law would suggest. According to the survey, a majority of American institutional investors reported that they have not invested in a corporation or reduced their stake in one because of their dissatisfaction with governance practices.

But governance practices to what end? As I will discuss in more detail in part 3, the two leading governance models are the stockholder-centric model that dominates in the United States and the United Kingdom, sometimes referred to as the Anglo-American model, and a stakeholder model that developed in the European social democracies and Japan, in which the responsibilities of corporate boards and managements extend beyond the stockholders to more or less all of the constituent groups affected by the corporation, from creditors to employees and suppliers, customers, the environment, and the community in general.

There is no question that American institutional investors promote the Anglo-American model with a vengeance.[20] The survey asked institutional investors to rank the priority of interests of different constituencies on a scale of 1 to 6, with 6 being the highest priority. American institutional investors gave stockholders a priority weighting of 5.7, almost 27 percent higher than the next interest group, the employees, 50 percent higher than creditors, 137 percent higher than the interests of suppliers, and of fully 175 percent greater importance than the environment. Now to be fair, these numbers are not out of line with the attitudes of institutional investors in Germany, Japan, and the United Kingdom, which at least for the first two countries might be surprising (but that's a discussion for part 3 of this book). The important point is that stockholder interests are clearly dominant, and one can at least speculate that the only other interests that appear at all significant in investors' estimation, those of employees and creditors, are significant because of their relationship to stockholder interests.

Stockholder interest is reflected in institutional investors' decision making as to where to invest their funds. According to the survey, the most important factors in U.S. institutional investment decision making are financial performance (92 percent), growth prospects (90 percent), management quality (80 percent), and stock performance (56 percent). In its 2000 *Survey*, Russell Reynolds reported that while financial performance still ranked first among U.S. investors at 90 percent, stock price had moved up to 73 percent, an obviously significant 17 percent higher. Stock performance is important and is unmistakably on the rise. Moreover, in light of the fact that corporate performance depends on earnings per share (and the fact that the investing community famously focuses on quarterly growth in this factor in predicting stock prices), one can reasonably conclude that the most important factor is anticipated stock performance and that the relatively lower rating given to historical stock price performance compared to financial performance is more a reflection of the lesser value placed upon that factor as a predictor of future stock price performance.

This trend is reflected in institutional investors' attitudes toward executive stock options. According to the Russell Reynolds 2000 *Survey*, 63 percent of U.S. institutions believed that director options ought to be priced at premia, "following observers who believe directors should be rewarded for returns only above those of a rising stock market."[21] Clearly the interest of the institutional investor is stock price, and the corporation that follows this concern is one that will place increasing pressure on its management to maximize that price.

Whether or not others perceive them as having exercised their potential influence, the survey reports that institutional investors themselves believe they are increasingly exerting influence on corporate managements. In 1997 and 1998, similar surveys reported that two-thirds of American institutional investors believed that they "exert at least a moderate degree of influence over top management."[22] In 1999 that number had risen to 73 percent. The vast majority of this "influence," however, consisted of voting in favor of a stockholder resolution, with relatively small (but still significant) percentages of U.S. institutions writing or orally expressing their views to management, and relatively insignificant numbers sponsoring stockholder resolutions, working with other institutions to influence the board, or attempting to exert more direct influence. But in the 2000 *Survey*, Russell Reynolds reported a decline in U.S. institutional activity in terms of voting on shareholder resolutions and expressing their concerns to management. As we will soon see, the types of stockholder resolutions that are by far the most common are directed toward easing the ability of stockholders to replace boards and take advantage of hostile bids for the portfolio companies—in other words, they're directed toward increasing stockholder value. And it may well be that the decline in institutional activity is itself a reflection of increasing institutional satisfaction that American corporate management has internalized institutional values and places stock value at the top of its agenda.

The survey did have one surprising result, particularly in these times of antigovernment sentiment. While 32 percent of institutional investors surveyed believed that they should be the actors to set standards for corporate governance, 46 percent believed that this activity should be undertaken either by stock exchanges, the SEC, or the government more broadly. It should be noted, however, that 68 percent of American institutional investors thought these guidelines should be voluntary.[23] While this is interesting in that regulation appears to be more attractive to institutional investors than one might think in the wild free market environment of the United States, the anomaly may well be explainable as an instance of regulatory capture; that is, either the institutions believe they can lobby self-regulatory organizations or the government to provide governance standards that favor their interests, or they assume that in the current political and economic environment governance standards are almost certain to reflect the current attitude of stock-holder-centrism that exists in the United States. In its 2000 *Survey,* Russell Reynolds found that only 35 percent of U.S. institutions believed that corporate governance codes have affected corporate behavior, although 46 percent reported their belief that they have reflected concerns held by institutional investors.

ONE, TWO, THREE, WHAT ARE WE FIGHTING FOR?

So let's take a closer look at the allegedly increasing activism of institutional investors. If the lion's share of the action is in voting for stockholder proposals, what kinds of things are they voting for? While I'll take you through a series of examples that might be slightly mind-numbing, the bottom line is that they all go to the bottom line: increased stockholder profit.

Let's start with the policies of pension funds. In the first place, we ought to expect pension funds, certainly those that are defined benefit plans,[c] to have a longer-term perspective than most other types of institutional investors, say, mutual funds, because they need to be able to have sufficient assets to pay out to their beneficiaries as retirement approaches—since the beneficiaries have nothing to gain if the fund earns more than they're entitled to, the funds are less concerned with portfolio gain than with ensuring adequate assets to pay the beneficiaries. Given that risk and return are di-rectly correlated, we should expect such investors to have a lower risk profile than mutual fund investors, who can come in and out

[c]A defined benefit plan is one that pays out a set amount to retirees over time. This contrasts with defined contribution plans, which pay out whatever amount the particular retiree earns. In 1999, defined benefit plans had $3.75 billion in assets compared to defined contribution plans, which had $1 billion in assets, although the latter have been receiving more in contributions and making larger payouts. *Profile Statistics at a Glance,* Pensions & Investments, January 24, 2000. TIAA-CREF, about which I shall talk shortly, is of the latter type, each retiree self-directing the investment of her portfolio and reaping the gains or suffering the losses upon retirement. CalPERS is the largest of the former type yet is known as one of the most active stockholders among all pension funds.

whenever they want, although not without tax effect, and, to a lesser extent, than defined contribution plans, in which maximization may be the goal. The growth of defined contribution plans, by the way, has far outpaced that of defined benefit plans, a fact reflected in the growth of mutual funds and the resultant exacerbation of the problem.[24] Almost everyone recognizes that socially responsible corporate behavior is, for the most part, in the best long-term interest of the corporation's goal of wealth creation.[d] There is evidence even, though not undisputed, that institutional investment in general has a positive effect on corporate social responsibility, which suggests that such behavior might be encouraged; I will discuss such evidence at the conclusion of this chapter.[25] And, again, though not undisputed, there is also some evidence that at least public pension fund managers are more concerned with issues like product quality, environmental protection, labor relations, and worker treatment than investment managers like those managing mutual funds.[26]

But that evidence goes only to investment behavior and its effects on social performance. Let's turn to institutional investor activism, which, as I noted, has been seen as the saving grace of the American system. Two major American pension funds, TIAA-CREF and the California Public Employees Retirement System (CalPERS), should by the nature of their constituencies be among the most active institutional investors with respect to issues of corporate social responsibility and accountability. Why would one expect social concern from these organizations? Well, TIAA-CREF is the largest pension fund dedicated to the retirement well-being of educators at all levels (including me). It goes without saying, I think, that teachers are not people who have, for the most part, chosen their occupation in order to become wealthy but rather are attracted to the calling for a variety of reasons, not the least of which is to be of service to others in an important endeavor. Thus, while one can assume that teachers care as much as anyone about having ade-

[d]Although for the reasons I discussed earlier, this argument works only up to a point. While it is an economic rather than a social or political argument, it is consistent with these arguments up to that point and is therefore worth noting here.

quate wealth for retirement, one is probably safe in assuming that teachers on the whole are more concerned with social issues than others.

TIAA and CREF, whose boards are composed of academics and public servants as well as business people, have adopted a *Policy Statement on Corporate Governance* which it claims to be an "evolving document" that is the joint product of its committees on corporate governance and social responsibility. The *Statement* does, in its eleven pages (net of an appendix on executive compensation),[e] note that boards of directors should be appropriately diverse in terms of gender, age, and race as well as experience; this can be considered an issue of corporate responsibility, although TIAA-CREF views it as an issue of corporate governance, theorizing that the more diverse the composition of a board, the less it will be beholden to management and the more likely it will be to improve corporate performance. Thus TIAA-CREF views even an issue that one would likely consider to be social as a wealth-enhancing device. The *Statement* notes further that "the leadership of the corporation should set a high standard of performance accountability and ethical behavior." And in a brief section entitled "Social Responsibility Issues," the *Statement* acknowledges a relationship between good behavior and long-term shareholder value and recommends that corporate boards have policies and practices addressing environmental impacts, equal employment opportunities, employee training, and the evaluation of "corporate actions that can negatively affect the common good of the corporation's communities and its constituencies." It concludes by suggesting that corporations "should avoid the deliberate and knowing exploitation of any of the non-shareholder constituencies."

Now this is not a great deal of space devoted to accountability and responsibility issues, at least if we ignore the stockholders for

[e]I should point out that this is the number of pages which printed from the copy of the *Statement* posted on TIAA-CREF's website, http://www.tiaa-cref. org/libra/governance/index.html, and that a different format might alter the number of pages. But the proportions noted in the text are at least informative.

the moment. And the standards set out are precatory, but then so are the balance of the standards — TIAA-CREF can't compel a board to do anything except through its voting and investment policies, although it seems to be the case, at least with TIAA-CREF, that informal contacts with management through letter writing are the preferred means of influence, and highly successful ones at that.[27] You might think I'm quibbling, that the fund is trying, and I should be grateful for its attempt.

But let's look at the rest of the statement. The balance of the eleven pages is devoted solely to issues of stockholder value. In fact, at the same time that TIAA-CREF professes a concern for non-stockholder constituencies, the *Statement* notes that these constituencies, unlike stockholders, who have only their vote, have the ability to protect their interests through contracting with the corporation. Even among academics who are committed to the stockholder-centric principle, the ability of constituents like employees and communities to protect themselves from corporate exploitation is a questionable proposition, a fact of which the *Statement* takes no note. But more to the point, this assertion strongly qualifies, if it does not negate, any expressed concerns for social responsibility except perhaps for the nonexploitation principle.

More important, however, is the fact that all of the other issues addressed by the *Statement* are indisputably about stockholder value. Many of the specific principles articulated are directed toward the prohibition or removal of a variety of antitakeover protections that might be used by management to fend off hostile takeovers. Moreover, virtually all of TIAA-CREF's reported corporate governance activity goes directly to these or related matters.[28] According to the Investor Responsibility Research Center, between 1995 and 2000 TIAA-CREF made only one shareholder proposal relating to social issues (and CalPERS, which I will next discuss, made none).[29] Corporations subject to hostile takeover obviously present the potential for increasing short-term stockholder value through the payment of control premia. But as our experience with hostile takeovers (indeed takeovers in general) shows, such short-term stockholder benefit often comes at the expense of other stakeholder groups: creditors who see the value of their debtholdings drop as leveraged acquisitions increase default risks, suppliers who see long-term relationships disrupted, employees who are laid off to cut costs that allow leveraging to occur and premia to be paid to stockholders, and entire communities that lose jobs and employers (which is one of the reasons that states passed constituency legislation and antitakeover statutes in the first place). If even a liberally oriented organization like TIAA-CREF is so focused on stockholder value, what are we to expect from mutual fund managers and private pensions?

So maybe TIAA-CREF is not an avatar of accountability, except to stockholders. What about public employee pension funds? Civil servants, like teachers, might also be expected to have a more significant public interest than the general population. And public pension fund managers are themselves civil servants who are paid only a fraction of their private institutional money manager counterparts, so one can suppose that at least part of the reason they take these jobs in contrast to private sector jobs is a commitment to public service.

Sometimes public pension funds do take positions that could be seen to reflect a clear interest in accountability. For example, Carl McCall, New York's state comptroller and head of its pension fund, recently wrote directly to the chairman of Coca-Cola, Douglas Daft, demanding that Coke quickly settle a lawsuit brought against the company by black employees alleging racial discrimination in Coke's employment practices. The nature of the suit and the action at least suggest a desire to hold Coke accountable for socially unacceptable practices. But even here, profit seems to be the ultimate target. The letter reportedly stated that fund beneficiaries were bothered by the suit's impact on Coke, and in addition to questioning the handling of the lawsuit complained about Daft's compensation package at a time when Coke's stock price had dramatically fallen.[30] There's little question that, despite the social patina, the motivation behind the letter was primarily financial and that financial performance is at the forefront of even these funds' institutional activism.

Let's take the largest of all American public pension funds, CalPERS, long known for its leadership in institutional activism.

According to CalPERS' *2000 Focus List*,[31] the fund was slated to make four shareholder proposals, two of which demanded that the targeted company's board chairman be an independent director, one of which demanded that a majority of the board be composed of independent directors, and the fourth of which proposed to declassify the targeted corporation's board. There could be a variety of reasons for these proposals. But one thing is obvious: they all aim to reduce the ability of management to keep itself in office. This in itself is not a bad thing. But it does strengthen the institution's hand in takeover contests, which, as I've observed, can be highly beneficial to stockholders and harmful to everybody else.

In addition to these formal proposals, the *Focus List* reports on meetings held by CalPERS with various portfolio companies and their results. There were six reported meetings, all of which were directed toward the same kind of independence demanded in the stockholder proposals. Not one had to do with issues of accountability to other constituents or responsibility for other behavior. From 1995 to 2000 CalPERS did not make a single formal stockholder proposal having to do with social issues. CalPERS' overwhelming concern is stock price.[32]

Moreover, CalPERS has published a substantial set of *Domestic Proxy Voting Guidelines* as well as a set of *International Proxy Voting Guidelines* (which I'll discuss later.) The third paragraph of the *Guidelines* leaves no doubt as to CalPERS' interests. It states that it will cast its votes against any proposal for representation of constituencies on the boards of directors of its portfolio companies and states in no uncertain terms, "It is concluded that the corporate board members' primary responsibilities should be to direct the companies in the interests of all of the shareholders." To be sure, the *Guidelines* do set forth "Social Responsibility Criteria" for boards to follow, but these are highly general, setting forth the expectation that managements behave "with propriety and with a view toward social considerations," with the further expectation that management behave above the minimum level set by law, and that the managements of companies operating in countries where human rights abuses occur adhere to "maximum progressive practices" to eliminate them. Much better than TIAA-CREF. But the section also acknowledges CalPERS' fiduciary obligation to maximize returns to the pension fund, which takes precedence over other concerns. In fact the *Guidelines* clearly are aimed at stockholder value. Like the TIAA-CREF *Statement*, the *Guidelines* spend most of their time setting out voting principles designed to keep portfolio corporations free and available for hostile takeovers and thus short-term stock price maximization. And although, as we've seen, CalPERS pays some lip service to social impact, the *Guidelines* make it quite clear that CalPERS opposes all management proposals to permit boards to consider the interests of stakeholders other than stockholders in the takeover context; and of course, in recent decades, takeovers have been the context in which constituent interests are most at risk. So while CalPERS seems to make some effort in articulating social concerns in its broader principles, it would be unreasonable to expect CalPERS to put itself out too much in pursuing social agendas when it comes to actual voting or influencing of the board. And it hasn't.

Greater institutional investor activism can reasonably be expected by the pension fund of the AFL-CIO, at least with respect to labor and employment issues. And the Office of Corporate Affairs and the AFL-CIO pension fund management have indeed been very active in pursuing corporate governance issues around the globe. In fact labor union pension funds have become the most active of all institutional investors, aided in part by the AFL-CIO's Center for Working Capital, established for the purpose of helping local unions use their pension power to make corporate managements more accountable to labor.[33] But while the AFL-CIO has made some formal shareholder proposals over the past three or four years, they are of exactly the same type as TIAA-CREF's and CalPERS': that is, they demand a majority of targeted company's directors be independent and raise issues of executive compensation, poison pills, other antitakeover devices, and the like. And it appears that local union pension funds are following its lead. They are raising traditional issues of corporate governance that reflect attempts to increase stockholder value, although occasional proposals for labor representation on the board and other employee and social welfare issues are made.[34] But the principal thrust of union pension activity is still stock price maximization.[35] As two commentators put it, "Labor activism is a model for any large institutional investor attempting to maximize return on capital."[36]

What about the rest? Well, not surprisingly, mutual funds designed for socially responsible investing often take an activist position on issues like the environment, labor relations, workplace conditions, workforce diversity, cultural impacts of corporate behavior, and the like based on their social screening criteria. One of the leaders has been Domini Social Investments, the first mutual fund to publish its votes; its voting record with respect to each of its portfolio companies is published on its website.[37] Domini Social Investments regularly submits shareholder proposals to be placed on its portfolio companies' ballots[38] at the same time that it regularly beats the S&P 500. Other social investment funds are not activist at all and are "social" only in that they employ some screening criteria for investment in their portfolio — the Vanguard Calvert Social Index Fund is an example. For the most part, America's 3,952 equity mutual funds (in 1999), representing more than $4 trillion in assets, have remained passive.[39] Mutual funds are hardly the place to look for help in ensuring corporate accountability.

So, what are we fighting for? Stockholder wealth. It's clear as day from the evidence available that to the extent that American institutional investors are active in corporate governance, they are concerned first and foremost with increasing the wealth of their funds. There's nothing wrong with this in and of itself. I certainly hope to amass a sufficiently large pension package to retire comfortably. But it is disappointing to see that those who have the power to act like real owners, to take the kind of active interest in the behavior of their businesses that an individual proprietor might, don't do so. The reasons they don't, of course, are their own fiduciary obligations to their fund beneficiaries and their own self-interest. But I return to the question posed and analyzed in chapter 4: Is wealth a value? If it is, should it be balanced with other considerations? Should a private pension fund sell its shares into a takeover or vote in favor of a merger that will result in many of its beneficiaries losing their jobs? Would these people really trade off their employment for a slightly higher return on their investments? Do they want a higher return as a result of bad corporate behavior? It's not really fair to expect these institutions to have any greater moral conscience than the corporations in their portfolios — after all, they're subject to the same problems of role morality we explored with respect to corporate directors. My point is simply that the institutional stockholder is not the place to look for hope of greater corporate accountability.

But there's another problem. If institutions simply behaved like long-term investors, seeking to profit well over time but not worrying about the short term, at least as long as they have assets sufficient to meet their current claims, their self-interest wouldn't be a problem. And the simple fact is that the size of institutional holdings does lock institutions into investments in a way that is usually not true of individual investors.[40] But as I showed earlier, many institutions, including the fastest-growing segment, still trade heavily, thus imposing the same kind of short-term pressure, if perhaps to a lesser extent, we've seen from individual investors.

The greater problem is the incentives of fund managers, and this is where differentiation by type of fund makes a difference. Here I reintroduce Peter, whom we met at the beginning of the chapter. Unlike public pension fund managers, who are civil servants working for a salary, or union fund managers, who have workers' interests at heart, Peter is compensated on what he produces in terms of fund value. Now. And therein lies the greatest source of short-term and thus irresponsible pressure from financial institutions.

THE PAY'S THE THING

So let's take a look at how institutional money managers are compensated. Needless to say, they make a lot of money. They average $660,000 per year. For that kind of money, they're expected to produce.[41] According to a recent survey by *Investment News*, the key to portfolio managers' compensation is beating identified benchmarks, like major stock indices. At the same time (this is the good news), investment managers are increasingly receiving equity stakes in their corporations as part of their compensation, a way of linking their pay to longer-term performance. This gives them an incentive to increase assets under management by high-pressure sales tactics — and the SEC recently caved in to allow advertising based on performance to help them out.

But the short-term remains dominant. How much you find in your annual bonus check depends upon what you have produced *now*. A survey conducted in 1999 by the Association for Investment Management and Research and Russell Reynolds Associates shows that of all investment professionals, including analysts, executives, marketing people, and traders, portfolio managers' bonuses are most closely tied to their individual performance, with analysts a fairly close second. Since bonuses can easily exceed 50 percent of salary, the incentive to perform is very strong indeed. The same is true for pension fund managers. And some clients of investment managers are including contractual penalties for underperformance.[42] Compensation depends on how you do in the short run, and that gives money managers and the funds they manage every reason to pressure corporations to increase their short-run performance at the expense of the long term. Remember Richard Mahoney's experience as head of Monsanto that I discussed in chapter 5? No surprise that the institutional activism we've seen is directed toward removing takeover barriers and increasing managerial vulnerability to the capital markets. Forgetting any incentives that institutions as institutions have to look good now, their compensation structures definitely push the short term.

Now you might say I'm overlooking an important point. After all, corporations must continue to make money if money managers are to preserve their levels of compensation. But this is not an answer. In the first place, high trading volumes suggest that the way for investment professionals to make money is to trade stocks that don't perform quickly enough for stocks that look prettier in the short term, thus exacerbating the effect. Moreover, psychological evidence more or less definitively suggests that most people are more inclined to go after short-term rewards than to be patient for the long-term.[43] Finally, a reasonably short focus isn't irrational for portfolio managers. A survey conducted by *Pensions and Investments* in 1999 concluded that the highest average portfolio manager compensation came between years eleven and nineteen of experience, which for most money managers covers their thirties, and that in fact average earnings declined with experience greater than nineteen years.[44] Nineteen years is a reasonably long time. But knowing you've got only nine years of maximum earnings potential while you're in the business does suggest that you are likely to make hay while the sun shines. By the time you hit forty, you're pretty much over the hill.

So? What do we do about it? Well, the solutions I've already suggested would alter the incentives of institutional investors quite severely; and adopting some form of my tax proposals might also help curb excessive institutional trading in vehicles which were built for long-term performance. We might also want to think about ways of limiting the amount of money manager compensation that is tied to short-term performance or to give favorable tax treatment for stock options in their mutual funds that are held for long-term periods. The idea is the same: Create incentives for long-term investing while retaining the efficient, centralized structure of American corporate law. Being locked in for the long term should sharply focus the institutional mind.

ABANDONING THE
STOCKHOLDERS

I have argued thus far that the key to unlocking long-term value in American corporations and to ensuring a governance and ownership structure that will provide for sustainable corporate productivity and profitability is to break the bonds that tie managers to stockholders and to create incentives to keep stockholders invested in the long term rather than as short-term speculators. The basic idea I have been promoting is to let managers manage; trust them to run their corporations in responsible and accountable ways, taking into account the moral and social propriety of their behavior as well as the profitability of their actions.

But the specter of relatively unconstrained management may be frightening. After all, the basic operating premise of American corporate law is that stockholders invest their money and in so doing cede control over the future of their investments to corporate management. This is the famous separation of ownership and control that Adolph Berle and Gardiner Means first observed in their classic book *The Modern Corporation and Private Property* (1932) as an empirical matter which then got turned into a virtue. One of the central problems they identified — the one that has dominated corporate governance discourse in America ever since — is that of ensuring that managers keep faith with the absentee owners of the corporation. Berle went on to write a series of articles arguing that managers should act as trustees for the stockholders, keeping their interests as the touchstone for all that they do. He needn't have worried quite so much. Berle was writing against the backdrop of the enormous corporate abuses of the 1920s, documented quite graphically in the hearings of the so-called Pecora Commission that was convened prior to the enactment of the series of securities laws passed by Congress during the 1930s. But what we have thus far observed about the structure of corporate law and the behavior of our equity markets shows, I think irrefutably, that managers have every incentive to worry about what stockholders think. Part of the reason is, of course, those securities laws themselves, which mandate disclosure of material corporate events, financial information in carefully prescribed form and at regular intervals, and a vigorous set of antifraud laws. Yet as successful as these laws have been in providing capital markets with tools to keep managers accountable, they have been aided by the structure and rules of corporate governance as well, leading to what I have observed so far to be an excessive and often destructive focus on stockholder welfare. This allows managers to disregard the enormous power they have over the lives and well-being of so many others who are affected by the corporation.

Berle's attempts to focus managers on stockholders did not go unanswered. His articles were challenged in a series of pieces by the Harvard professor E. Merrick Dodd, who claimed that managers were professionals and part of the responsibility that went with such professionalism was to consider the interests of all people upon whom managerial actions had potential impacts. His argument was, in essence, a progenitor of the more contemporary debate that I've reflected so far as to whether management should account for the interests of corporate stakeholders other than stockholders, an argument that is grounded not only in the morally correct notion that with power comes responsibility but also in the economic observations I've focused on with respect to long-term sustainability versus short-term stock price maximization.

Berle came from the rough and tumble of Wall Street, where he had observed the most primal behavior of which man is capable without resorting to violence. Dodd was sheltered in the ivory tower of Cambridge, and in many ways his ideas reflected the notions of that class, notions that can be traced back to such "best men" as Henry Adams, John Hay, and Henry Cabot Lodge,[1] that relied upon the breeding and values and education of a superior class to fulfill its civic responsibility, whether that responsibility was exercised in the pulpit, the law office, the classroom, the physician's clinic, or in business. For business was a calling too.

We've long since passed the point where arguments about a better class are generally acceptable, and while Dodd's ideas have a certain attraction they can also be seen as breeding racism, anti-Semitism, classism, and misogyny. But the core idea remains: with power goes responsibility. It is a bedrock notion in our Constitution; it is a core moral idea in our society. And in order for the powerful to exercise responsibility in a manner that allows us to hold them accountable, they must be free to make their own decisions.

That's the argument. It is the argument that I've built so far in calling for devices to permit managers to manage free of undue short-term pressure. It's the argument that will deprive managers of the defense that they are just doing their job, just following orders, when in their pursuit of higher stock prices they make decisions and take actions that harm others.

But my argument does leave a fairly gaping hole. If we free managers from stockholder pressure and release the tethering of managers to stock prices, then we risk allowing them to serve themselves, to satisfy their own interests, justifying whatever they do as being in the long-run interests of their companies. As any good lawyer knows, it's not difficult to construct plausible arguments to support almost any action short of outright stealing.

I started with the assumption that most managers, like most people, want to do the right thing. And despite the stories in the popular press about various corporate abuses, especially in the realm of executive compensation, I continue to make the assumption that most people, most of the time, will in fact do the right thing. But we have two issues to address: What is the right thing (sometimes it's not obvious)? and what do we do when managers clearly do the wrong thing (like steal)? And so we must take a moment before continuing the argument to add a necessary qualification to my proposal to free up managers. We must be sure that laws and norms exist that ensure that in serving the corporate entity and its various constituents managers will understand their basic obligations and face penalties if they fail to fulfill them.

There are laws already in place that are designed to do this. In addition to the federal antifraud and insider trading laws, state corporations laws are full of rules coming under the general rubric of fiduciary duty that are designed to ensure that managers serve the corporation's interests and not their own. But as much as the structure and rules of corporate governance fail nonstockholder constituents, fiduciary law has evolved over time to the point that it fails the stockholders too. Judicial rhetoric still resounds with the high morality of fiduciary obligation. But judicial practice and the legislation that has followed it have for the most part left stockholders without meaningful remedies when good managers turn bad (or when bad managers are selected). Thus in order to free managers to behave responsibly and accountably toward the world in which they live, we need to ensure that tight protections exist to prevent them from using their newfound freedom as an excuse to rape, pillage, and steal in the corporate bastion.

PROTECTING THE VULNERABLE

Fiduciary duty is a fairly rare animal in our law. As I noted earlier, American social, political, and legal philosophy is largely based upon the idea of personal autonomy, the notion that we are free to do as we like as long as we don't unduly intrude on the rights of others. The way this is reflected in our law falls more or less into two categories. First, as is commonly noted, American law is a law of prohibition: it tells us what we can't do, rather than what we have to do. We have few positive obligations other than to pay our taxes and serve in the military if drafted. We don't have to vote; we don't have to rescue others in distress; we don't have to engage in any sort of public service (except for the aforementioned draft). Citizens of other nations have some or all of these obligations, but it is considered inconsistent with our constitutionally guaranteed freedoms to require us to do much of anything. On the other hand, it is consistent with those freedoms to allow others to enjoy their freedom as much as we enjoy ours. Thus we are prohibited from hurting others, from taking their property, from discriminating on irrelevant bases like race and gender, and from interfering in general with their pursuit of happiness. This structure of a jurisprudence of prohibitions is obvious to any law student and to anyone else who takes a moment to ponder the array of our laws.

The second category, which mirrors the first, is private association. We can pretty much befriend whom we like, marry whom we like (except, regrettably, in the case of homosexuals), and do business with whom we like. Many of our associations are informal and don't rise to levels where they are recognized by law. But some of those associations are more formal, and that is where the rubber meets the corporate road: they take place within the institution of contract, a series of rules and norms that in American society come under the general rubric of freedom of contract.

Freedom of contract means that as long as two parties are engaging in legal activities, they can structure whatever deals between themselves that they like. They can sell or buy, provide or procure services, borrow or lend, all on terms of their own making. And if one party chooses not to comply with the contract, the law backs up the wronged party by ensuring that the bargain is kept. But it does not rewrite the bargain. The parties are presumed to have wanted the deal to which they agreed.

Sometimes this arrangement looks unfair. Sometimes prices fluctuate between the time a contract is signed and the time it is executed. In long-term supply contracts or loan agreements, which are a species of what is referred to as relational contract, one party might get hurt badly because the price of oil dropped way below the price at which the parties contracted or because interest rates increased above the fixed rate on the loan. But courts won't interfere with the substance. The reason is that we assume the parties know their interests better than we do, that the risks they take are risks they have chosen to take, and that their contract is very much an exercise of the personal autonomy we so prize.

In order for this attitude to be legitimate, it must rest on certain underlying assumptions. And it does. The basic assumption, one that pervades our more public constitutional jurisprudence as well, is that most people are roughly equal — that is, they are equally able to make the autonomous choices that result in agreement. Equality in the realm of contracts is based partly on knowledge and information (or at least an equal ability to obtain it) and partly on bargaining power. And the assumption of rough equality is often borne out in reality. Corporations that publicly issue bonds or borrow from banks are, like their lending counterparts, accustomed to the activity, sophisticated financially, and represented by competent counsel.

There are circumstances, though, even circumstances that originate in contract, in which rough equality is absent. There are many examples in which one party to a relationship is decidedly not equal to the other. Parent-child relationships come to mind, as do lawyer-client, doctor-patient, trustee-beneficiary, and manager-corporation. These relationships are characterized by circumstances in which one party has greater knowledge or expertise than the other and both know it, or greater power than the other, and each has willingly entered into the relationship in that knowledge. People hire lawyers because of their expertise in an area in which the client has limited or no knowledge. They hire doctors to make them well or save their lives in circumstances in which their own abilities fail them. Children rely upon their parents, although involuntarily, for food, shelter, education, and safety. Beneficiaries rely upon trustees to manage their property in an honest, prudent way. And corporations and their stockholders rely upon management to serve the collective interest and not their own in the decisions they make.

These relationships are between people who are, on the one side, expert or powerful and, on the other, vulnerable to that expertise and power. Whether the vulnerable party has voluntarily ceded control of his interests to the powerful party or the situation arises as a matter of simple fact, the risk exists that the powerful party will in some way abuse the trust reposed in her by the weak party. These relationships, which we classify as fiduciary, are valuable. They enable some people to benefit from the expertise of others and often provide a means of livelihood for the experts. But they are subject to abuse. Because the control lies in the hands of the powerful party, it has the opportunity to take advantage of the vulnerable party. As a result, and in order to control for the possibility of abuse and to provide a remedy when it happens, the law has developed an area in which affirmative obligations to others exist: fiduciary duty.

The basic premise of fiduciary duty is simple: the powerful party, or fiduciary, is required to act in the best interests of the vulnerable party. This requirement involves more specific rules, like prohibitions against self-dealing and obtaining profits by virtue of the fiduciary's position and the injunction to perform obligations with care. In some areas of the law, this tells practically all you need to know about fiduciary duty, and it is rigidly enforced. But corporate law is different.

LETTING THE FOXES RULE THE ROOST

Fiduciary doctrine in corporate law started out much the same as other forms of fiduciary law. It used to be, rather a long time ago, that directors and officers who faced a conflict of interest were prohibited from acting upon or profiting from it upon pain of being required to disgorge anything they received from the transaction. It didn't matter whether the deal was good or bad for the corporation — for example, an officer could have sold needed real estate to the corporation at a fair market price — he'd still have to return the profits to the company.

The reason was simple: the essence of a fiduciary relationship is trust. It is based on the idea that the vulnerable party can avail himself of the fiduciary's time and expertise and, backstopped by legal rules punishing violations of that trust, be confident that the fiduciary could be trusted. Whether or not the transaction was fair (or even a really good deal) wasn't the question — it was the breach of trust that was relevant. Once the fiduciary profited because of her position, the basis for trust was gone and that not only damaged the relationship but suggested that such relationships were dangerous unless the vulnerable party watched the fiduciary very carefully, a response that would destroy the whole efficiency of the relationship in the first place.

There was another reason it was sensible to prohibit these transactions. It inheres in the concept of fairness. What is fair when you're dealing with the sale of property, or giving a family member a job with a salary, or taking an opportunity that might (but might not) be profitable to the corporation? Appraisers of various kinds of assets differ notoriously in their estimates — lots of markets don't even come close to the relative efficiency of the stock market. And how do you assess your son's talents relative to those of other job applicants? Kind of hard to do, especially when blood ties are involved. In order to permit such transactions to occur, courts would have to get into the business of performing such evaluations every time a manager acted on a conflict of interest. And courts have long professed their lack of expertise in business matters, which has led to the widespread development of the business judgment rule I discussed in chapter 3. The only alternative would be to let the board of directors, or those members of the board who themselves had no financial interest in the transaction, engage in a process designed to replicate an arm's-length transaction by serving, in a sense, as an independent committee. As independent parties would, they would hire appraisers and vote (without your participation) on your son's hiring. Rather a risky business, given, first, the very close relationship that board members of corporations typically have among themselves and, second, their well-known similarity of background and perspective.[a]

But this is precisely what corporate law has done. So let's take a tour of corporate fiduciary duties to see how the law has left the stockholders at the mercy of directors.

[a]The Russell Reynolds 1999–2000 Board Practices Survey examined data on 12,139 directors of the more than 1,200 public companies in the S&P 1500. It found that 7,721 were independent of the companies, meaning they had no personal or professional ties, 2,541 were employees of their companies, and 1,877 were affiliated, meaning they had some professional ties to the companies. The average director's age was fifty-nine, with more than one-third falling between fifty-seven and sixty-five and three-quarters being in their fifties and sixties. Only 7 percent were members of a minority group, and only 9.3 percent were women. While the study reports a significant increase in independent directors, it remains the case that they tend to be drawn from the same pool of people.

In order to understand the difficult legal position stockholders are in, it is first necessary to understand the ways in which corporate managers can adversely affect corporate and stockholder fortunes. We begin again with the understanding that fiduciary duties are designed to protect the vulnerable party in a relationship from the fiduciary's abuse of power. Now of course we've already seen the power that stockholders can exert on managements' behavior through the ordinary functioning of the capital markets. But our look at fiduciary duty will take us inside the black box of the corporation.

Fiduciary duty operates to neutralize conflicts of interest. There are essentially two kinds of conflict in corporate law, vertical conflicts and horizontal conflicts; everything else is a variation on them.

Vertical conflicts are probably the easiest to understand, and they provide the background for the traditional, long-standing rules of corporate fiduciary duty. Vertical conflicts arise when managers conduct the ordinary business of the corporation: make investment decisions, sell and buy assets, hire employees, compensate themselves, and pursue or reject a variety of business opportunities. They arise, in other words, from managers' duties to run the corporation on a day-to-day basis. I call them vertical because that best describes the relative position of the managers and the corporation they serve; the managers have power to which the corporation, lacking power of its own separate and apart from the actions of the managers, is subject. It is a classic hierarchical relationship and therefore can be visualized as a vertical line running from managers to the corporation.

The kinds of harm that arise from vertical conflicts are basically a category that Aristotle described in the *Nicomachean Ethics* as harms to be redressed by corrective justice. While they have technical names like self-dealing, corporate opportunity, and waste, in nontechnical terms they all involve some sort of theft from the corporation by the managers. Managers are able to steal in this way precisely because of their position of power over the corporation — that's why the duties that redress them are fiduciary. Vertical conflicts are the kinds of conflicts that are redressed, if at all, by the derivative suits I described in chapter 5. In other words, although stockholders might initiate the suit, any damages collected are paid to the corporation itself because it is the corporation that is harmed when managers take advantage of these conflicts and steal wealth that properly belongs to the corporation.

Horizontal conflicts are a relatively new development in corporate fiduciary law, although they have analogs in much older doctrines of trust law that require trustees to deal fairly with multiple beneficiaries of a trust. The Aristotelian analog to the harms caused by horizontal conflicts is the concept of distributive justice, the idea of giving to each his due. While vertical conflicts arise because of the power that managers have over the corporation, horizontal conflicts come about because managers or some other powerful person within the corporate structure (like controlling stockholders or directors who own substantial amounts of the company's stock) have the opportunity to favor their interests *as stockholders or other financial claimant* over the interests of the other stockholders. The laws dealing with vertical conflicts, as they originally were conceived, derive from the idea that managers have no legitimate interest in the corporation's property other than agreed-upon compensation. In contrast, in horizontal conflicts, the manager-stockholder or director-stockholder or controlling stockholder does indeed have a legitimate interest by virtue of his stockholdings. The question in these kinds of cases involves determining whether the powerful stockholder has taken more than his due, to the detriment of the other stockholders.

With this broad, somewhat overgeneralized classification in mind, let's take a look at the fiduciary law that governs in each category.

Vertical Conflicts

Let's say a well-known oil company wants to sponsor worldwide radio broadcasts of classical music, including opera, and also run a major website for classical music fans. Texaco has been sponsoring Metropolitan Opera broadcasts for years, but my story is hypothetical and based on a real case involving a corporation in an entirely different line of business.[2] Let's also assume that Texaco's president is married to a well-known opera singer — call her Maria. She's not Jessye Norman, but she's good, and she's sung at the Met as well as La Scala and other famous opera houses throughout the world, usually in supporting roles. The company, Oilco, believes that this will distinguish it in a business that is basically one that sells commodities and in which brand name differentiation is therefore difficult to achieve. The assumption is that a classical music audience is an elite, well-educated audience that tends to buy big gas-guzzling cars, luxury SUVs, and the like, and that capturing their business is likely to increase profits.

The Oilco board meets, and the vice president of marketing presents the plan, which has been developed with the aid of a famous marketing company. Different types of music will be featured each night, and the website will contain interviews with a variety of classical music stars. The marketing v.p. names a number of performers who have agreed to participate, including Maria. He notes the amount of compensation to be paid to each, including the fact that none of the performers will receive more than their customary pay per performance. The board knows that the president is married to Maria, but he reminds them just the same. The presentation completed, the board votes to approve the show and commits 2 percent of the company's net revenues for the next three years to the project.

How do you solve a problem like Maria? There doesn't appear to be anything wrong with what the board has done. The president is well compensated, and his family hardly needs the money. Maria gets plenty of gigs on her own, so she doesn't need the work. And she's not getting special prominence or being paid more than her normal rate.

But there is a conflict of interest. After all, no matter how straightforward this arrangement looks, she is the president's wife. So how do we know that Maria's deal is fair to the corporation? Remember that the board's standard of behavior is based on the business judgment rule, which operates to keep courts out of business decisions. But one exception is the case of conflicts of interest. The reason is that when a board acts on a conflict of interest, we cannot know for sure whether it was really acting in the corporation's best interest even though their action incidentally happens to benefit someone else — in this case the president's wife and presumably therefore the president — or whether it is acting to give special advantages to these people.

The old solution was to prohibit the deal entirely, in technical legal terms, to make it voidable. Maria simply can't perform or maybe she can perform for free, but even that's open to question given the fact that Oilco is paying for the show and it will presumably at least not hurt, if it doesn't help, Maria's career. The idea was that by acting on the conflict, the board's motives were obscured, and since we can't examine their heads we don't know why they were doing it. Besides, by acting on the conflict, the board gave reason for stockholders to call their good faith into question and thus breached their trust. Prohibition was seen as the best way to resolve ambiguities and to maintain faith with the stockholders.

But the rule was inconvenient and, some think, inefficient. In the first place, earlier in the last century there were many directors who sat on the boards of companies that did business with companies they ran. The cross-business might well have been beneficial to both corporations. Why should we stop good deals from happening? Besides, these directors might bring a lot of knowledge and expertise to a company, and to prohibit these transactions might be to exclude these directors and their expertise from the board. Finally, sometimes a director or manager (or his sisters and his cousins and his aunts) might have talents or property that would be useful to the corporation; thus to prohibit dealings between them might well be to deprive the corporation of important benefits.

So, in this area, as in so many others that are beyond the scope of my discussion, the legal solution was to dispense with this inconvenience. Instead of prohibiting the transaction, first courts and then legislatures held that self-dealing could occur as long as it was fair to the corporation.

What does fairness mean? Well, let's take a look, for example, at the modern definition in Delaware's fairly typical self-dealing statute (by the way, all states have them). It begins by telling us that transactions aren't voidable because of conflicts of interest if certain conditions are met. The first, and essential, precondition is that the conflict and the circumstances of the deal be known to or disclosed to all of the directors. Seems reasonable enough: had they no knowledge of the conflict, the board could be taken advantage of. Now once the board has knowledge, it is free to approve the deal provided that a majority of the disinterested directors approve the deal (regardless of whether the "interested directors," a term that would include the president in Oilco's case, actually vote). This holds true even if the interested directors are too few to make up a quorum.[b] And that's all you need. Voila! The conflict is sanitized because the board approved it. Never mind, as I pointed out before, that there's probably a close relationship among the inside and outside directors. Never mind the de facto power that the president has to make sure friendly directors are nominated. That's all it takes.

Now say for some reason you can't get disinterested director approval or you want to be really sure that you're safe. You can put the matter to the stockholders. All the statute requires is that a majority of stockholders approve the deal, and stockholders are notoriously complacent, as we've seen. It doesn't even require that the approving stockholders be disinterested, so if our president has a major block of stock he gets to vote (although case law in Delaware has developed the requirement that the approving stockholders be independent). But this isn't hard to meet.

Look what's happened so far. If you plan right, the matter never

[b]So, for example, if a corporation's board were voting on an executive stock option plan and had ten directors, five of whom were company executives who would receive options and five of whom were outside directors who had no affiliation with the company, the five interested directors would be disqualified from voting. A normal quorum of the board would be six, or a majority, but there is no quorum of disinterested directors. Under Delaware law, if three of the five outside directors approved the plan, it would satisfy the statutory test. Some jurisdictions, New York, for example, don't permit board approval of these deals when there is less than a quorum of disinterested directors.

has to leave the boardroom; and if the case is litigated, all the board needs to do is provide minutes showing that it was informed and that it considered enough evidence to determine that the deal was fair. The directors themselves get to determine whether they have breached their fiduciary duty. The foxes are guarding the henhouse.

But what happens if for some reason you can't get director or stockholder approval? Well, the board has a defense. If a stockholder brings a derivative suit seeking to void the deal, the directors will win if they can prove that the transaction was fair to the corporation.

But what is fair? Well, the case of Oilco is pretty easy: we have a market price for Maria's services, and as long as the radio show is otherwise a good idea, there doesn't seem to be very much danger in letting it proceed. But what if a director wanted to sell a piece of real estate to the company? Fairness depends on the court's resolution of a battle of expert appraisers, each of whom will try to establish his own idea of a fair price. But there will undoubtedly be a range. And the more unique the asset, the wider the range is likely to be. When the court picks a number, it will almost certainly be somewhere within that range.

Now look what's happened. If the director were to sell the property to a third party, the third party would presumably negotiate hard to get the lowest price. But we can't be sure that the corporation has done this with its own director. So it may well be that the fair price is higher than our director could have gotten in tough negotiations with a third party. But that's okay because all that is required is a fair price. If the fair price paid by the corporation is higher than the price the director could have gotten on the market (we'll never know for sure), then the interested director has made some extra profit on the sale at the expense of the corporation. So even when we apply a substantive fairness test to the deal, we are, in some measure, permitting managers to profit at their corporations' expense. And if they play their cards right and get director approval, they don't even have to prove fairness to a court. They have to show only that they did their best to ensure that the price was fair. They have the power, in other words, to create for themselves a property interest in the corporation where none existed before. That's a far cry from fiduciary law, aimed at keeping faith with the stockholders. There are a lot of rules like this. I've given just one important example, but they all follow the same basic pattern.

Now Just Try to Get to Court

As if that weren't bad enough, it gets worse. As I noted, vertical conflicts are challenged in derivative litigation. But there are enormous obstacles to bringing a derivative suit. A salmon swimming upstream from the middle of the Pacific Ocean probably has a greater chance of spawning than the average stockholder has of getting her day in court. Here's why.

Derivative litigation is an interesting device. Remember that the vertical fiduciary duties we've been talking about, referred to in corporate law as the duties of care and loyalty, are owed by the board and the managers as well to the corporation itself. But boards have almost unlimited legal power, delegated by the state through its corporations statute, to run the corporation. This creates an interesting problem. If the board violates these duties, who is going to sue to enforce them? It hardly seems likely that the board is going to cause the corporation to sue itself.

So courts developed an interesting device, called the derivative suit, to get around this sticky problem and make sure that the duties can be enforced. Derivative suits are designed so that stockholders, and only stockholders, can bring a lawsuit in the name and the right of the corporation, thereby acquiring the chance to enforce the duties by sidestepping the board of directors. I've described this briefly before. Technically, the derivative suit is actually two suits in one: the first is a suit by the stockholder against the corporation to cause it to sue a third party, in this case one or more of the directors. The second is the actual suit by the corporation against the third party. The combination of these two actions, and their obvious extraordinary nature in violating the basic precept that the board manages the corporation, make it rather a complex animal. And especially because it is an exception to the norm that directors run the corporation, a number of limitations and conditions need to be fulfilled before a stockholder-plaintiff is permitted to have her day in court. Only one of these will concern us here: the requirement that, prior to initiating the suit, the stockholder make a demand on the board.

What exactly is it that the stockholder must demand? She must demand that the board cause the corporation to bring the lawsuit that the stockholder thinks ought to be brought. This demand requirement serves two purposes. The first is conceptual. It is, in a sense, a requirement that the stockholder pay homage to the board, that she recognize the board's supreme authority. Thus by asking the board to bring the action itself, the stockholder is, in effect, holding her right to sue in abeyance until the board makes its own decision, thus at least theoretically preserving the rule of board governance. The second reason is practical. It may be that the board agrees with the stockholder and will in fact cause the corporation to bring the suit itself. If it does, then there's no need to complicate corporate law, and the stockholder can quietly go home and let the board do its job. Now this might happen if the stockholder thinks that the board should sue a third party — one example might be a major customer who refuses to pay its bill, and for some reason the board doesn't try to collect it. But these kinds of suits are very infrequent. The far more common derivative suit occurs when the stockholder thinks the board has screwed up. And how likely is it that the board is going to receive the stockholder's demand and say, "Yes, we've done wrong, and we shall correct our misbehavior or sue ourselves"? It could happen. It probably has happened. But it's not very likely.

One approach that courts could take is to say that once the stockholder has made a demand and the board has refused to accede to it, the stockholder is free to sue. They haven't done this, and for good reason. If stockholders were able to usurp the board's power whenever they didn't like what was going on, there'd be an awful lot of litigation, and it would interfere tremendously with the board's ability to run the corporation, which, after all, is one of the things that makes American corporate law work. On the other hand, when the board is the group being sued, common sense tells us that it's unlikely to accept demand. So instead, courts have developed rules that determine when demand can be excused because the board is the defendant and when the board is allowed to reject the suit even though the stockholder might have a point. The upshot of these rules is that it is very difficult indeed for stockholders to have their day in court.

Let's consider how Delaware does it. There's some reasonable variation among the states in the way they approach this problem, but because of Delaware's importance in the world of corporate law it seems like a reasonable exemplar. The general rule is that the stockholder-plaintiff has to make demand. So the first question is when it is that demand might be excused because, say, the directors have a conflict of interest in that they're the defendants. There's a simple answer to the question: Demand is excused when it's futile, that is, when it's so obvious that the board is going to reject the demand that there's no point in making the stockholder go through the exercise in the first place. We'll see that even if the stockholder is excused from making demand, the board still has a device that may allow it to get rid of the lawsuit. But for now let's focus on what it means to say that demand is futile.

According to Delaware law, demand is futile when the facts alleged by the plaintiff are such that "a reasonable doubt is created that: (1) the directors are disinterested and independent and (2) the challenged transaction was otherwise the product of a valid exercise of business judgment."[3] We can dispense with the second part quickly. A board's decision has to be virtually ridiculous — not just unreasonable but irrational — to fail the second part of the test.[4] So let's look at the first part. What exactly does it mean to say that the directors are not disinterested or independent?

Disinterested is easy. It requires that the directors have no direct financial interest in the challenged transaction. In order for demand to be futile, it's not enough that one or even a few of the directors have a direct financial interest; as we'll see in a minute, as long as there are some directors without such an interest the board is considered sufficiently untainted to maintain the demand requirement. It's also not enough that directors are paid for their services and could lose their jobs in the next election if the suit is successful — even though directors of public corporations are generally well compensated, the courts don't consider this a disqualifying interest. So this one is easy to measure, and, except in suits in which the plaintiff is challenging the way the board compensates itself, awfully unlikely to result in demand futility.

There's another way plaintiffs can show director interest: that is if there are facts that create a reasonable case that the directors, by their actions, are trying to entrench themselves in office. This is almost impossible to show in the case of ordinary business transactions. Where it comes up is in cases of hostile takeovers and proxy fights, where we have a whole different set of rules that go beyond this discussion.

So what about directorial independence? In order to show that directors are not independent, the plaintiff has to show that one or more of the directors who are interested in the transaction (as defined above) completely dominate the other directors so that they are largely deprived of their ability to make up their own minds. This does sometimes happen.[5] Most directors are serious people themselves, and it would take an awful lot to show that they lack any independence because of a Svengali-like interested director. Moreover, most American boards now have a majority of independent directors, who have no other affiliation with the company. Where that's the case, stockholders will never find demand excused. For, as the Delaware Supreme Court put it, "Approval of a transaction by a majority of independent, disinterested directors almost always bolsters a presumption that the business judgment rule attaches to transactions approved by a board of directors that are later attacked on grounds of lack of due care."[6] In lay terms, this means that if a majority of the board is composed of outside directors, no matter how they've been chosen, what kind of relationship they have with the other directors, including the interested director, or how much incentive they might have not to rock the boat, the stockholder has to make demand. End of story.

So demand is almost never excused. But it gets worse. Often a stockholder-plaintiff needs the tools of court procedure, called civil procedure in the trade, in order to get enough information to allege the facts that would lead to demand futility. The trick is that you can't get much procedure until you've brought a suit. And you can't bring a suit without either making demand or establishing that demand is futile. So why not simply allege demand futility, engage in some discovery, and then allege your facts? There's a very simple reason. Delaware has stymied you: if you bring a suit alleging demand futility and you turn out to be wrong, your case gets dismissed because you didn't make demand and you get thrown out of court! So why not make demand just to be on the safe side? Because under Delaware law, once you've made demand, you are deemed to have conceded that demand is not futile — you lose your chance to allege demand futility![7] So you're demand if you do and demand if you don't! (Sorry, I couldn't help it.)

The next thing is, What happens when a stockholder does make demand? As I noted earlier, that can't be enough to let the stockholder go marching on, or else the board's role in running the corporation would be seriously compromised. Instead, we have a series of rules governing when the board, after receiving demand, can refuse it and dismiss any suit the stockholder brings. There are two types of circumstances governed by slightly different rules: the first is when demand is required; the second is when demand is futile. As we'll see, if demand is required (and what I've said already suggests that in Delaware you're mostly stuck with making demand), it's easy for the board to dismiss the suit. It's more difficult if demand is futile, but since we've already seen that demand is almost never futile, the basic conclusion is that stockholders can almost never bring derivative suits. It's bad enough that fiduciary duty is so weak, but what's worse is you can't enforce even the weak duties that exist.

If demand is required, made, and refused, the rule is simple enough: the board's decision to refuse demand and dismiss the suit is respected and will be upheld by the court unless it was wrongful. Of course this gets us into the question of what wrongful means, and the answer to that is simple too: a decision is wrongful if in making it the directors' have not exercised their duties of care and loyalty. In other words, as long as they can show that they haven't acted irrationally and that they are disinterested and independent, they get to dismiss the suit even if the entire board has been sued! So if you have to make demand (and we've seen why, at least in Delaware, you almost always have to make demand), you in effect have no chance of bringing your suit if the board chooses to dismiss it, as it almost always will.

What about those rare cases in which demand is futile? If demand is futile because nobody on the board is disinterested or independent, the stockholder will be allowed to proceed. But as we've seen, that almost never happens. Usually there are at least a few directors who are disinterested and independent, and the board can add new directors who have nothing to do with the lawsuit if there are vacancies on the board after the suit has been brought. In either case, the board, that is, the entire board, including the interested or dependent directors, can delegate its power to a committee consisting of the disinterested and independent directors. Once they've done so, the committee, as long as it fulfills its duties of care and loyalty, can recommend dismissal of the suit to the entire board. The court will respect that decision if (1) it determines that the committee truly was disinterested and independent and fulfilled its duties of care and loyalty, and (2) if the court decides (and this step is entirely optional with the court) that dismissing the suit is in the best interests of the corporation — in other words, whether it agrees with the committee's decision.

So here's the end of our rather long tale. In Delaware at least, about the only time a stockholder is going to have a chance even to bring a lawsuit to enforce the rather insipid fiduciary duties to which directors are subject is when that board is disqualified by conflict of interest from making the decision itself and can't requalify itself by using an independent committee because the court chooses to look at the substance of its decision and decides it is wrong. That doesn't happen a whole lot. We might as well not have fiduciary duty at all.

Who Cares?

I've spent a lot of time on vertical duties and their enforcement (or nonenforcement) mechanism, the derivative suit, for one major reason. Managerial stealing is not that huge a problem. Petty theft might occur, petty, that is, in contrast to the corporation's overall financial position. Overcompensation is a somewhat greater problem but also more visible and thus more subject to public and market pressures. Some theorists argue even, and have been supported by courts, that we really don't have to worry about these issues at all because stockholders should be well diversified, and whatever managers steal from one company will be offset by the honesty and higher profits of another. But the key problem that our weak fiduciary duties cause is a lack of trust.

Trust is the key to permitting a corporate world in which managers take the money of absentee owners and have essentially complete legal freedom to determine how it's invested. Of course it's the rare stockholder who knows most of the managers and directors of his company, or even one for that matter. It's not rational to trust people you don't know, although over time you can develop trust by watching their good performance. Fiduciary law makes trust rational, not only by setting out the rules of the game so everyone knows what's expected of them, but also by providing a legal backstop when managers breach that trust. Vertical fiduciary duties and the mechanisms of the derivative suit have mostly taken that backstop away. Trust becomes irrational, and your only protection is to hold a diversified portfolio and hope that the market punishes errant managers. The only way the market knows how to do this is through stock prices. And that returns us to the managerial focus on stock prices and short-term management. So you see how it's all related.

Horizontal Conflicts

I've just subjected you to a substantial portion of my basic course on corporations, and I don't intend to try your patience very much longer with technical details about corporate law. But I do want to spend a little time talking about the other kind of conflict that fiduciary duty deals with, horizontal conflicts of interest. Recall that in horizontal conflicts, the issue is not one of stealing by people who have no legitimate interest in the corporation's wealth. Rather, the issue here is how the corporate pie gets sliced up among people who do have real financial interests in the corporation: that means stockholders, including managers who are stockholders, an increasingly important issue given the sharp rise in compensation through stock and stock options, preferred stockholders, and controlling stockholders. Of course others have an interest too, in particular, creditors and employees, but as I've already explained, these people are excluded from the rules governing the corporation.

Horizontal conflicts present less of a problem than vertical conflicts, in part because they tend to be more transparent and in part because the rules designed to deal with them are more protective of stockholders than those governing vertical conflicts. They also matter less in this context because my point in this chapter is that freeing the directors in large public companies from stockholder control will work only if we strengthen the laws protecting stockholders from directors' misbehavior. Horizontal conflicts are not about directors' misbehavior as such. Rather, they almost always arise when there is a single stockholder or group of stockholders who control the corporation.[c] This presents a different situation from that of the kind of corporation on which I've focused, that is, one in which directors may own shares but in which no single stockholder is dominant. Nonetheless, a few words on horizontal conflicts may be in order just for the sake of completeness.

The distinguishing aspect of horizontal conflicts is that they present cases in which the fiduciary has a legitimate financial interest in the corporation, usually as a stockholder, but pursues that interest in a way that gives her benefits she doesn't share with the other stockholders. For example, the controlling stockholder might own Class A common stock and the other stockholders might own Class B common. She may cause the board to declare a dividend only on the Class A common and not on the Class B, or might cause the corporation to repurchase the Class A but not the Class B, typically at a price not available to the other stockholders.

The fairness test governs horizontal conflicts of interest just as it does vertical ones. Of course it presents the same kind of valuation problems as appear in the vertical context, but since the stock-

[c]A controlling stockholder isn't necessarily someone who owns a majority of the stock; to be a controlling stockholder merely requires the practical ability to elect a majority of the board, which, for a variety of reasons, can often be accomplished even if the stockholder owns less than a majority of the stock.

holder clearly has preferred herself, courts seem more inclined to scrutinize expert valuation opinions than they do in the vertical context. In any event, because of the obvious disproportionate treatment of a group of stockholders by a more powerful stockholder, courts and legislatures have been less easily able to find ways to privilege theft. The simple procedural devices applicable in vertical cases won't do. There are, of course, nuances and refinements to the way courts handle these matters, but for present purposes I've said enough.[8]

Tender offers present a special set of cases, but the technicalities and details of takeover law could fill an entire book. Suffice it to say that takeover law is reasonably well developed at this point, and that while it may present a number of problems of its own it does not create a serious impediment to the kind of board independence I am advocating. We could easily free the board within the structure of existing takeover law without incurring serious adverse consequences.

**THE DILBERT SOCIETY?
AMERICA'S CORPORATE
WORKERS**

American corporate law ignores workers. They don't figure into the structure of the corporation or its legal duties. But there is no one group of people more identified with a corporation and more responsible for its day-to-day conduct than corporate workers. Ensuring corporate accountability means making the worker the central actor in the corporate structure as the only real person who can make a difference. And as popular culture from Dagwood to Dilbert shows — backed up by management and behavioral studies and comparisons from countries like Germany and Japan — the way workers are treated within the corporation has a dramatic effect upon their behavior. Workers who are made to feel responsible and accountable, who identify with the goals of their employer, and who are made to feel like important contributors with independent ideas are far more likely to care about the corporation and to take an interest in its behavior than workers who are treated as nothing more than living machines designed for the production of profit. As one manager put it, "Being at a good company is like having a good wife. . . . When you get used to a certain level of freedom and excitement, you don't want to leave." This is a feeling most workers lack, and the legal and financial structure of corporations is an important part of the reason. Maximizing stockholder profit means treating the worker as an expense. It means endowing the worker with a purpose that we have already seen does not have intrinsic value and is likely to be unrewarding. It means turning the worker into something like that by which *Forbes* magazine rather obnoxiously describes itself: "Capitalist tool." If you think I'm exaggerating, read all the new, purportedly worker-friendly scholarly literature which has rediscovered the worker as "human capital."[a]

Proctor & Gamble is one of many corporations to recognize recently the importance of making work meaningful and treating workers like people. One way it did so was by giving all employees access to its CEO to suggest innovations and by awarding stock options for the best ideas. It has set up a website where employees can post their ideas and has dispensed with its employee rule books. Continental Airlines, a corporation previously known for its maltreatment of workers, is another example. It's now also abandoned its employee rulebook. More important, it has made its workers part of the decision-making process. Chairman Gordon Bethune recently considered outsourcing the ticketing function to save money by reducing Continental's workforce. Instead, he offered the employees an opportunity to come up with a way to reduce costs and save their jobs. They did and not only kept their jobs but were treated as valuable assets, as an important part of the decision-making process.

At the same time, according to a Challenger, Gray and Christmas report, the boom in mergers and acquisitions in 1998 increased layoffs by 99.8 percent over those in 1997 — almost 600,000 workers laid off as a result of mergers and acquisitions alone. And we've already seen examples of CEOs like Coke's Douglas Daft making more and more money as they lay off workers. Former NationsBank CEO and head of BankAmerica Hugh McColl was paid about $45 million in stock in addition to $3.75 million in salary and bonus in 1999, while approximately 19,000 bank employees were laid off as a cost-cutting measure. (By the way, BankAmerica's stock price dropped about 17 percent in that same year.) The CEO of GTE, Charles Lee, got a $10 million incentive bonus and a $4 million

---

[a]To my knowledge there has been no such thing as human capital in this country since January 1, 1863, as enshrined in the Thirteenth Amendment to the United States.

implementation and retention bonus, and he is eligible to receive a $7 million long-term performance bonus in addition to stock options and pension contributions. Bell Atlantic CEO Ivan Seidenberg received a $14 million retention and implementation payment as a result of the Bell Atlantic/GTE merger. In January 1999, GTE announced that it would attempt to increase earnings per share by 13 percent by reducing expenses by $600 million, primarily through job cuts. When FleetBoston Financial Corp. took over BankBoston Corp., Fleet CEO Terrence Murray was paid $20.2 million and its president, Chad Gifford, $15.6 million. FleetBoston announced it would lay off almost 7 percent of its workforce, or 4,000 workers. Some 16,000 employees were laid off when Exxon and Mobil merged, and 10,400 after the Travelers/Citicorp deal.[1] And the beat goes on.

Despite the introduction of new management techniques, workers remain highly vulnerable while managers profit. Besides, large-scale layoffs are one of the fastest ways to boost the bottom line and establish a quick increase in stock prices. On average, stock prices rise 8 percent when a downsizing is announced, although the evidence is that this does not translate into better long-term profitability. When profitability does improve, gains are often not shared: witness the airline industry, which demanded and got substantial concessions from its workers during the recession of the early 1990s but has yet to share its newfound prosperity with them.

Corporations continue to treat their workers not as assets but as costs. And why not? That's the way accountants treat them. Costs need to be monitored and controlled. That's why GM shut down an entire town when, despite tax concessions from the town and promises not to do so, it closed its Willow Run plant and consolidated operations in Arlington, Texas.

Those workers who survive layoffs often are treated with suspicion and resentment — and of course they're suspicious and resentful themselves. Witness, for example, the recent introduction of the Fool Proof Time Clock, a new device which reliably clocks in employees by measuring their hand size. In my recent scholarly work I have, as I mentioned in chapter 5, called the corporate legal structure that results in this treatment of workers the American monitocracy.[2] And as I have demonstrated, workers who feel untrusted are not likely to be loyal, dedicated, and trustworthy themselves. They are, instead, likely to look out only for themselves.

Equally important, workers typically lack ownership interests in the corporations for which they work, except for the rather attenuated pension fund shares discussed in chapter 7. And we know how important ownership is to establishing feelings of commitment to the enterprise. Finally, it can't help but demoralize workers to know that in 1999 the average CEO earned 475 times the pay of the average blue collar worker, with 1999 average raises of 17 percent compared to average blue collar raises of 3.4 percent and white collar raises of 3.5 percent.[3]

The premise of this chapter is that the mandate of stockholder profit maximization encourages managers to treat workers poorly, both to the disadvantage of the workers and of the corporation as a whole. I will look at two essential components of the problem: worker treatment and its effect not only on the individual worker but on our social and political structures as well, and the possibilities of worker ownership as a solution. While I tend to favor the latter, it is certainly the case that worker treatment and its consequent social ills can be significantly ameliorated even within our current system of investor capitalism. It is to that end that my concluding suggestions will be aimed.

LET MY PEOPLE GO

It may seem vaguely odd to begin a chapter on workers in corporate America with a discussion of a century-old Supreme Court opinion dealing with the discredited doctrine of substantive due process.[b] But *Lochner v. New York*[4] is central to our discussion, first, because it is the most famous of a series of cases decided at the turn of the twentieth century that establish a social policy which dominated until temporarily halted by the New Deal and which revived

---

[b]Because the doctrine itself is discredited and not especially germane to the discussion I won't discuss it. The point of discussing the case here is the social philosophy that underlies it.

in the 1980s and remains with us today; and second, because it is based upon a conception of the autonomy of the American worker which still retains currency. The case involved a challenge to a New York statute which limited the working hours of bakers (at the time a dangerous and unhealthy profession) to no more than ten hours a day and sixty hours a week. The Supreme Court held that the law was invalid because it limited the bakers' freedom of contract. After all, if bakers chose to risk exhaustion or ill health in order to make more money, that was their decision, and the state ought not to be in the business of interfering with contracts freely arrived at between consenting adults.

Of course this was nonsense. Bakers didn't have a whole lot of choice. If the baking industry demanded that they work long hours, that's what they had to do. It is specious to suggest that the bakers could have pursued another trade; recall the student I discussed in chapter 5 who suggested that one made a choice to be a steelworker much the way he had chosen to go to law school. Working conditions for most trades at the time were far from optimal from a human point of view.[5] The point, of course, is the Supreme Court's implicit assumption (or, more likely, its social policy construction) that workers were fully autonomous in their relations with their employers, that they were fully capable of negotiating for themselves and, if they didn't like the terms offered, of working elsewhere or in a different trade. Such an assumption was contradicted by Adam Smith in his observation that, at least as far as wage negotiations go, the masters have by far the greater advantage over the worker.[6] I assume that it doesn't require the brilliance of Smith or a whole lot of evidence to make the assertion that the Supreme Court's observation was just silly, not to mention destructive.[7] Working-class Americans at the time were highly vulnerable to the whims of their employers and had very little choice as to the nature and terms of their working lives. Far from being autonomous, they were weak and exploited. Worker autonomy was a myth upon which the Supreme Court was relying, the very same myth I have argued is alive and well today. The Court chose to assume liberal autonomy where nothing but vulnerability existed.

Vulnerability is what it's all about. I have elsewhere discussed in great detail the relations between autonomy and vulnerability in American society and the power of the latter to lead us to caring behavior. In the context of this book, vulnerability takes on a more focused meaning. For what I discuss in this chapter really is concerned about vulnerability within organizations and, to a real extent, vulnerability of organizations to those of whom they are made.

According to the Department of Labor's Bureau of Labor Statistics (BLS) Household Data Survey for February 2000, 76 percent of employed Americans worked for private industry.[8] As of 1996, the latest data available to me, almost 63 percent of those worked in firms of one hundred or more people.[9] If nothing else, this implies that the overwhelming number of Americans work for someone else and mostly within some sort of hierarchical structure. Although many companies, especially in the service and high-tech industries, have flatter organizational charts than classic manufacturing companies, the clear implication is that almost everyone has a boss. Almost 16 percent of employed Americans work for federal, state, and local governments, all of which are hierarchies. Only 7 percent of Americans reported being self-employed. Thus it is obvious that most people work within organizations.

Naturally people are subject to vulnerabilities before they enter an organization, whether it be civil society or Microsoft. This is the essential insight of Thomas Hobbes's classic state of nature, in which the rough equality of all makes each subject to the predations of the other. For Hobbes the solution was the state, ruled through laws emanating from a ruler with extraordinary enforcement power and designed to protect the relative autonomy of each. But while Leviathan may have been the cure for state-of-nature vulnerability, it created its own vulnerabilities, as citizens of the state were subject to the authority of the ruler and the collectivity.

The modern corporation presents a Leviathan-like organization in precisely this respect. Working and living within an organization itself create vulnerabilities. Boards are vulnerable to takeovers and stockholder removal as well as to the disapproval of the markets. Managers are subject to dismissal by the board or their superiors. And the lower down on the food chain you go, the more fungible the work you do, the more subject to dismissal you are — whether for cause or by layoff. You are an instrument of production. And when you're not needed, you're let go.

Well, maybe not that fast. You might have a union to protect you, although only 9.4 percent of privately employed American workers belonged to unions in 1999.[10] Or, you might say, my employer's reputation would be hurt too badly by promiscuous layoffs such that it would be difficult to hire new employees, and that offers protection. But reputation is a marginal thing. It didn't stop the massive layoffs that occurred in the 1980s and 1990s and are still occurring today. Reputation didn't stop the last bastions of genteel over-employment, major New York law firms, from shocking young lawyers who traditionally had job security (at least until the partnership decision) by laying off hundreds them in the late eighties and early nineties to keep partnership draws high. And when times got better at corporations and law firms alike workers came back in droves. To paraphrase Willie Sutton, that's where the jobs are. So relying too heavily on reputation alone is a dangerous thing.

Feelings of vulnerability increase the more you are monitored. What does it feel like to have someone looking over your shoulder all the time? and looking carefully because he fears that if you don't perform, he will lose his job? Henry Ford is quoted as saying, "The average man won't really do a day's work unless he is caught and cannot get out of it."[11] Not an attitude that makes you feel comfortable or trusted.

Why subject ourselves to this kind of vulnerability? Most of us have no choice. Organizations are where the jobs are. Make no mistake, you could strike out on your own, as many have, to make your own job and your own fortune, which of course has its own vulnerabilities, including exposure to those with whom you do business. Such social vulnerability is an inescapable fact of life. My point is that within the corporation, especially the corporation so directly and unyieldingly tied to stock price with the attendant internal monitoring that occurs, vulnerability or at least feelings of vulnerability are enhanced.

So what do we do about it? Well, one suggestion I will now para-doxically pursue is that we ameliorate this vulnerability by employing a different form of vulnerability — trust — to replace the monitoring that characterizes American corporate life.[12] Trust is an important social fabric, binding people in common enterprise, encouraging cooperation and group goals at the same time that it leads people to accept the decisions of higher authorities in a way that simple command does not. It helps to create feelings of dignity and autonomy. It also, as we will see, enhances productivity. And where true trust reigns, these feelings are not the result of some sort of Marxian false consciousness but instead are real because the trust that creates them is real. Trusted workers are, in short, human workers. And trust in the workplace has the capacity not only to make richer working lives but to spill over into civil society as well, enhancing the cohesiveness of social and political institutions.

Twenty-nine years have passed between Studs Terkel's classic *Working*, which documents the generally unsatisfactory work lives and attitudes toward work of ordinary Americans, and Thomas Petzinger's *The New Pioneers,* which reports upon his study of innovation and entrepreneurial power throughout the American economy.[13] But despite appearances and real, indisputable improvements, the truth for most Americans is not a lot different from what it was when Terkel wrote or, at some level, at the time *Lochner* was decided. That very same employee vulnerability exists today, although it is masked by strikingly low unemployment and the much-publicized bargaining power of the knowledge worker, especially in the high-tech sector of the economy. It's easy to be fooled into thinking that things have changed.

Maybe I'm getting old, but I recently read with some horror of the twenty-three-year-old trainee at Salomon Smith Barney, writing on behalf of all five hundred of his young colleagues (though at the request of the firm), to demand improvements in working conditions in order to prevent a mass exodus from investment banking to the high-tech sector. Among the young associates' demands were an on-site concierge, more money for meals (and we're not talking McDonald's), better laptop computers, use of the firm gym on weekends, a nurse room or rec room where the analysts could relax, reimbursement for clothing and other personal items bought on business trips, "a relaxation of the firm's dress code, more social events and corporate credit cards 'where the analyst never sees the bill' " but gets the sky miles or reward points or whatever. And the firm caved — to people in their early twenties making an average of $70,000 per year and anticipating compensation in the millions just five years after they're employed![14] Donaldson, Lufkin & Jenrette has been signing new graduates of Ivy League business schools to two-year contracts worth $700,000 to $800,000.[15] I'm just jealous, you say? You bet I am! But the point is that stories like these and the tales of dot.com millionaires (and billionaires) that have moved from the financial press to the popular press lead easily to the conclusion that all is well in the world of work.

Things certainly have improved, at least for the moment, although the continuing popularity of Scott Adams's *Dilbert* might suggest that not everybody finds their work life completely fulfilling. As I write, unemployment has been at a thirty-year low, and stories abound of employers unable to hire sufficient workers, let alone workers of the caliber they want.[16] Coupled with these are stories about how corporations are attracting and retaining employees — not all of them are as munificent as Salomon Smith Barney, but they include increases in pay and perks. At start-up ArsDigita, employees who recruit ten programmers to the company are given a Ferrari. SmallOffice.com gave its forty employees a vacation in Maui.[17] And you can get a Mercedes if you work for Novosoft and exceed your goals[18] or a Harley-Davidson motorcycle if you are one of the two employees of DoubleClick to bring in the highest number of recruits.[19] But even as I write, the week of May 29, 2000, the government announced a slight increase in unemployment figures, signaling a possible slowing of the economy, at least in part as a result of the Federal Reserve's increase in interest rates. Will the new age of worker power survive increasing unemployment? or is it simply a function of necessity breeding niceness? Has the average American worker become sufficiently autonomous to strike the kind of free bargains assumed by the *Lochner* court?

Of course it's hard to know. Peter Drucker has identified two classes of workers: knowledge workers, who in effect have replaced machinery and money as the true capital of industry in the information economy and who can take it with them wherever they go, and service workers, who clean toilets and take out trash and provide the unseen, unpleasant infrastructure of the information economy.[20] Knowledge workers have real bargaining power; without them, their employers have nothing. Employers know this and have resorted to a variety of tactics from on-site child care to simply being nice in order to keep them happy.[21] Service workers, who formed at least 13 percent of the employed American population in 1998, don't have it a whole lot better than toilet cleaners and burger flippers ever had.[c] The inflation-adjusted minimum wage in 1997 was $5.15, just 66¢ higher than it was in 1954.[22] And while the dot.com kids and investment bankers are driving Ferraris to firm-paid lunches or being coddled by the company nurse, 24 percent of all "full-time blue-collar and service workers employed by midsized and large firms did not have rest breaks in 1993," the most recent data available, nor did 51 percent of part-time workers.[23] According to the most recent data in the BLS *National Compensation Survey*, the average hourly earnings of a worker in private industry in the Middle Atlantic region (the highest-earning region of the nine used by the bureau) was $16.47, and the average hours worked was 35.8 per week. This produces pretax earnings of $589.62 per week, or, assuming a full fifty-week work year, annual earnings of $29,481.30. The comparable figures for the lowest-earning region, the West South Central region, were $12.97 per hour for 36.4 hours and an annual $23,605.40.[24] The poverty level for nonfarm families of four in 1997 was $16,400, and 125 percent of the poverty level was $20,500.[25,d]

And it's not just that the absolute figures are strikingly low. Substantial evidence supports the conclusion that, for the past several

[c]The BLS statistics may somewhat understate the number of what we might consider service workers, as it defines "service worker" to include only five categories: health, food preparation and beverage, personal, cleaning buildings and grounds, and protective services. And I'm not even talking here about blue collar workers, who, as the following text shows, aren't doing very well either.

[d]The government treats persons living below 125 percent of the poverty level as an important indicator of financial well-being in its own right. See *Statistical Abstract of the United States, 1999*, table 760.

decades, hourly pay in constant dollars has either flattened or declined. When this is combined with the fact that almost two-thirds of the increase in American gross domestic product from 1979 to 1996 went to the top 5 percent of families, the result is, as Richard Freeman and Joel Rogers put it in their book *What Workers Want* (1999), that "the level of income inequality in the United States has skyrocketed, making the country's economy the most unequal in the developed world."[26] They note, citing data from the Organization for Economic Cooperation and Development, that whereas the top 10 percent of American workers earn on average 5.6 times more than the bottom 10 percent, the comparable proportions for the European Union and Japan are 2.1 and 2.4, respectively. William Greider and Robert Kuttner each compellingly point to the globalization of corporate production as a source of downward wage pressure for American workers and little improvement for lower-paid workers in other countries.)[27] So much for an egalitarian society.[e]

Although life has improved through minimum wages, social security, unemployment insurance, and intangibles like improved health care for those who are insured or can afford it, it is my thesis that the stock-price maximizing structure of the American corporation will, in a time of increasing unemployment (which seems to me certain to happen), return us more than we care to think to the old ways. It's simply in the structure.

By saying it's in the structure, what I mean is that the monitocracy goes deep into the corporation. This has a number of implications for corporate behavior, implications which may well be masked by worker scarcity but which are part and parcel of the American em-

---

[e]While on average after-tax family income in the United States increased 9.5 percent from 1977 to 1994, the top 1 percent of families found their income increasing 72 percent, the next 4 percent had a 25 percent increase, and it went down from there, with only 25 percent of the lowest 80 percent of families seeing any increase at all (a paltry 4 percent) and the rest experiencing declines from 1 percent to 16 percent (for the lowest quintile.) Isaac Shapiro and Robert Greenstein, "Trends in the Distribution of After-Tax Income," Center on Budget and Policy Priorities, August 14, 1997.

phasis on individual autonomy and the lack of group cohesiveness, especially in the economic realm. The first is that in worsening economic times we can expect to see a return to relatively poor treatment of workers, a relic of Taylorism,[f] accounting rules, and American social attitudes. We are, after all, not far removed from that age, and I will next discuss the embeddedness of this way of thinking. A second implication arises from this old style of management and that is the nature and function of trust as social capital not only in enhancing economic efficiency but also in helping to create a society in which people care about one another, about economic justice, and about the quality of their lives beyond making a simple living. Finally, I will discuss the relation between the corporate monitocracy and broader social issues, in particular, the fate of civic virtue when the work environment is one of relative tyranny and vulnerability. This naturally leads to a discussion of the wisdom of worker ownership and to some suggestions for reform.

SOCIALISM IN THE CAPITALIST TOOLBOX

In his book *A Preface to Economic Democracy* (1985) the political scientist Robert Dahl pointed out the socialistic nature of the American corporation,[28] an irony especially notable in that nothing has come to represent American capitalist success so much as our business corporation. Dahl's reasoning is simple and compelling: nothing so embodies the command and control ideal of socialism as the hierarchical managerial structure of the American corporation. A famous American law school casebook studied by generations of law students described the legal structure of the corporation as an inverted pyramid, with ultimate power resting in the stockholders, delegated to the board of directors, and from there to the officers.

[f]Taylorism, the production and management system of scientific management pioneered by Frederick Winslow Taylor, stresses the difference between planning and doing. Managers make the decisions; workers carry them out. The classic Taylorist artifact is the assembly line, but as David Levine points out, it is inherent in the way McDonald's employees, data entry clerks, and textile piece workers perform their tasks as well.

While countless writers have suggested, with some reason, that the real power lies with management, the theory I have detailed so far suggests that power over corporate behavior rests in the capital markets—and that means the stockholders, as we have seen them. The pyramid was a useful heuristic and accurate as far as corporate law goes, for as I've already pointed out stockholders, directors, and officers[g] are the only constituent groups of which corporate law takes any real notice.[h] But had the pyramid been redrawn to reflect the reality of corporate operations, it would have had to point deeper: it would have had to go through layers of management to middle-level employees and down to the lowest level of corporate worker; from the chief operating officer to the people who work in the mail room and clean out the trash at night. Of course it could have been redrawn in a different geometric form to include relationships with creditors, suppliers, and customers, but that's beyond the scope of my point here.

Anyway, redrawn in this more realistic way, the pyramid metaphor is a good one, not only because it correctly depicts the structure of legal power but also because, like an inverted pyramid, it shows an increasing narrowing of focus, an increasing beam that cuts through the layers of the corporations and shines most directly on the people who show up for work every day. Drawn this way, the inverted pyramid correctly depicts the monitocracy that dominates American corporate thinking.

What do I mean by this? One answer was given by David Gordon

[g]Here I'm using the technical legal term—not the broader concept of managers—in which officers consist of a president, treasurer, secretary, and perhaps vice-presidents, all as set forth in the corporation's bylaws. These are people with generalized legal authority to act in certain ways on behalf of the corporation. The concept of management is much broader, encompassing a wide range of employees who are given job-specific authority and who run the corporation on a day-to-day basis.

[h]I've already mentioned stakeholder statutes, about which there exists a vast body of scholarly literature. But for the reasons I've set forth so far as well as a number of other reasons, these have had no significant practical effect on corporate law and don't seem to have had much effect on corporate behavior either.

in his book *Fat and Mean* (1996).[29] Gordon details the extraordinary top-heaviness of American corporations, even taking account of the spate of white-collar layoffs that so horrified corporate America in the early 1990s, claiming that what he calls "the bureaucratic burden" is "one of the most stunning features of the U.S. economy."[30] Using BLS figures from 1994, he claims that 17.3 million American workers—almost as many as worked in the entire public sector, federal, state, and local—worked in nonproduction and supervisory jobs. And he found that this enormous level of supervisory employment was sustained and even grew during the heavily publicized downsizing of white-collar workers in the early 1990s. Using the same statistical base Gordon used (although a simpler and arguably more conservative methodology), I calculate that, including government employees, in February 2000 at least 40,806,000 workers, or slightly over 33 percent of the nonagricultural workforce, were supervisory in some way.[31] It doesn't appear that things have improved.

By Gordon's own admission, his data arguably overstate his case. The BLS statistics don't break employment down into sufficiently fine detail to enable one to separate what might be called real managerial jobs from an employee who simply has the power to tell another employee what to do. To some extent this doesn't matter. My point (and his) is that excessive supervision creates a management style of discipline and culture of distrust that is destructive of the social fabric of the working environment. But if these data are subject to some question, they are not the only information available.

Gordon's data are supported, indeed amplified, in work performed by the sociologist Erik Olin Wright in his well-known *Class Structure Survey,* the most recent data for which are from 1991.[32] In contrast to Gordon's methodology, which relied heavily on government statistics (which Benjamin Disraeli, referring to statistics in general, told us are worse than "lies and damned lies"), Wright and his colleagues actually surveyed workers about their jobs and the responsibilities that went with them. Of course pollsters well know that the way in which questions are formulated can bias answers, as can peoples' motivations to look good. But Wright's questions were fairly pointed, for example, "Do you have the power to fire another employee?"and therefore seem pretty reliable. They found that 38.9 percent of surveyed nonfarm workers spent time supervising others or telling them what to do, and that 36.3 percent claimed their jobs were supervisory or managerial.[33] Maybe some of them did exaggerate a bit. But no matter how you cut it, that seems like an awful lot of managers.

Gordon's thesis is that the monitocracy carries with it a managerial style he calls the stick, that is, a confrontational and aggressive form of supervision in which worker compliance is obtained more by threat than by positive incentive, and that this has produced, among other by-products, a variety of social ills, from the destruction of family life to increasing income inequality. His argument is persuasive, if not indisputable. But while these conclusions are important and imply a particular view of corporate accountability, they don't go to the heart of the argument I'm making.

Another study does exactly that, as it shows that the American trend of managers managing managers managing managers is only increasing. Michael Useem's interesting and timely book *Executive Defense*[34] takes an interesting approach to the corporate restructurings of the eighties and early nineties by relying upon interviews with a wide variety of sources and detailed studies of seven corporations in seven industries. In addition to concluding that stockholder-centrism is, as a real-world matter, the order of the corporate day— confirmation of the theory I've been at great pains to construct— Useem spends a sizable portion of his book analyzing what this means for managers.[35] His conclusion is that the stockholder-centric ethic has penetrated deep into the internal structure of the corporation. For a variety of reasons he concludes that the rise of stockholder interests gave managers more latitude to operate corporate businesses as they saw fit, at the same time that their new freedom was measured scrupulously and unforgivingly by the market. The basic function of senior management became the hiring and supervision of lower management, and the basic function of managers overall became that of managing managers—all to the end of increasing stockholder wealth. While managers were evaluated for compensation and promotion on the basis of a variety of factors,

Useem finds virtually all of these to be linked in some way to "shareholder value," which he generally treats as dividends plus capital gains per share divided by beginning share price; and when management compensation was tied to shareholder value in this way, Useem noted, it was the best predictor of corporate behavior.

What Useem saw is not all bad. For example, skill in people management became a greater concern of managers as they tried to fulfill the corporate mandate to the stockholders. And a focused concern with shareholder value enabled management to create incentives that motivated other managers to achieve the corporate goal.

But there was an ominous consequence for my argument: an obsession with share prices. Useem spoke with the chief operating officer of one corporation whose compensation package was designed so that about 70 percent of his annual compensation was in shares of his company. "When asked how often he checked his company's price, he said 'every morning, every night, and . . . probably about ten times a day.' " Useem goes on to report that at this company "management obsession with stock performance was reflected in the entry to the executive office building, where the visual field contained only two objects: a receptionist desk guarding the portals and a display posting a number. Updated three times a day, the posting contained the current price of the firm's shares."[36]

The ethic of stockholder wealth maximization has produced real benefits for managers. Stock options and other forms of incentive-based compensation have made lots of executives very rich. According to one recent study, the average corporate chief executive officer has about $75 million in stock options. Having such munificence put away for a rainy day, the *New York Times* concluded, "a chief executive makes more in a single day than the typical American worker does in a year."[37] The same report observes that the heads of "new economy" companies averaged $720 million in stock, in addition to an average annual compensation of $27 million. But what has the new economy done for other workers, who on average earned $33,000 in 1999? The answer appears to be what William Greider calls "wage arbitration," the movement of production from high wage regions to lower wage regions, aided by the globalization of capital and product markets as well as free trade agreements imposed by rich nations on poorer ones.[38] While Greider does not link this movement as closely as I do to the profit motive, it is implicit in his argument that the search for higher corporate profits has led corporations in wealthy nations like the United States to move jobs out of the country and into poorer ones where production costs are dramatically lower. The result is a worldwide competition for jobs and wages, with the laws of supply and demand in a relatively free global market tending to equalize wage levels at those considerably lower than American workers demand. Thus the American worker bears much of the cost of stock price maximization, as jobs disappear and wages stagnate. Challenger, Gray and Christmas reported layoff announcements in 1999 running at 40 percent higher than in 1998. One scholar notes that approximately 13 percent of the American workforce was displaced between 1991 and 1993, 15 percent between 1993 and 1995, and 12 percent between 1995 and 1997. That's a lot of workers put out of jobs.[39] And according to the Census Bureau's *1999 Statistical Abstract of the United States,* the real minimum wage increased by only 66¢ between 1954 and 1997.

Of course the true egalitarian should applaud Greider's observation because national boundaries arguably ought not to define human equality. If workers in poor countries now find themselves with jobs and better wages, we should applaud this and understand that a more equal world is not only a fairer world but a more stable one as well. Not so fast. Workers in poor countries are not dramatically benefiting from the global commodification of the labor market (Kuttner describes it as a "spot market") but instead are being doomed to stasis in a system which, left unregulated, will not bring them higher level jobs and upward mobility. But for my immediate purposes, and before anyone starts celebrating the final unification of the workers of the world, I should point out how unconvincing this argument should be to American workers. Of course greater world equality is better as a moral matter, or so I shall assume, and more stable. But notice who is bearing the cost. There is no evidence — quite the contrary — of a decline in executive compensation, and what I've already said makes it clear that in fact the richest Americans are continuing to get richer. And it's not just the executives. To the extent that the globalization of the labor market leads to stagnant and decreasing American wages, it does so in the name of rewarding American capital. I know capital in other wealthy countries benefits too, but none more so than America, and it is upon America that this portion of the book is focused. It may be that some American workers will eventually see some of this reward to capital in their pensions, assuming they participate in defined contribution plans rather than defined benefit plans. Federal Reserve Board statistics show that in 1998, 54 percent of American households participated in retirement plans sponsored by their employers, of which 18 percent participated in defined benefit plans and 33 percent in defined contribution plans.[i] But looking to your rewards in retirement when you find it almost impossible to make ends meet, as the data I've given suggest most people do, is cold comfort indeed. It would of course be one thing if the wealthy had to bear some of the burden—and my earlier suggestions on increased taxation of capital gains would produce revenues that could be used for things like worker retraining, education, including aid to lower-income workers to send their kids to college, and even simple distribution or tax cuts for lower-income workers at levels where it is needed. But in the current state of affairs, things seem terribly unfair indeed. And it's largely as a result of our drive to maximize stock prices.

Maybe this picture is too bleak. There might be an upside to stockholder-centrism for employees. Perhaps corporate managements understand that one way to increase profitability is to make sure that workers are well trained. If so, then workers benefit too because their job skills are enhanced and the upward potential of their careers is increased. Certainly Useem believes this to be the case in the managerial ranks. But what about the average guy? Things are improving: corporate training expenditures are up 26 percent since 1993, but that's nothing compared to capital market

[i]Only 11 percent of workers with incomes under $10,000 and 33 percent of workers with incomes between $10,000 and $25,000 participated in these plans, while 77 percent of those with incomes between $50,000 and $100,000 did.

performance, and there's a long way to go before decent treatment of workers becomes widespread.[40]

TRUST ME

The reign of the stockholder and the monitocracy it sustains creates another dark side for workers. That is the erosion and disappearance of trust in the workplace. Trust is important. It can make operations more efficient by cutting down on the need to supervise people. But then what would all those managers do? Trust is also important in its own right, as a mechanism to bind people together in a way that sustains cooperation and community, thereby giving them a sense of belonging and of being cared for. It also makes them care. Writing for *Directorship* magazine, the consultant Jordan Lewis advises boards on the importance of trust in ensuring that employees are cooperative and, as a consequence, more productive; he notes further that such benefits are felt at all levels from the board to the shop floor.[41] Strong psychological evidence supports the assertion that people who believe they are trusted in fact act in more trustworthy ways than people who do not. Trust creates trust; trust sustains trust. And mistrust leads not only to alienation and disaffection but also to untrustworthy, even destructive behavior. Adam Smith included the level of trust required in a particular occupation as one of five factors affecting the wages of the worker.[42] And it might be argued that the more you can trust workers, the more you can pay them, especially if, as evidence suggests, increased trust increases productivity.[43]

Trust is a multifaceted concept, but in our context I want to focus on two aspects of it: trust that you are doing your job, and trust that your boss is treating you fairly. Consider Mary Morse, a software engineer working for a company called Autodesk in California, where she's been employed for two years. Every week or so she is recruited by other Silicon Valley companies, some offering her much greater compensation: one promised to make her a millionaire. Morse always declines these offers. The reason is simple: she works for a boss who is nice to her, who cares about her professional development and career ideals, and who understands that she is an individual with hopes, goals, and aspirations. In contrast, the interviewer at the company that would have made her a millionaire showed complete disinterest in the kind of work she wanted to do or at least move toward, telling her that if she came to work for the company she was going to do precisely what was assigned to her.

David Sulik, a superintendent at an International Paper factory, has learned the benefits of being nice and attentive to his employees, a lesson that has been stressed by his own bosses. As reported in the *New York Times,* Sulik criticizes his subordinates less, compliments them more, and talks with them more frequently. As a result, Sulik says, "I think they trust me more than in the past." The results of a recent Gallup Poll of two million workers at seven hundred companies were reported in the same article and concluded that both an employee's productivity and the likelihood of her remaining in her job were determined by her relationship with her boss. Only 11 percent of employees surveyed who were satisfied with that relationship said they were likely to look for new jobs, in contrast to 40 percent who were dissatisfied.

Employers don't seem to have gotten the message very well. Fifty-six percent of those surveyed felt that their employers didn't really care about them or their careers, and 55 percent reported that they had no strong loyalty to their companies.[44] The message is clear: trust breeds loyalty, and loyalty retains productive workers.

Trust is important. It keeps valuable employees where they are. It cuts down on the costs of supervising employees. And it makes employees work harder. But you can't fake it. According to the economist Robert Frank, whose work follows the moral sense theory of Adam Smith, in order to be genuinely trustworthy you have to internalize the value of trust. The fact that there may be payoff for trustworthy behavior is important, but if that's your only motivation, you will be inclined to break that trust at the margins. And as the philosopher Annette Baier has written, trust, once broken, is very difficult to regain.[45]

Substantial psychological evidence supports the conclusion that trust is an important business asset. For starters, high trusting people are more likely to restrain themselves, voluntarily to restrict their own consumption of common resources, *even when others aren't doing so.* In other words, they are not out to maximize their own gain from limited resources but understand the cooperative nature of the endeavor and are willing to act in accordance with that understanding.[46] We'll look at what can happen when people are not trusting or trusted in a moment. But there's more. The psychologists Tom Tyler and Peter Degoey found that trust makes it more likely that people will accept the decisions of higher authorities and obey group rules. And the astonishing thing is that this seems to be true even when they perceive that the decision maker is not entirely neutral. As they put it, "People seemed willing to forgive surface features of racism and sexism . . . if they felt that the authorities involved were basically motivated to act in a benevolent manner. It was the trustworthiness of the intentions of the authorities. . . , not surface features" that determined peoples' reactions. They also found that when employers conveyed their sense of trust by treating their employees respectfully and neutrally, employees were almost five times more likely to behave in a trustworthy manner.[47]

That's a fairly striking conclusion and suggests that perhaps Kant was right: the only good thing is a good intention. But whether or not that's entirely true, it is evident that trust can substantially cut down on supervision and lead workers to identify more closely with their employers' interests. There's a lot more psychological evidence supporting these ideas, but I'm not going to go through it all here.[48] The point is that trust is important. It's not even that difficult to build trust within an institutional setting like the corporation. All you have to do is care — and show it.

What happens when, as the monitocracy presumes, you don't trust your workers? Sometimes they just go sullenly about their work, doing what they have to do to get by and no more. But sometimes they're destructive. They contaminate products, undermine their coworkers, destroy computer programs and create viruses and bugs, defame their employers in tabloids, and generally sabotage the corporations.[49] And their employers don't set very good examples either. According to recent surveys conducted by the Ethics Resource Center and KPMG, ethics on the job are suffering as well. The center's National Business Ethics Survey reported that approximately one-third of the 1,500 public and private workers surveyed claimed personally to have witnessed misconduct at work, including employers lying "to employees, customers, vendors or the public," abuse of employees, theft, and lawbreaking. The KPMG survey of 3,075 employees reported over 75 percent claiming they had seen employers break laws or violate company standards over the preceding six months.[50]

Sometimes it's even worse. What happens if you can't trust your boss not to take it out on you if you give him bad news? You don't give him bad news. And this sometimes results in disaster. For nineteen years, Boeing Corporation failed to report the existence of fuel-tank defects that seemed to be the cause of the explosion of TWA Flight 800 in July 1996. One explanation for the nondisclosure was the employee culture of Boeing, which had been roiled by massive layoffs.[51] It's not hard to see in that environment why you wouldn't want to tell your boss the bad news.

Trust and caring arise from worker participation. So, by the way, does increased productivity. David Levine, in his book *Reinventing the Workplace* (1995), surveyed the available empirical evidence, looked at specific examples, and concluded that substantial productivity gains could be achieved simply by treating workers as if they mattered.[52] And Freeman and Rogers have found overwhelming evidence that in effect what workers want is to be reassured of their importance to the firm. But there is a substantial obstacle to effective worker participation, and that is the fact that employees will work harder (which participation generally requires), share ideas, and cooperate with one another and management only if they trust management to share the gains rather than use them to siphon off more money for themselves or lay off workers who become less critical to the enterprise with increased productivity.

There's a lot of talk in the popular and scholarly literature about worker participation, but as Levine sees it it's not all that simple. In the first place, the type of participation matters. Establishing works councils to be informed of corporate finances and discuss worker issues, as is common in European corporations, or simply putting worker representatives on the board of directors is not enough. This consultative participation, as Levine calls it, not only has no long-term positive effects but can have even negative effects. It's the kind of participation that was fairly common in the United States in the eighties and nineties in the form of what were called quality circles. Levine points out that managers liked them because they gave workers the impression they were being listened to. But as Robert Frank and Adam Smith told us, people aren't that easily fooled — and neither were the workers. No false consciousness here!

The kind of participation that really matters is substantive participation: that which involves employees in actual work teams in which they have a great deal of latitude to organize and perform their work with very little supervision other than general directives regarding work requirements. These are the kinds of participation that Petzinger reported as being so effective in his study. But, as Levine points out, substantive participation is not by itself enough; after all, when you give workers this kind of responsibility, you are asking them to work harder, to work in ways that may increase efficiency and possibly make some workers obsolete, and produce gains that they personally may never see. Trust is the glue that binds workers to the enterprise, and it's a crucial additive to participation.[53] What else do you need?

Well, in the first place, Levine tells us that it's important to involve workers at higher levels of decision making. As I mentioned, this kind of consultative process by itself doesn't result in greater productivity but, when combined with the substantive forms of participation, has an important positive effect. And this makes sense in light of the evidence I've already discussed. Recall the psychological evidence that people are more likely to be trustworthy, which includes doing their jobs honestly and well, if they believe they have good relationships with their bosses and that they are treated fairly. But you need even more.

Levine found that in order for worker participation to increase productivity, workers also needed to be assured that they were sharing in those productivity gains.[54] As Levine put it, "Some kind of sharing of rewards from involvement is a key element of almost all participatory systems." And, indeed, he found substantial correlation between participation and gain sharing. There are a number of ways that gains can be shared. Employee stock ownership plans (ESOPs) are increasingly common in the United States, approximately 9,500 U.S. companies, mostly privately held, having one.[55] But ESOPs alone are not enough. The companies that enjoy real productivity gains combine them with substantive worker participation. Another important method is to reduce the pay differential between managerial and workers' salaries. It should be obvious as to why this is beneficial, but some die-hard neoclassists would view the practice negatively because it can be seen as robbing managers of the incentive to produce greater wealth for all. Of course this argument overlooks the fact that incentives are also necessary to encourage workers to produce greater wealth for all, too. It also overlooks the negative effects that such substantial differences can have on employee morale.

As Levine explains it, there are three principal benefits to salary-differential reduction: it helps foster an atmosphere of trust among workers; it creates incentives to work for group goals, which, as we have seen, is a consequence of increased trust itself; and it helps to foster cooperation. Drawing on the work of the famous organizational psychologist Morton Deutsch, Levine notes that any increase in democratic and egalitarian structures within the organization increases cooperation and productivity.

In order for participation to translate into productivity, workers have to be comfortable that any criticism of existing practices or efficiency gains won't lose them their jobs — a fact stressed by Freeman and Rogers. In fact job security is so important that Levine claims the relation "between labor participation and avoiding lay-offs appears to be causal, not merely correlational."[56] The desire for job security encourages employees to monitor each other and to share information. It also increases the motivation provided by group-based compensation and social approval within the workplace. Not surprisingly, Levine found that companies with higher levels of employee involvement offer greater job security. And of course they provide more job training as well — consider the example of Mary Morse, whom I discussed several pages earlier.

As to my earlier speculation that much of the contemporary improvement in the treatment of workers is at least in part a function of a tight labor market, Levine reports that in the business downturn of the late 1980s and early 1990s, worker participation decreased. Gains there are, but there is always concern for the bottom line. Unless worker participation and the treatment of workers as assets rather than costs are institutionalized — that is, unless we can take our eyes off our corporations' stock prices "every morning, every night, and probably ten times a day" — it seems unlikely that these gains will last. And not only will that be harmful to workers as people; as we have seen, it can also hurt long-term productivity.

It's not just the workers who need trust in order to be both more productive and happier people. Trust is required at the board level, at higher management levels, and throughout the corporate structure. In the first place, the higher up trust exists in the organization, the better it will be modeled for those lower down.[57] It's hard to expect middle managers and plant workers to trust one another if they see nothing but competition and controversy at the top. And as I made clear earlier in chapter 5, trust is required at the level of the capital markets as well. It's hard for a board of directors to instill trust within an organization if they themselves believe they are not trusted. Of course as I also pointed out, this is precisely what our corporate structure leads them to believe.

The relative absence of trust in the workplace is an understandable and possibly inevitable consequence of our monitocracy. Cooperative corporate systems like those of Japan and Germany exhibit substantially higher levels of trust throughout the corporation, and the ethic of cooperation is pervasive from the shareholder level down to the shop floor.[58] Well, you might note, these are countries in which cooperation is a cultural norm, at least more so than in the United States. You might also argue that trust in these societies tends to be exclusionary — you have the problem of the in-group and the out-group. And of course you'd be right, although as Tocqueville observed and as is still the case, America is a nation not only of individuals but of a countless variety of organizations to which people willingly give their time and energy. Although civic cooperation has declined in America, the root of it has always existed.[j] But indi-

---

[j]For a detailed discussion, see my *Stacked Deck: A Story of Selfishness in America.*

vidualism always seems to grab pride of place, and perhaps no more so than in business, where we seem to believe that a different ethic prevails. Jordan Lewis reports that at Motorola, "internal friction was so rampant for so long that staffers labeled the company 'a federation of warring tribes.'" I guess at least there was teamwork within the tribes. But Lewis's explanation lays the blame on individualism. As he writes, "Underlying these troubles was a practice of emphasizing independence and entrepreneurial machismo over interpersonal strengths in selecting people as business heads."[59]

Perhaps "business is business." But if we believe that to be the case, we are fooling ourselves. If business is business, it is so because we have artificially constructed a different ethic around business than around our daily lives outside of work. While I believe that this is true to some degree, I am also concerned that the American ethic of autonomy, which I described in the beginning of this book as having reached a pathological state, is even more pronounced in the business arena. But as the examples Lewis enumerates and the evidence I have presented show, we can cooperate if we want to. Trust is the glue of that cooperation, and it's not only healthy for business; it's healthy for our society as well.

CIVIC VIRTUE BEGINS AT WORK

Monitocratic management has serious negative consequences for American society. For most of the first eighteen or twenty-two years of their lives, most Americans are in school, learning in traditional classrooms run by the teacher. Although lessons in democracy and civics are taught and older students are offered such opportunities for institutional participation as relatively autonomous student governments and clubs, school life takes place within a fairly sheltered institutional environment. When we graduate to work, most of us enter, at least as a matter of the statistics we've seen, the American monitocracy. Our work success, indeed, our job security, depends more or less upon doing what we're told and making our bosses happy, which includes making them look good to their own bosses. Promotion is competitive, and compensation depends upon how well you play the game. While the corporate conformity of the 1950s seems largely behind us, conformity continues to play an important role for most Americans. And that means doing the job you're told as well as you can, a job determined increasingly by corporate efforts to maximize stock prices.

What does this mean for our broader society? Probably quite a lot, but there are two aspects upon which I'd like to focus. The first is the ethic of the work environment; the second is the opportunity to become a fully participating member of society.

I've already discussed the ethic at some length. Let me simply add here Schumpeter's observation that the rationality of the profit motive and self-interest, which he sees as independent of capitalism, is stretched by capitalism through accounting practices and measuring things in units of money. The result is that numerical valuation winds up affecting capitalist society's view of life, including things we generally think of as being immeasurable, like aesthetics and spirituality.[60] If the corporate watchword is wealth in the form of higher stock prices, then the employee's role ethic is wealth as well. Recall the company that posts its stock price at its door three times daily. Workers arriving at that job have no doubt as to what their purpose is. It is not to make the best product they can or to provide the best services available. It is to maximize corporate profit.

One of the most controversial areas in which this effect can now be seen is managed health care by private corporate health providers. I have no doubt physicians have always been concerned with their income, judging at least by my doctor's improved financial well-being over the years as a result of my and others' illnesses. But doctors are professionals, and presumably money is not the only draw to their profession; my doctor is also a humane and caring man who takes the time to understand and treat me as a person and incorporates that understanding into his treatment. Corporations are, as we have seen, artificial constructs with artificial purposes. And their employees, including the doctors who work for them, are charged with fulfilling that corporate purpose.

Now I don't want to go overboard. Obviously if the doctors in a given managed care company consistently provide bad treatment, patients will choose other providers and profits will dry up. But the problem is not a particular company or even the particular individuals who suffer before other health care consumers get the message. The problem is that all managed care corporations have the same incentive to maximize profit while competing for the same pool of patients. As a result, one can expect the quality of health care or at least the time and attention given to each patient to diminish. And a study by researchers at Harvard and Public Citizen concluded exactly that.[61]

But the problem involves more than just theory. You see, health care professionals employed by managed care companies have strong incentives to cut corners on their treatment in order to enhance the bottom line. If a doctor provides care that is not covered by the plan and not approved by the managers, the doctor will not be paid for his services. Participating doctors are also subject to "gag clauses," which preclude them from informing patients of treatment options not covered by the plan but available from other providers. Contracts between managed care companies and doctors often include clauses that award bonuses if care costs are kept below a specified amount or that withhold a portion of the doctor's fees and return it to employees who keep costs below a stated target. Needless to say, while they might originate in a legitimate realization that health care costs have gone out of control owing to excessive treatment, these perverse incentives to save money can and often do compromise the quality of care.

Cynthia Herdrich went to her doctor at the Carle Clinic, an HMO in Urbana, Illinois, complaining of abdominal pain. This organization gave its doctors a share of the annual profits. Rather than immediately determine the cause of Herdrich's pain, her doctor delayed testing for eight days until tests could be performed more inexpensively at the clinic. Herdrich's appendix ruptured.[62] Jacob Howard was born with a vascular malformation of which his pediatrician was aware. Nonetheless, when Jacob's mother called the doctor to inquire about Jacob's high fever, the doctor refused to authorize her to take him to the emergency room (which authorization was required for reimbursement) but to wait until morning, when the doctor could see him during normal hours. The next day, Jacob died.[63] Patrick Shea had a family history of heart disease, which he described to his doctor in a visit following a business trip during which he had suffered severe chest pain. Over the course of several visits, Shea reported feelings of dizziness, short breath, chest pains, and muscle tingling. The doctor decided it was unnecessary to refer him to a cardiologist, although Shea did not know that the managed care company of which the doctor was a member offered its doctors financial incentives to keep specialist referrals down. Several months later, Shea died of a heart attack.[64]

These are the bad cases. I'm sure there are ways in which managed care is very beneficial and reduces health care costs — or at least the American Association of Health Plans, the trade organization for the managed care industry, thinks so.[65] The important point for my purpose is what the corporate goal of profit maximization does to employees like doctors. It replaces a professional ethic, indeed a professional purpose, of patient care with a goal of stock price maximization, a goal embedded in the very compensation structure used in the managed care industry.

Few jobs have the life and death implications a physician faces. But if doctors are being turned into profit machines, imagine the effect on workers who do not take professional oaths and who are far removed both from the consumers they ultimately serve and the consequences of their behavior on those consumers. It doesn't take much to imagine a profit-conscious, cost-conscious worker at GM deciding not to install a cheap safety device or cutting corners in order to save costs and speed productivity; or higher-level managers behaving in similar ways. As with managed care companies, consistently poor products or services might lead consumers to shy away from some companies. But the systemic embeddedness of the stock price maximization ethic suggests, as it does in health care, an overall lowering of the level of quality and for obvious reasons: if everyone is concerned about stock price, the company that incurs the additional time or cost to produce better quality will be punished by the capital markets. It might ultimately be favored by the product markets, but that's a longer-term proposition. In the meantime, a rising market lowers all standards, and the company that tries to rise above the tide risks some period of competitive disadvantage relative to the rest of the fleet. Perhaps it could survive that period. But perhaps not. What manager wants to take that risk?

So there's a lot more than simply nice treatment of workers at stake. The ethic of stock price maximization has the capacity to put us in harm's way when we most need help from corporations. If it can turn doctors' incentives, imagine what it can do to workers who are not professionally sworn to another goal. It can lead to unsafe cars, unreported aircraft defects, devastating pollution. Wealth is not a value. By making it the predominant, if not the only, value in our corporate structure, it has the capacity to infect our other values as well.

But there's another problem. Think of all Americans leaving school and joining the corporate workforce. Think of them spending about half their waking hours inside the institution Robert Dahl described as the most socialistic in the world. More than that, he also pointed out the importance of economic fairness to sustained democracy. What does our current situation imply for society?

Despite the success of American political democracy, it's hard to imagine that it will long continue in an environment of sustained economic inequality. When I use the phrase "economic inequality" here, I mean more than just the extraordinary inequality of income and wealth distributions to which I earlier referred; I mean more than distribution of economic resources. I mean power over economic resources as well. That power is not just the ability to invest and redeploy capital: it is the power to put that capital to use in the workplace. It is the opportunity to take that capital and make of it something more valuable than wealth. Of course, as I've noted earlier, returning profit to capital investors, to stockholders, is critically important in order to sustain business, the economy, and the overall American standard of living, although of course this doesn't answer the question of how corporate profits ought to be split up within society.[66] But as our foray into workplace participation shows, it is vitally important to the quality of American life, including economic life, that workers show up each day with purpose and power. Economic democracy includes giving workers choices and giving workers powers.

Dahl was as concerned with economic distribution as with economic and political participation. I have elsewhere written about distribution; my concern here is with participation. As Schumpeter pointed out, democracy and capitalism aren't necessarily inseparable.[67] Capitalism, in its simplest definition, seems to require some form of private property and some form of markets.[k] The concepts are probably endemic to capitalism; the forms they take are not fixed, as history and contemporary examples demonstrate. The Scandinavian social democracies operate under economic systems different from the German model, in which social welfare is important but greater emphasis is placed on worker participation in the corporate system; the German in turn differs from the British model, in which an American-style corporate capitalism coexists with a substantial degree of social welfare.[68] And all differ from the model in some Southeast Asian nations, in which authoritarian political rule and the repression of basic freedoms coexist with relatively unfettered economic life.

Democracy, in its modern form, is about universal political participation. It requires a measure of liberty and a measure of equality. I realize that both of these working definitions are gross oversimplifications. But the point is clear enough. There is no reason to think that private ownership and free markets are absolutely necessary to political liberty and equality except to the extent that, as John Rawls so famously observed, some degree of economic well-being is surely necessary as a practical matter to permit people to participate in the political process,[69] and that, as Michael Walzer

---

[k]Adam Przeworski, echoing Adam Smith and to some extent Locke's theory of property rights, adds to this the definitional requirement that "the optimal division of labor is so advanced that most people produce for the needs of others." Przeworski, *Democracy and the Market: Political and Economic Reforms in Eastern Europe and Latin America* (Cambridge: Cambridge University Press, 1991), 101. While the insight that capitalism depends on a well-developed labor market is interesting, I question whether it is essential to defining capitalism or merely an outgrowth of a system of private property and free markets.

has shown, modern life to a large degree wrongly conflates money and power.[70] But that's it.

If we have an economic system — and modern American corporate capitalism is as good a candidate for this as any — in which participation is limited to those with capital or ready access to capital, and the amount of capital that one has determines the extent of one's participation, then a significant proportion of the population is robbed of its ability to participate in economic life other than as consumers, which hardly seems like a role designed to foster human freedom and dignity. Because Americans spend about half of their waking hours working within the capitalist system, the effect of that participation has to have a substantial effect on activities in the rest of their lives. If, as Dahl pointed out, American workers are trained in command and control, and their full and equal participation in the political and social community is voluntary and on their free time, it seems likely that the training most of us receive is not in participation but in obedience. It's difficult to be a cog in a wheel from nine to five and then arrive home ready to become an active and empowered citizen in the political process. It seems that one of the most important consequences of the way we structure work is to rob us of our feelings, if not the reality, of political autonomy, our feelings of equal liberty to take part in civic life.

The kind of division of labor that orders people into fairly distinct, if not immutable, class structures that permeate American social and institutional life also robs us of the participation of a vast number of highly talented people, people whose talent is unrecognized because of circumstance and class structure.[71] Although the American system of universal education (however grossly unequal) and theoretically open opportunity is less stratifying in theory than European and Asian models that track children into professional and vocational educations at an early age, it is far from perfect. It denies the reality that talent, while perhaps undeveloped and latent, exists in abundance throughout the workforce. Adam Smith, who was right about so many things, noted this at the same time he applauded the increased productivity brought about by the division of labor:

The difference in natural talents in different men is, in reality, much less than we are aware of; and the very different genius which appears to distinguish men of different professions, when grown up to maturity, is not upon many occasions so much the cause, as the effect of the division of labour. The difference between the most dissimilar characters, between a philosopher and a common street porter, for example, seems to arise not so much from nature, as from habit, custom, and education. . . . By nature a philosopher is not in genius and disposition half so different from a street porter, as a mastiff is from a greyhound, or a greyhound from a spaniel, or this last from a shepherd's dog.[72]

I don't know much about dogs, but Smith's point about people seems obviously right. Not everyone can be a nuclear physicist. But our contemporary corporate capitalism hardly leads most people to, as the Army ad puts it, "be all [they] can be." Train a man to be a porter, and a porter he becomes. Train a man to be a philosopher, and that is what he will be.

The point, of course, is not that we should all be philosophers (or porters), but rather that we should understand what it means to say that a man is a porter or a philosopher, what it means for a man to be a porter or a philosopher. There is no reason why in training the porter we cannot train him to develop his natural talents in a way that makes his work more meaningful, no reason that he cannot be allowed to employ his natural talents to use as much discretion as possible in his work, and no reason why empowering him to do so will not raise his self-respect and work fulfillment as well as his sense of place in the community.

Worker empowerment through worker involvement has the capacity substantially to change the equation. If workers are active participants in defining their own goals, in structuring their own jobs, in making their workplaces something of themselves and their own, the effect on the political process is likely to be healthy. Workers who are people at work are more likely to be citizens at home. After all, Athenian democracy was only for the leisured class, that group of people who not only had the time to participate in the process but whose lives were lives of self-determination. It was only the idiot of this class who removed himself from community life, who failed to participate in politics and civic affairs. Nonparticipating workers are idiots in this original Greek sense to the extent their lives in the workplace are overdetermined — because we make them so. Can we expect more of them in civil and political life? And if we, by training if not by policy, disenfranchise such a substantial proportion of our population, can we truly call ourselves a democracy? Capitalism and democracy may not be necessary bedfellows. But capitalism done badly can destroy democracy.

GIVING THE WORKERS THE STORE

One approach to resolving the problems I've discussed in this chapter is to make workers owners. The legal scholar Jeff Gordon usefully points out that employee ownership takes a variety of forms, from partnerships to stock ownerships to ESOPs and worker cooperatives, among others, and that it is helpful to think of them as being arrayed along a spectrum.[73] And as Peter Drucker argues in *The Pension Fund Revolution,* workers largely *have* become owners of American business through the enormous amounts of their collective wealth invested in pension plans. While his point is well taken and while I agree that some pensions are beginning to wield their power, they are doing so largely for the purpose of increasing stock prices, a goal not likely to ameliorate the problems I've identified. Moreover, much of the activism engaged in even by the labor unions is aimed at removing devices designed to make companies takeover proof, thus making them easier targets. While it is entirely possible that this might increase aggregate worker wealth, one has to wonder whether, given the choice, the average worker wouldn't rather avoid being axed in a takeover than have a little more in his retirement fund.

In any event, this is not the kind of ownership that is likely to make workers feel empowered. It may be positive as a matter of economic distribution, but it has little consequence as a matter of the policy concerns I've raised. The kind of ownership represented by pension money is passive group ownership; even if the fund is activist, the investor-worker remains at two levels of remove from the action and has no real power to exercise a voice. And the pension trustees are themselves legally obligated to look after the financial well-being of the plan for its beneficiaries. Not a formula for empowerment and participation.

ESOPs have become popular over the past several decades, partly as an antitakeover device (they are controlled by management-appointed trustees) but also as a means of giving workers a direct stake in their companies by leaving a portion of their future wealth to be determined by the company's performance. The number of ESOPs in the United States grew from two hundred in 1974 to ten thousand in 2000, approximately 10 percent of these in public corporations.[1] ESOPs own about $262 billion in corporate assets; fifteen hundred of the companies sponsoring ESOPs are majority-owned by their employees and five hundred are fully owned.[74] Like pensions, ESOPs are a form of collective ownership. But worker participation is not a natural consequence of ESOPs, certainly not at the shop floor level and not even at the higher level of corporate governance like the election of directors. ESOP stock is held in trust for the workers, and trustees tend to be appointed by management. Thus, while as a matter of economic distribution and worker incentive ESOPs may be beneficial, they don't really solve the problem of worker participation.

Another alternative form of worker ownership is the worker co-operative, in which each worker is both an owner and a participant in the business. The most famous and successful of these is the Mondragón cooperative in Spain, as reported by William Foote Whyte and Kathleen King Whyte in their book *Making Mondragón: The Growth and Dynamics of the Worker Cooperative Complex*. Mondragón grew from one cooperative of 23 workers in 1956 to 19,500 workers in more than one hundred coops and related organizations in the late 1980s. Businesses ranged from the manufacture of kitchen equipment, electronics, and machine tools to printing,

---

[1]Even if ESOPs were a good answer to these problems, this number is discouraging, for it is the publicly held corporation that is at the mercy of the capital markets and driven to the stock price maximization ethic far more than the privately held corporation needs to be.

metal smelting, and shipbuilding, along with a central cooperative bank and a social security cooperative. While Mondragón suffered its problems, the example of such a substantial and successful experiment in worker ownership and democracy is striking. Each worker had his own capital account, but the rule was one person, one vote. While worker cooperatives are notorious for turning their workers into traditional capitalists who then go on to employ substantial numbers of nonowners in their businesses, Mondragón kept the number of nonowner workers to 10 percent. Worker cooperatives are known to be very industry-specific throughout the rest of the developed world (the American plywood industry comes to mind), but Mondragón was a well-diversified, far-flung industrial conglomerate. Even in Mondragón, however, worker participation was limited. Workers there elect representatives to the supervisory boards of the individual firms comprising the larger enterprise as well as to a social council that deals with worker concerns. Industry groups are governed by a higher council appointed by the managers of the constituent firms. And each Mondragón cooperative is required to be affiliated with the Mondragón central bank. Finally, the disposition of profits is carefully restricted by a set of rules that govern their distribution.[75] So even in the exemplary success story, worker participation in governance is limited, although it is clear that the fact of worker ownership and participation provides substantially greater empowerment than that possessed by a GM line worker.

Mondragón's worker-owners sought profits. And for the most part, they received them. But the choice of the cooperative form reflects, in the Whytes' words, "the choice . . . not simply between acceptance or rejection of the profit motive. The choice may be between considering the pursuit of profits as the sole or primary driving force or considering profits as a necessary limiting condition—a means to other ends."[76] Of course that's what I've been talking about, and Mondragón to a large extent exemplifies the means-to-an-end choice. Dahl observes that, as an economic matter, "self-governing enterprises have a greater resiliency than American corporations."[77] And Przeworski surveys the evidence that shows worker cooperatives have higher worker productivity and better economic distribution than the traditional form of corporate organization.[78]

Mondragón is not unique. While worker cooperatives may not be the dominant form of business organization in most industrialized countries, they are not insignificant. Italy has a cooperative sector that employed 428,000 workers in 11,000 firms in 1981; in 1986, there were 1,300 cooperatives in France with 34,000 employees; and during the period 1976–81, some 14,000 cooperatives employing 223,000 people were created in the European Community.[79] In 1994, a report showed that there were more than 53.7 million coop members in the European Community, over half of whom were participants in other industries.[80]

There's a large literature on worker ownership debating the extent to which it increases productivity or profitability or both, where it most effectively does so, and how stable such businesses are.[81] I'm not going to take the space to review it here. Suffice it to say that worker ownership, at least in the Mondragón sense, is unlikely to become a part of the American economy any time soon, however beneficial it might be. Far more promising at the moment are attempts to include workers as part of the corporate calculus in a way that recognizes them as vital and important resources. Doing so will not only make work more rewarding but will also change the equation that depresses the wages of workers and promotes their general social disenfranchisement.[82] It is to that end that my suggestions are aimed.

Before getting to them, let me dispel one other myth. Workers, it is often said, don't want the responsibility of making decisions. They tend to be risk averse and fear the personal and financial repercussions of being wrong. There may be some truth to this. But as Freeman and Rogers suggest, perhaps it is more correct to say that workers do want participation if they can be given some assurance that they will not be fired or mistreated because they have dared to criticize authority. Workers take risks every day, in some occupations, the risk of severe injury or death. It's silly to think that workers care more about their jobs than about their lives, even if choice or circumstance leads, or forces, them to take dangerous lines of work. The kind of risk that participation represents is a risk that workers will be given the appearance of freedom without the reality. Remember that under the monitocracy one of the functions of the worker is to make his boss look good. No rational worker would risk suggesting a change that would either show up his boss and thus incur the boss's enmity or result in adverse consequences. Of course there will be cases in which workers, just like managers, make mistakes, and financial consequences will result. But surely there are ways of constraining the risks to prevent workers from exposing their entire welfare when they seek to innovate. We have done that for stockholders through limited liability and for managers and directors through directors' and officers' liability insurance and statutes that absolve them from financial consequences for negligence. If we can protect directors and managers because we think they need leeway to take risks without risking themselves, surely we can do the same for workers. Under such a regime, it's hard to imagine why workers would fear participation.

THE VALUABLE EMPLOYEE—THE VALUED EMPLOYEE

My principal proposal to make the worker central is to change the accounting rules to treat employees as assets instead of liabilities. Treating workers as assets has a number of implications, including better treatment and higher pay. This has both business and social benefits. The business benefits are clear: corporations that treat workers as valuable are more likely to produce more skilled, better trained, and happier workers. As a social matter, they are more likely to invest more in their workers, too, including the investment in their pay, a fact which might begin to ameliorate the dramatic gap between executive compensation and workers' wages and, in addition, reverse the present trend toward even greater inequality. All of these factors may lead to greater worker participation in their corporations—improving worker skills and treating workers as valued members of the corporate community may encourage managers to invite worker input into all levels of running the business. Finally, treating the worker as a valuable member of the corporate community is also likely to have the positive effect of increasing the satisfaction of work and creating the environment of civic virtue with which Dahl was concerned.

My suggestion for accomplishing these goals is to change the tax laws and the related accounting rules to require corporations to capitalize workers' salaries above a stipulated amount. Obviously some portion of an individual worker's compensation would properly be taken as a current expense, because it would reflect the worker's monthly (or quarterly or annual) contribution during that financial reporting period. The precise amount of compensation to be capitalized could be developed either on a companywide or an industrywide basis reflecting the average compensation for workers. All capitalized compensation would be carried as an asset on the balance sheet and depreciated over time.

The depreciation period could be determined in a number of ways. For example, it could be measured as the average tenure of an employee within a given corporation or industry. If more uniformity seemed desirable, tax regulations could specify a uniform depreciation period based upon similar kinds of statistics for workers in various industries or classes of occupation.[m]

The details become complex. What, for example, should we do if an employee whose "excess" pay has been capitalized leaves before the end of the depreciation period? One possibility would be to require that the amount of undepreciated pay be taken as an ex-

[m]Determining the depreciation period by some classification of job within an industry has the disadvantage of ignoring the possibilities of job shifting and promotions to different job classifications within a given corporation. This might have the perverse effect of discouraging promotions from within if it diminished the allowed depreciation period, although I suspect that the aggregate numbers of such promotions among different classes of job from year to year would not be all that significant. Nonetheless, the risk is strong enough that I would prefer to see depreciation periods set without regard to job category. It could become a problem if American corporations began to adopt work models like that in Japan, where employees are regularly shifted among jobs; but the issue could be revisited if the American workplace were to change in that direction.

pense in the year the employee leaves. This could have a punitive effect on corporations that experience high turnover, but precisely because of that effect it might encourage corporations to create work environments and provide financial incentives that induce employees to stay. It's not obvious to me that this approach is as easy to implement as one in which depreciation continued over the stated period regardless of turnover (and this latter approach would be consistent with the concept of taking an average worker's tenure as the depreciation period to begin with), but I favor the former approach precisely because it creates greater incentives for managers to focus on the welfare of workers and to encourage them to remain with the company as well. Another set of issues, which I've implicitly raised, is whether measurements should be on a company-specific, industry-specific, or national basis. I prefer the company-specific approach because it most directly internalizes the costs of high worker turnover to corporations that provide less desirable workplaces. The corporation that has longer-tenured workers will have a longer period of depreciation and consequently less effect on the bottom line.

A related issue concerns the treatment of undepreciated compensation in the event of layoffs or plant closings. Here again, I favor an approach that requires all undepreciated compensation to be taken as an expense in the year of termination. While this would make even necessary layoffs and plant closings more expensive, it would help to ensure that these events occur only when the marginal benefit from them exceeds the marginal cost. As a result, we could expect to see worker displacement for the purpose of transferring wealth from workers to stockholders occur less frequently and thus only in circumstances in which economic necessity dictates. If the requirement of immediate expensing of undepreciated amounts would unduly burden a company, we might want to allow for appeal mechanisms for companies that believe they have legitimate reasons for layoffs or plant closings. But such an accounting change would go a long way to diminish much of the promiscuous worker displacement we've seen over the past several decades.

Capitalizing workers' salaries would also make it easier for corporations to raise wages without having to worry about immediate adverse effects on stock prices. Wage premia, which would help to attract and retain the best workers, would have less impact on a corporation's bottom line and therefore on its stock price than under the present system of treating them as current expenses. The fact that a company pays higher than average wages could then itself be seen as a signal of management's commitment to the long term and might even have a positive effect on stock prices.

What is true for compensation would also be true for worker training costs. Capitalizing such expenses and allowing depreciation over a given period would encourage managers to invest in worker training and well-being. The issues are less complex than capitalizing compensation, but the salutary result is the same.

In order to ensure that my suggestion is effective with respect to lower-level workers, we might want to have different rules for executive compensation, defined either as certain types of job categories or salary categories. The disproportional amount of pay that executives already receive might, in some corporations, lead my reform to provide instant corporate benefits without much need to adjust worker salaries. There are several ways to hit the target. One would be to disallow depreciation in corporations in which the ratio of highest-to-lowest paid employee exceeds a certain amount. This might encourage executives in such corporations to increase worker pay to adjust the ratio or, somewhat less likely, to cap their own pay. The problem this approach creates is that it may lead some corporations simply to forego the compensation depreciation, thus depriving their workers of the benefits my proposal seeks to achieve.

Another and, I think, better approach would require some additional changes. First, Congress should repeal the law limiting the deductibility of executive salaries over $1 million. It should be replaced with a law requiring that all executive pay — probably over a reasonable stated amount, say $150,000 or some other capped amount that we could base, perhaps, on what we consider to be an appropriate executive-to-worker pay ratio — is to be taken as a current expense, that is, none of it would be capitalized. The result would be that excessive executive compensation, not worker compensation, would adversely affect earnings per share. At the same time, I'd suggest that the law not permit any executive compensation above that amount as a tax deduction. Thus, executives that overpaid themselves would harm their companies in two ways: first, by diminishing earnings per share and, second, by creating a business expense without a tax advantage to soften its blow.

We still have to worry about stock options. My proposal creates at least as great a risk as does current tax law that executive pay would shift to stock options. This wouldn't be a bad thing if it didn't carry with it the problems that options currently do, the problems we looked at in chapter 5. The way to prevent such dilemmas brings us back to the way I suggested that we deal with excessive trading. Amend the tax laws so that stock issued pursuant to executive option plans would be punitively taxed if the executive sold the stock in too short a period. It is reasonable to expect executives, especially executives who are richly rewarded with a piece of the corporation, to have a long-term horizon for the corporation and their contribution to it. Thus we could impose, say, a 75 percent tax on stock sold within five years of exercising the option, with a sliding scale reducing it to normal capital gains taxes after perhaps ten years.

There are other details to consider here, too. Do we want to exempt the estates of executives who die before the favorable tax rate kicks in? or do we want to require the estate to complete the holding period to give executives every possible incentive to look to the long term? What about managers who are fired during the punitive tax period? Should it depend upon the reason they're fired (unsatisfactory performance)? And what if managers sell the company during the punitive tax period? Should they be presumptively subjected to unfavorable tax treatment with an opportunity to appeal by showing the economic value of the sale for the business as a going concern? or should the period automatically terminate? These are important questions, but the need to resolve such details doesn't detract from the soundness of the basic idea.

What should be clear from this chapter is that much of our social, political, and economic well-being depends upon the condition of American workers. These suggestions go directly to the problems I've identified. They require a shift in our thinking about workers as well as some crucial legal modifications. And they're not without some risk, for there may be unintended adverse consequences. But the current system doesn't work very well for an awful lot of hardworking people, even in times of low unemployment. It's important to our future as a nation to try something new.

III

**AMERICANS
ABROAD**

CAPITALISM, SOCIALISM, AND DEMOCRACY

I begin this transition from analysis of the flaws of the American corporate system to a brief examination of other systems with a tongue-in-cheek nod to the great economist Joseph Schumpeter. For I certainly lack the space, time, and insight to fully engage in the kind of study of the relations among capitalism, socialism, and democracy that he did. I do think it is important, however, in order to place in context what has come before and to set the stage for my conclusion, to reflect upon the relation between capitalism and democracy and the relation of both to the corporate system. For if you remember nothing else, remember that capitalism is a many-splendored thing, that capitalism and democracy are not coterminous (and that we therefore need to consider what our goals in the world are and why), and that corporate capitalism done our way is by no means the only workable form, as China and Singapore demonstrate. Adam Smith, who might be considered the ur-theorist of modern capitalism, was himself appalled by corporate capitalism, although for reasons that may not be as relevant today as they were in his time.[1]

These are issues which have been at the forefront of international consideration since at least the fall of the Berlin Wall and the collapse of communism. The most immediate impetus, of course, was to attempt to advance the economies of formerly communist countries, to help them achieve economic independence from the former Soviet Union, and to bring them into the capitalist frame-work encompassing the Americas, Western Europe, and much of Asia. This is not the place to take the measure of that process, which is still going on; neither will I assess other developments, such as the stunning and culturally insensitive failure of attempts to impose the American corporate system on Russia, the system of Czech voucher privatization which led to the transfer of much of Czech industry to foreign hands, the success of Poland in fits and starts, or the rather invariant march toward capitalism of Hungary. But it has been more than a decade now, everybody more or less agrees that capital-ism of some form or forms is indeed to be the order of the day, and so I will begin by taking the hegemony of capitalism as a fait accom-pli and a desirable one at that.

I've already spent some time on the fundamental definitions of capitalism and democracy. Most people would agree that capitalism requires some form of private property and some form of markets, although the particular ownership and market forms are not fixed. Some theorists have added the system of labor that accompanies capitalism as a definitional point. The economist Adam Przeworski, in his study of the transition economies and polities of Europe, suggests that capitalism includes the existence of a labor market sufficiently specialized that most people produce "for the needs of others," thus adding a neoclassical aspect to the basic definition.[2] Samuel Bowles and Herbert Gintis also include labor as part of capitalism, but in rather a different way. They point out that one of the most overlooked aspects of capitalism, at least from the perspec-tive of liberal theory, is that capitalism is as much a system of em-ployment as it is of exchange. As they put it, in a way that is impor-tant for our discussion, "The capitalist enterprise exists precisely as a system of authority within a system of markets."[3] In so doing, they explicitly connect the economic system of capitalism with politics, thus bringing it from the private realm in which modern economic theory locates it to the political realm, in which a more realistic view of the world would suggest that it, or certainly corporate capitalism if not capitalism *simpliciter,* belongs.

In any event, nobody really doubts that capitalism and politics affect one another. Even Schumpeter, who saw modern democracy as a "product of the capitalist process," believed that democracy and socialism could coexist, and that there was no inevitable connection between capitalism and democracy.[4]

So the question to be considered when we, as Americans, look at the rest of the world is, Why do we care what the rest of the world looks like? Obviously there is a deep and important preliminary question as to whether we have any right to influence the rest of the world, but I think we're heavily enough involved to allow the assumption that, at least as far as we think our own interests are concerned, the question is off the table.

I also want to avoid the important discussion of the nature of human rights and our role in assuring they exist throughout the world. There is, it seems to me, a perfectly legitimate question of whether each nation should be allowed to determine for itself what human rights appropriately consist of and what the nature of its society should be. I hardly mean to suggest by this that I'm agnostic on the nature of human rights. Torture, murder, genocide, misogyny, bigotry, oppression, and intolerance are not things that I find especially attractive. But there are, I suppose, degrees, and if we're honest with ourselves we will admit that there are even degrees in the United States. Certainly there are theocratic states like Iran and states in which there is an established religion, de facto if not de jure, in which much of what defines the rights and roles of people is determined by a collective belief in revealed truth. Unless we are prepared to insist that all members of that society are plagued by false consciousness, their belief in such truths leads to institutional, political, and social structures that are distinctly divergent from those of modern liberal society. And, as I noted, the United States contains subcultures which deny the premises of modern liberal society. The Christian right, for example, would like its values to dominate society, and Hasidic Jewry simply wants to separate from society to be free to practice its cultural and religious norms. Who's to say whether they are right or wrong? We won't know until the final day of reckoning. Meanwhile, liberalism requires tolerance, at least within limits, and it seems as though that tolerance ought to extend to the international sphere as well.

As modern liberals, however, we believe that one of the principal ways basic human rights as we understand them can best be protected is through democratic systems of government. And while democracy, like capitalism, is variously defined, among its salient and, it seems to me, invariant characteristics are the equal rights of all citizens to participate in the processes of selecting a government and the basic liberties necessary to form one's ideas about what constitutes good government. It's difficult to oppress people when they are empowered to choose their own government, and when the government is answerable to them.

It's too easy, though, to conflate democracy and capitalism. Listening to public and political discourse in the United States with regard both to domestic and to world affairs, one might be pardoned for believing that our economic success (if we leave aside our distributional problems) is our very reason for being. "It's the economy, stupid," might well be taken as the signal American watchword of faith. And even if we are capable of theoretically and intellectually separating the two realms, our politics are, as a practical matter, so bound up with our system of corporate capitalism that to separate them would appear to pose the same challenge as undoing an omelet.

Wealth is not a value. We tend to forget that our lives are not lived for the sake of money, and even if there are those who, consistent with the liberal tradition of self-determination, choose to believe that it is, it is hardly either an attractive or a constructive goal for our society. Robert Dahl writes, "Democracy requires neither opulence nor the material standards that today prevail in advanced industrial countries. It requires instead a widespread sense of relative economic well-being, fairness, and opportunity, a condition derived not from absolute standards but from perceptions of relative advantage and deprivation."[5] We are indeed a capitalist society. Capitalism, however, provides not the ends but the means for our liberal democracy. As we have seen from our foray thus far into American corporate capitalism, those very democratic values of fairness, opportunity, and relative equality remarked upon by Dahl are severely jeopardized by the means as they threaten to swallow the ends, if not to make their attainment impossible.

While Dahl referred broadly to advanced industrial countries, it is not the case that all advanced industrial countries treat material wealth as the end, at least in anywhere near the degree that Americans do.[a] The German constitution, to take just one example, states that "property imposes duties. Its use should also serve the public weal."[6] While I will, in the following pages, have occasion to describe how capital markets and particularly the effect of American capital are perverting this aspiration, it is clearly the case that German corporations and corporate actors have long believed that their principal purpose is to produce goods and services that better society and that social welfare and worker welfare are fundamental justifications for corporate wealth. Japanese corporations, although under the same kinds of contemporary pressures, have understood one of their primary purposes as being to provide employment for Japan's people. Needless to say, these functions are very different from maximizing stock price, and while corporations in all countries recognize the need to profit in order to fulfill their goals, the very differences in goals imply a much more constrained view of means, even given the importance of profit.

Michel Albert divides the corporate world into the Rhine model, in which he includes Japanese corporations as well as continental corporations, and the neo-American model. One of the ways he distinguishes them is by suggesting that "the neo-American model is based on individual success and short-term financial gain; the Rhine model . . . emphasizes collective success, consensus, and long-term concerns."[7] Following this, one might think it appropri-

---

[a] It is also not the case that all materially wealthy countries treat democracy as a goal. Greider notes that Singapore's per capita income exceeds that of Great Britain's, yet that country is governed by a highly repressive regime. As he puts the issue, "The ideological confusion within capitalism poses a crucial question about the nature of global convergence: Will nations gravitate toward civil democracy something like America's or will they decide instead that success in the marketplace requires the productive efficiency of a regime more like Singapore's?" Greider, *One World*, 36–37. While the following pages question Greider's assumption that some form of convergence seems inevitable, at least with respect to the nature of corporate capitalism, his point is well taken and reminds us that, after all, there were productive efficiencies in Nazi Germany as well.

ate to understand American capitalism as individual capitalism, and European and Asian capitalism as collective capitalism. Of course this would be an oversimplification, as Europeans and Asians (as well as Latin Americans and Africans) have an interest in their own success and well-being, but the oversimplification could be excused as a matter of emphasis.

But it's not just oversimplification. For while American culture and American capital markets are, for all the reasons I've discussed, wildly individualistic, the American *corporate* culture is aggregative. It is the most powerful focal point for wealth and work in the world. As a consequence, one might think of the American corporate capitalist system as being in one sense intrinsically collective. After all, the Latin origin of the word "corporate" is "to make into a body."[8] One might argue, therefore, that the corporation is intrinsically collective, intrinsically communal.

Well, if you've stayed with me to this point you know that, although there is truth to this aggregation with respect to the corporation's position in the broader world, it is also true that what goes on within the corporate structure belies that communality. But there's more. You see, by incorporating and thus creating an individual out of many, we have endowed our corporate actors with all of the power and rights with which we endow our citizens, the very people whom Smith contemplated as being at the core of a more individualistic corporate system, an individualistic system that worked precisely because the actors are people and are endowed with all of the moral autonomy I've argued has been stripped from the corporation. The corporation is indeed a collective. But as Bowles and Gintis put it, "The most powerful form of collective organization in contemporary capitalism — the modern business corporation — is stripped of its communal status in liberal theory. It is ignored in neoclassical economics, treated as a quasi-individual in law, and considered 'private' in public discourse. Its status as a form of social power is thereby obscured and its reality as the terrain of class conflict is systematically slighted."[9]

Not quite. In fact contemporary neoclassical economics, by deconstructing the corporation into a system of markets organized within the shield of limited liability, has to some extent attempted to correct for this by restoring individual action within the corporation. But it is a fiction and fails to describe the reality because it adopts for its maxim the same goal of wealth maximization that we have attributed to the corporation. In so doing, it reifies economic actors, that is, people, in exactly the way I have claimed that we have reified the corporation. It thus denies the complex humanity of people, as it does the complex social and political aspects of the corporation. Because the corporation itself is artificial and because we have given it privileges, it will naturally tend to obscure this humanity unless we consciously understand it to be composed of people and therefore to collectivize all of the motivations and interests of people, rather than to treat it as a thing that embodies a single human character. In other words, the American corporation, instead of being made in our image, has remade us in its image.

This inversion has important social implications. The difference in the corporate models that exist throughout the rest of the developed and developing world is that they start with the recognition that the corporation is a human affair with human actors, human aims, and human ends. They privilege, even within the corporation, the relationships that we have stripped from them by leaving its conduct to the capital markets. American corporate capitalism is the aggregation of collective economic power without the tempering influence of collective human power. It is a capitalism that, as we have seen, left to its own devices, can outpace us as citizens in a democracy. And as we shape our institutions, so they shape us. The shape that we have taken from our corporate capitalism is the shape of rational economic actors, each making the maximization of wealth our goal. Instead of controlling it, we have allowed it to control us. And in so doing, in taking away our power to direct the corporation to improve our society, we have devoted our society to improving the corporation, and that, as we have seen in America, means increasing our wealth. We have taken the collectivity, the society, and made it monolithic in a way that other capitalist cultures have not. We have created a risk that capitalism will thrive at the expense of democracy. In considering the values we export to the rest of the world, we must consider whether we are exporting our corporate capitalist system for the sake of democracy or democracy for the sake of capitalism. If the latter, it seems likely that democracy will not long last. In a democracy, the state is, however imperfectly, us. It reflects our hopes and dreams, is an aggregate of our individual attempts to live lives of value and meaning. In American corporate capitalism, the economy is the stock-price maximizing corporation. If we permit our capitalism to dominate our democracy, it is those lives of meaning we are sacrificing.

Other capitalist countries understand this. Vaclav Havel famously proclaimed that the Czech economy would be "capitalism with a human face." The very fact that he felt the need to describe the brand of capitalism to which he aspired in that way suggests how inhuman the dominant world capitalism—American capitalism—has become. Not surprisingly, when the Czech Republic looked to reform its corporate law in a capitalist tradition, it turned not to the American model, but to the German. Not surprisingly, when American advisors persuaded Russia to adopt American-style corporate law, the Russian economy tanked.[b] Japan, bowing to pressures from American capital, has loosened the system of lifetime employment, which has resulted in major social dislocation. And West European democracies, also yielding to the might of American capital, are experiencing the introduction and proliferation of devices like the hostile takeover, with all of its socially distorting consequences, that are inimical to the values of community that characterize these societies.

There are a number of dangers in our exportation of American corporate capitalism through the power of our capital markets. One is that our proteges might best us. In their fascinating book *Chaos and Governance in the Modern World System,* Giovanni Arrighi and Beverly J. Silver draw parallels between the seventeenth-century collapse of Dutch commercial rule to the financial hegemony of England and the twentieth-century collapse of England to the

---

[b]Of course there are complex reasons for this, including a legal system and market system that were inadequately developed to rely upon a law that so heavily depended upon self-regulating and transparent markets. But the gross insensitivity to a culture of authority and collective dependence led to the creation of a system that was antagonistic to core Russian values.

American century. One of the signal hallmarks that the end was near for each of the economically dominant nations was the excess of investment capital with insufficient domestic opportunities, leading to the investment of that capital abroad, which enabled the next-dominant country to expand and overtake the former.[10] The recent dramatic increase in American investment abroad parallels these earlier developments, and while Arrighi and Silver might not have a complete explanation for changes in financial leadership, this factor has some real explanatory force. The more we instruct the rest of the world in our methods through our capital, the more we compel them to adopt our system in order to have access to our investments and the more likely it is that we will find our future prosperity becoming dependent upon a power that has not yet reached its ascendancy.

There is another risk. The cheetah population is dying out and can be saved, if at all, only through science. The reason is that cheetahs are, as a result of inbreeding, more or less genetically uniform. If one cheetah becomes infected with a deadly disease that it is unable to fight, the chances are good that all cheetahs will disappear. So it would be if there were a uniform world system. When Japan and the rest of Asia suffered economic decline in the 1990s, the American economy did not collapse because our system differs from theirs. When the Russian economy failed, we were able to sustain our own. In the event that we reshape the world in our own image, we run the risk of the cheetah: financial collapse in one region could well lead to the downfall of others.

Finally, there is a more human risk. Although travel and communication have tended to homogenize world culture, that is, make it like ours, one of the glories of the world still is the diversity of approaches to life from country to country. We benefit and learn from such variety. It is precisely that diversity that led to the development of our federalist system of government and is the rallying cry of conservative federalists in the United States today. To the extent that we destroy that diversity, to the extent that we homogenize economic systems to the same degree that we are homogenizing culture, the opportunity for each nation to learn and improve through experimentation is lost. That is a serious risk indeed.

AMERICA RIGHT *AND* WRONG: GROWING U.S. ECONOMIC IMPERIALISM

The *New York Times* recently reported at length on the war of attrition being waged against European business by American takeover artists and other cowboy capitalists. Operating in cultures in which patient capital and responsible management long have been the rule, cultures in which the ethic of autonomy is balanced by notions of individual and social responsibility, these U.S. businessmen, according to the *Times,* aim "to cut costs, increase profits and then sell out." And why Europe? Because "years of corporate downsizing and other measures have made it harder today to squeeze new savings out of already-lean American companies." Lean? — or anorexic?

Telecom Italia abandoned plans to spin off its wireless division. Angry stockholders complained that their rights were being violated. And who were these angry stockholders? American institutions in the main, demanding that stock prices be maximized. The chief investment officer at our old friend TIAA-CREF went so far as to write a letter to the Italian government complaining that minority stockholders were being taken advantage of and threateningly predicting that the credibility of the entire Italian stock market would be damaged. Maybe he was right. But the hand of stock-price-maximizing American capital was all over the deal. As one report put it, "The juggernaut known as the global market is responsible, in several ways, for expanding shareholders' power in Europe. So much of America's foreign investment capital has poured into equities in Western Europe — nearly $1 trillion . . . that American reverence for shareholder value and shareholder rights has inevitably influenced the attitudes and priorities of investors and companies alike."[1] While this commentator suggested that complete convergence of European and American forms was unlikely given the strong European stakeholder orientation, the pressure of American capital is increasingly hard to resist.

One of the most knowledgeable observers of corporate financial structure, Carolyn Kay Brancato, recently wrote, "The economic power and corporate governance influence of US investors in global markets is [*sic*] undisputed. US institutions control the largest proportion of global investment."[2] And she's got the numbers to back it up. According to the *Institutional Investment Report* she prepares for the Conference Board, American institutional investor financial assets were over "ten times those of France and Germany and almost four times those of Japan." American institutional assets comprised 66.8 percent of the total in five major economies.[3] She further notes that TIAA-CREF itself "represents much of the stock market capitalisation of some Asian countries."[4] While 49.2 percent of American institutions' equity investments were made by pension funds, including heavy participation by TIAA-CREF and by stockholder value activist CalPERS, money managers comprise a large and fastgrowing segment as well. And this capital is highly concentrated. Sixty-six percent of foreign equities held by American investors toward the end of 1999 were owned by the twenty-five largest American pension funds investing in international stock, and "the largest 20 active equity managers with international holdings have portfolios . . . [representing] slightly more than 67 percent of . . . total foreign equity investments held by all U.S. investors in 1998."[a] American influence is further compounded by the dramatic growth of equity issued by foreign corporations in the United States.[5] American capital is a major export, and its push to unlock stockholder value throughout the world is very powerful indeed.

[a]Brancato notes differences in turnover rates from a relatively low 16 percent for indexed funds to over 95 percent for aggressive growth funds.

A report in the *Economist* in April 2000 analyzed the trend of European corporations toward deconglomeration. Big, powerful European conglomerates were being broken up by their management. Why? The *Economist* reporter explained it as rationalizing businesses that were built for growth and stability and applauded the move. What did he mean by rationalization? Maximizing stock prices. As the reporter somewhat arrogantly put it, "At long last, the message is sinking in."[6] He applauded the restructuring of Siemens, which aimed to destroy "the company's culture of complacency and concentrate on financial performance, installing a former investment banker as finance chief. Some 60% of top managers' pay has been linked to targets for return on capital."

The former World Bank chief economist Joseph Stiglitz recently commented on the disaster that has been the privatization of East European economies. He contrasted the approach of what he calls "shock therapy," which became the method of choice and was largely pushed by the United States and "international financial institutions" (presumably including the World Bank and the IMF), with the "gradualist" method advocated by "specialists in the study of these countries and comparative economic systems, and those who believed there was more to a market economy than 'free markets.'"[7] The economic and ideological imperialism of American advisors resulted in a disaster in Russia, where an American-style corporate law was pushed, adopted, and failed, failure elsewhere, and a false start in the Czech Republic, which initially appeared to be one of the bright spots for privatization.[8]

Is capitalism specific to certain cultures? It doesn't seem so.[b] Poland and Slovenia moved at their own pace and, despite some setbacks, have been relatively successful in their transition to capitalism.[9] But perhaps the brand of capitalism that a nation adopts is more culturally specific than Americans are willing to admit. As Stiglitz put it, "The failure of the transition is not a failure of economic theory, but it is a damning indictment of those who rely on

[b]At least if what we mean by capitalism is something other than the very specific idea, put forth by Max Weber, of acquisition for its own sake.

simple textbook models or naive ideology."[10] At least the advisors were thinking and well intentioned. Capital markets don't think.

The ideology of the American free market system is, as I discussed in the beginning, based upon the tenets of Enlightenment liberal philosophy taken to extremes. Whether or not we have perverted that philosophy, however, it is not universal. It is, historically, a peculiarly Anglo-American doctrine.[11] In his fascinating book *American Exceptionalism,* Seymour Martin Lipset claims that the full development of liberal philosophy is uniquely American.[12] Enlightenment attitudes in France, most notably in the philosophy of Jean-Jacques Rousseau, stressed an identifiable common will. German policies of social solidarity developed and were implemented by Otto von Bismarck and, while taken to extremes that led to disastrous consequences, have remained intact in a more constructive way as Germany has reformed. Strong family ties, apparent in the ownership structure of Italian corporations, characterize Italy. And it hardly needs noting that the Anglo-American (really Scottish) Enlightenment was no part of East European or Asian culture or, for that matter, the cultures of Africa or Latin America.[c] Yet it is this brand of market capitalism, based on the primacy of individual choice, individual autonomy, that we are exporting to the rest of the world. It's not terribly hard to predict that, even if there is some move toward convergence, it is a convergence that is unlikely to last, at least without causing some serious damage to other cultures and economies. And if it doesn't last, these cultures may pay a very heavy

[c]One commentator interestingly notes the divide in Eastern Europe between countries that have more successfully moved to capitalism and those that have not as corresponding to the divide between those who were historically under Hapsburg rule — with its "tradition of education, administration and commerce, backed by a middle-class that looked west" — and those "whose history is bound up with Byzantium and Orthodoxy." "Europe: Flickers of Economic Light," *The Economist,* September 5, 1998, 47. Leaving aside the whiff of cultural superiority implicit in the comment, one notes that the point does suggest that the successful introduction of capitalism depends at least in part on sensitivity to traditional and cultural norms.

price in their attempt to retain or regain their cultural integrity in the wake of potentially significant social dislocation.

Others have observed the trend toward cultural convergence in the media, product markets, and increasing world taste for American popular culture.[13] My point is that there is a deeper aspect to the culture that is embedded in our very style of capitalism, a culture that we have the power to push in light of the strength of our capital markets, but a culture we should be wary of exporting and others should be wary of accepting. As Lipset puts it, "[The American Creed's] emphasis on individualism threatens traditional forms of community, morality, and thus has historically promoted a particularly virulent strain of greedy behavior,"[14] an attitude which does not characterize much of the rest of the world. The problem is that capital markets are increasingly dominating the will, if not the power, of foreign governments and cultures to resist.[15] Do we really want the world to look like us?

Maybe Telecom Italia's minority stockholders were being hurt. And maybe big, diversified conglomerates are not a good idea. Certainly American managers have decided that they're not. Maybe a former investment banker will turn out to be a good manager for Siemens' stakeholders and for German society as a whole, although one suspects that the choice of an investment banker results from a decision to maximize stock prices. But the relevant point for our purposes is the emphasis on stock price maximization, an emphasis clearly resulting from the pressures of American capital. Corporations built for growth and stability may not return the highest profit to capital. But they do maintain employment; they do continue to provide the goods and services on which consumers depend. And what one commentator sees as a "culture of complacency" can also be seen as a culture of community and cooperation in contrast to the highly individualistic culture of both American managers and workers reported by Lipset.[16] It is possible, is it not, that the desire to maximize stockholders' wealth is not a universal value?

Nor is it at all clear that the drive to maximize stock price is effective. We've already seen the extent to which that pursuit in a globalized capital market has damaged the prospects of American workers. As Jeff Faux and Larry Mishel write, the greatest increases in income inequality during the 1980s and 1990s occurred in the strongest adherents to the American way, the United States and Great Britain. Moreover, while social safety nets have protected the displaced in other capitalist economies, poverty grew by 2.4 percent and 5.4 percent, respectively, in these countries from 1979 to 1991. Faux and Mishel point out that globalization of the stock price drive has not only diminished American workers' incomes but has done little to improve overall income growth and productivity. They compare the relatively stagnant 1970s and the booming 1950s and 1960s to the 1990s and find that per capita income growth in the latter period was actually somewhat less than in the seventies and considerably less than during the growth spurts of the fifties and sixties. As I have argued, the diminution in workers' compensation has been to the benefit of capital. And the power of the global capital markets has given capital greatly increased bargaining power over labor.

Faux and Mishel find that American productivity growth has been the same "sluggish" one percent during the 1980s and 1990s that it was during the seventies, and they cite OECD figures to show that U.S. productivity is no better than that in Germany, Belgium, France, Italy, and the Netherlands.[17]

Europe offers fresh new blood, and American investment bankers and buyout specialists like Goldman Sachs, Morgan Stanley, Lehman Brothers, and KKR have participated in some of the biggest European acquisition fights, including Banque Nationale de Paris' attempt to buy Paribas and Société Générale and Olivetti's bid for Telecom Italia. The new hostile activity in Europe, catalyzed by Americans, led *Business Week* to predict at least a $1 trillion mergers and acquisitions business on a continent long known for corporate stability.

These corporate gunslingers have been meeting some resistance from European executives raised in cultures that emphasize responsibility and schooled in long-term, humane, responsible European corporate practices. But it appears that the American way is winning, aided by the fear of takeover, stock market envy, and the allure of gargantuan, American-style executive salaries. (Not lost on them are such examples as Michael Eisner, whose 1998 payyear amounted to $575.6 million, and even Margaret Whitman, hired as eBay Inc.'s CEO in February 1998, who finished the year with $43 million following the company's initial public offering.) Legal "reforms" that make takeovers easier and strengthen minority stockholder rights have been adopted in Italy and Germany and are being considered in France.[d]

WATCH ON THE RHINE

It won't come as any surprise to readers that basically two models of corporate capitalism dominate the Western world.[e] The first is the model I have been describing throughout this book, the Anglo-American model, which, with some legal and cultural variation, characterizes the corporate economies of the Anglo-American world; the second is the West European model. (In speaking of an Anglo-American model, I recognize that England and Canada, for example, have more far-reaching social welfare programs than the United States and that Australia has a stronger labor tradition, features that ameliorate the harshness of the system in those countries. Such differences have led Michel Albert to distinguish the American system from that of the rest of the English-speaking world and term it a "neo-American model." Nevertheless, I will refer to the

[d]While it might appear on the face of things that minority stockholders' rights are a good thing, many European corporations are characterized either by ownership of a control block in the hands of founding families (Italy, France, Germany) or by banks which either own shares outright or act as depositories for stockholders and have the power to vote the shares (Germany.) There is no doubt that this limits the power of minority stockholders. But the minority stockholders weren't complaining until American capital became minority stockholders in these countries, presumably because the stability of the ownership structure provided social benefits like corporate survival and continued employment.

[e]I hope Japanese readers will forgive my inclusion of their economy (but not necessarily their culture) as part of the Western world, for surely west is the principal outlook of the Japanese economy. And including Japan as a Western corporate state is not unprecedented. See Michel Albert, *Capitalism vs. Capitalism*.

Anglo-American model because, for my purposes of analyzing disparate corporate systems, the two are more alike than they are different, even if important social differences make the British, Australian, New Zealand, and Canadian models less damaging to their societies.)[18] The Anglo-American model is one in which corporations are run for the sake of capital, with boards of directors and managements that are held directly responsible to capital, primarily through a series of laws and practices that attempt to ensure board independence from management (and from labor, too, for that matter) and prohibit management from serving itself at the expense of capital. As we have seen, these laws are relatively ineffective in enforcement, if not in symbolism. This model is characterized also by transparent capital markets to which corporations are responsible for providing information and rough capital market equality ensured by laws prohibiting fraud and insider trading. Although this litany of laws might suggest that the Anglo-American model is a highly regulated one, the reality is that corporate law does relatively little as a governance matter. Most of the work is done through federal regulation of capital markets and takeover markets, which themselves provide little regulation beyond the (very important) requirements of disclosure and the prohibition against fraud. The very structure of the model, not to mention the norms which have come to govern it, demands stock price maximization as the corporate goal.

The West European model is, at least traditionally, rather dissimilar from the Anglo-American. I borrow Albert's term "the Alpine-Rhine model" of Germany, Switzerland, and Scandinavia (in which he includes the Japanese model) to refer to it. I will casually use it to refer to the rest of Western Europe as well, for while Spain, France, and Italy have unique differences, there is commonality in the social and societal aspects of the model, which clearly juxtapose all of them with the American tradition of investor capitalism. And while there are considerable variations among the corporate laws of the countries that utilize some form of this model — French boards and managers, for example, are selected in a manner very unlike German ones, and the Japanese method differs from both of these — I believe that the technical legal characteristics of these corporations are less important than the social and cultural forces that have shaped them. The clearly distinguishing feature of countries which adopted the Alpine-Rhine model is that all of them treat the corporation as serving social goals beyond simple stock price maximization, and all of them are situated in cultures in which cooperation and community are highly prized.[19] This is a matter as much of ownership structure as of law, with substantial bankholdings characterizing German corporations, heavy government involvement in France, strong family ownership in Italy, and the famous system of crossholdings known as *keiretsu* in Japan. Under the pressure of American capital, law reform efforts under way in these countries are attempting to break these concentrated ownership structures and make them look more like the American, regardless of the negative aspects of that structure.

Albert, envisioning an ultimate battle of capitalisms throughout the world and predicting the ultimate success of the "more efficient," "more equitable" Alpine-Rhine model, notes, "Each of these models [the neo-American and Alpine-Rhine] belongs to the liberal capitalist family by right, yet each carries an inner logic which contradicts the other. The battle may ultimately come down to a confrontation between whole value-systems, and on its outcome will be decided the answers to such issues as the individual's place within the company, the function of the marketplace in society, and the role of law and authority in international economic affairs."[20] Precisely so.

Yet it appears that Albert, writing in 1993, was too optimistic, at least in the short term. What I have shown so far unmistakably suggests the increasing dominance of the American model. In order to explore this further, we must distinguish between claims about legal and structural differences between kinds of corporations and attitudinal differences. While I have been at great pains to point out that the legal structure of the American corporation is a major, if not the major, facilitator of the ethic of stock price maximization, I have been careful to emphasize that this approach itself is a consequence of American social thought and attitude and that it is law and structure which make it possible. Indeed, even in the

United States, the law and structure predate the attitude, even if the latter is implicit in the former and even if the attitude can be traced to our earliest days as a nation.

There are marked legal differences among the world's corporations, but there is some debate over how important they are in terms of creating stockholder power over corporate managers and, as a derivation of that, capital power. For while issues like the manner in which the board is elected and management is appointed and the structure of the board and management groups suggest real divergences in attitude, for the most part board election is a stockholder matter.[21] Consequently, one might expect that all corporate systems in which the ultimate residual power lies with the shareholders would exhibit the same type of attitude toward stock price and stockholder welfare.

As I have so far suggested, they don't. One reason may be the extent to which corporations in a given system rely upon equity markets for their capital. In Germany, where, despite a complex language that creates new words out of multiple roots, no word exists for "stockholder value," banks, not stockholders, are the principal source of capital. Corporations and banks form webs of cross-stockholding in Japan.[22] This may be changing, especially in Germany with the enormous influx of American capital into the German stock market and the substantial merger activity it has generated. Moreover, as a result perhaps of cross-border mergers such as that of Daimler-Benz with Chrysler, German corporations as well as other foreign corporations are increasingly availing themselves of American capital markets. To the extent that things are changing, it is apparent that legal structure alone is not an impediment to a corporate attitudinal shift toward stockholder value.

More important than law, perhaps, is ownership structure. As I've noted, American corporations, at least the relatively large American corporations with which we have been concerned, tend to be characterized by a separation of ownership and control. That is, stock is fairly widely dispersed in the hands of far-flung investors, and while the rise in institutional ownership I discussed in chapter 7 has had some effect on this by concentrating ownership, we have seen that, for the most part, institutional stockholders continue to behave in the relatively passive way that American stockholders always have, thus suggesting no great change from the norm.

But not all corporate systems have dispersed ownership structures. Quite the contrary, in fact. Rafael LaPorta and his coauthors conducted an extensive and detailed survey of the ownership structure of corporations in twenty-seven wealthy countries and concluded that, in both large and medium public corporations, widely dispersed ownership is quite rare. In fact, the German model of ownership concentrated in banks is rare, too. Far more common in these countries is a system in which families or the state own controlling interests in the major corporations. Thus the American model as an ownership model, and as a structural and normative model, is relatively uncommon.[23]

As La Porta and his colleagues see it, the corporate ownership structure in various countries is not unrelated to law. But the specific laws that they find correlative with ownership structure are laws governing minority stockholder rights. Not terribly surprisingly, they find that concentrated ownership is greatest in those countries which provide weak legal protection for minority stockholders and least prominent in countries that provide strong minority stockholder rights. (These rights include not only the right of each share of each class of stock to be treated equally, but also, and perhaps for these purposes most important, equal rights to have access to control premia in the market for corporate control. In blockholding countries, control blocks tend to be sold privately, and minority stockholders remain as a sort of permanent capital, at the mercy of controlling interests.) And La Porta et al. do not see any likelihood of ultimate convergence upon an American-style model, largely because of the intractability of entrenched controlling corporate interests.[24] Interestingly, the countries with weak minority stockholder protections principally are those whose legal system is based on civil law, while the countries with strong protections are those whose legal system is based on common law, which of course are the anglophonic countries.

I don't want to carry the point too far, but not unexpectedly minority stockholder protections appear in countries which lay greater emphasis on individual autonomy. After all, to say that minority stockholders have important rights in a system in which almost all stockholders are minority stockholders is to say that the individual stockholder matters, that the system is designed for him. In societies that place a greater stress on the collectivity, on the community (and in which, perhaps not coincidentally, stock ownership is most heavily concentrated), it shouldn't be terribly astonishing to see the individual subordinated to the common good by a relative lack of rights. This of course puts the best spin on the picture.[f] It implies that concentrated ownership makes for stable ownership, and that allows the corporation to be run in the long-term interests of the workers, the consumers, and the society. And it is also no surprise to see that these ownership structures tend to correlate with countries that have greater social welfare programs and provide greater downside protection than the anglophonic

---

[f]To put another spin on it, La Porta and his colleagues found that those countries which provided greater stockholder protection had larger capital markets and greater access to external (that is, foreign) capital (both debt and equity), and that companies with higher capitalization rates also had faster growing economies. These stockholder protections generally correlated with whether a country's laws were based on common law (the anglophonic countries) or civil law (most of the rest of the world). Rafael LaPorta, Florencio Lopez-de-Silanes, Andrei Shleifer, and Robert W. Vishny, "Legal Determinants of External Finance," *J. Fin.* 52 (1997): 1131. Faux's numbers suggest that American productivity growth has in fact not been significantly greater, if at all, than the anglophonic countries in recent years despite larger capital markets. Moreover, LaPorta's findings are not conclusive of the issues I raise in this book, even if they are correct. While he and his colleagues speculate that well-developed capital markets might have some relationship to trust (which I will take up later), it may well be that more developed corporate social values in civil law countries limit minority stockholder protections in favor of the greater stability and growth that relatively invulnerable protections against capital markets allow. In other words, wealth maximization might not be a value in such countries, and the sacrifice of minority stockholder interests could well be the price those societies are willing to pay in order to maintain a greater communal and social conscience within their corporations, particularly with respect to issues of employment and the meaning of work.

countries in which the model of widely dispersed stockholding exists. Corporations that have concentrated ownership are, whatever the law—unless it is simply confiscatory—relatively takeover-proof, and management in such firms has less fear of being ousted because of poor stock price performance than that in corporations ruled by capital markets.

The dark side, of course, is that controlling stockholders, especially in countries with weak minority stockholder protections, are able to divert corporate resources to themselves, to the exclusion of minority stockholders. In the academic literature on comparative corporate governance, this is generally decried as a bad thing, and, from the perspective of the American corporate system, it is. But it need not be viewed as necessarily bad, at least when "side payments," or bribes, in common parlance, made by managers to controlling stockholders are kept within reason. For while such preferential treatment might well divert some wealth from minority stockholders to controlling stockholders, it is possible and not at all unreasonable to regard those payments as the price of a system which prizes values of stability and continuity over maximizing returns to stockholders. If indeed these structures are more stable, they are so both because of the wagon-circling effect of controlling interests and because minority stockholders are adequately, if not maximally, compensated. Controlling stockholders may very well act as real owners, with broader notions of corporate success, than the American stockholder we saw in chapter 6. And if minority stockholders are willing to accept adequate, and not maximal, compensation, it presumably is because they, too, value the social result of a system of stable, long-term corporate ownership.

It is true that minority stockholders in many of these countries (Germany, it seems, in particular) are beginning to become restless and more demanding of rights and value. But that is a fairly recent development—remember, there's no German word for "stockholder value")—roughly coterminous with and surely deriving from the extraordinary growth in American equity investments abroad. There was no great outpouring of minority stockholder sentiment abroad until American capital became involved.

This book is not the place to go into an extensive examination of comparative international corporate law or of the legal systems of nations and the advantages and disadvantages of their structures over that of the United States. For what I have said so far should make the point clear: the overwhelming power and influence of American capital are changing everything, creating nearly irresistible pressures on corporate systems throughout the world to replicate the U.S. model for the benefit of American investors. To the extent that I am right in claiming that the American system disserves even American investors in a society in which at a minimum it accords with social and cultural norms, however distorted, it is a short step to conclude that the exportation of American corporate irresponsibility serves nobody's long-term interests. It is time that we stop to look at what we are doing, at home and abroad, curb our desire for ever more wealth at the expense of a healthy world, and develop more considered and sustainable approaches to reform.

CONCLUSION

The state of American corporate capitalism is the product of a structural and a legal system grounded in a uniquely American tradition and suited to that tradition. That system, however, while conceptually sound and consistent with our democratic ideas of power and responsibility, has gone seriously awry. The fault lies with nobody in particular and everybody in general. For the system has grown and developed in a way that reflects not careful, considered planning, but instead the unthinking forces of a relatively unconstrained capital market. It is both our benefit and misfortune that the corporate structure is highly sensitive to these market pressures: benefit because when market actors are thoughtful and controlled and corporations are restrained by considered social policy, they are extremely efficient at allocating resources in ways that lead to the production of desirable goods and services; misfortune because our personification of the corporation and our consequent unwillingness to regulate it allow selfish and unreflective capital markets to take the place of considered policy making. The result has been not policy, but reaction, and reaction by boards and managers who are constrained both by law and human instinct to bow to these pressures rather than to resist them.

The consequence has been for American corporations to develop a widespread, if not universal, focus on the short term, a focus aimed at raising short-term stock prices at the expense of long-term planning, a focus which results in an unsustainable rush to make money now rather than to plan for the future, a focus that results in the displacement of the costs of that short-term vision on workers, the environment, creditors, suppliers, consumers, and entire communities, a focus which indeed has affected the way we think about ourselves and our society and thus has perverted and threatens to overwhelm our democratic tradition and has led to the pursuit of individual gain over the desire for greater societal well-being. These are results that no thoughtful person should want, and yet every thoughtful person is trapped in the dilemma of foregoing economic betterment for the sake of principle or going along for the ride. Government largely has forsaken its role as solving this collective action problem through regulation, and business leadership is as caught up in the cycle as the rest of us. The structure is not intrinsically bad, but its oversensitivity to these pressures has led us to a bad place. Nobody is in charge.

The solutions I have suggested are not to change the structure except around the edges. Centralized corporate management is part of its great efficiency. But the unconstrained corporate ability to profit any way you can leads to immoral and irresponsible behavior. And the structural roles we have created for corporate managers allow them to deny accountability, to fall back on the old defense that they are only following orders.

Nobody doubts that long-term management is better than short-term management, that foregoing some wealth today will bring greater, more sustainable wealth tomorrow. Nobody doubts that long-term management leaves greater room for responsible and accountable behavior, preventing problems like environmental degradation and economic inequality instead of leading to the much more costly social alternative of cleaning up the messes after they've been made. Long-term management is better for all of us, from the wealthiest executive to the janitor who sweeps the factory floor.

How do we curb the power of the market? How do we ensure long-term management? I have made a number of proposals, most of which are aimed at overcoming our collective action problems by creating incentives for communal restraint. But the most important solution is not legal; it is normative. At a time when our professions — medicine, law, and even teaching (with the introduction of corporate sponsors into classroom instruction) — have remade themselves ever more in the model of profit-maximizing business, it is time that we turned to business as a profession. It is time that we freed corporate managers to do the right thing, to provide exactly the kind of economic leadership that our corporate capitalism ideally leaves it to business leaders to provide. It is not something that we can fairly expect them to achieve in a legal system that treats them with distrust, that assumes that they will steal or slack off if not constantly watched or pressured by markets. It is not something we can fairly expect them to achieve if they are constrained by structure and markets to focus on the bottom line here and now in order to keep their jobs and ensure their own welfare and that of their families. It is something we can fairly expect only if we free managers to do what it is they do best—manage our business economy—and free them with the knowledge that we will hold them accountable for the means they choose to accomplish that end. It is something we can achieve only if we free them from the need to be slaves to the market, to be chained to the bottom line.

Freedom. Freedom to behave in accordance with the liberal ideal. Freedom to act as a natural human being, situated in society and in a moral and ethical environment that allows all of us to make our choices and that holds us to account for the choices we make. Freedom that comes only if we break with the notion that corporations are people, and instead demand that they be run by people. The only alternatives I see are our eventual self-destruction or extensive regulation of business by government. Neither alternative is attractive. It's time to change our attitude toward corporations so that they behave like us, instead of allowing ourselves to behave like them.

NOTES

INTRODUCTION

1. For an analysis of the development of the ethic of stockholder value, see Allan A. Kennedy, *The End of Shareholder Value: Corporations at the CrossRoads* (Cambridge: Perseus Publishing, 2000).

2. Gretchen Morgenson, "A Company Worth More than Spain?" *New York Times*, December 26, 1999, sec. 3, p. 1.

3. John Tagilabue, "Resisting Those Ugly Americans: Contempt in France for U.S. Funds and Investors," *New York Times*, January 9, 2000, sec. 3, p. 1.

4. Judith Miller, "Globalization Widens Rich-Poor Gap, U.N. Report Says," *New York Times*, July 13, 1999, A8; *United Nations' Human Development Report 1999* (Oxford: Oxford University Press 1999).

5. *United Nations' Human Development Report 1999.*

6. Short-termism in American corporate life is a subject of lively debate. One of my principal goals here is to explain how short-termism is structurally embedded in our economic life. For an economic analysis of the short-termism of American business, see Michael E. Porter, *Capital Choices: Changing the Way America Invests in Industry* (Washington: Council on Competitiveness, 1992). Porter's study was supported by the Council on Competitiveness and the Harvard Business School, and his conclusions are endorsed by the council. See also a summary of these conclusions in Michael E. Porter, "Capital Choices: Changing the Way America Invests in Industry," in *Studies in International Corporate Finance and Governance Systems: A Comparison of the United States, Japan, and Europe*, ed. Donald H. Chew (New York: Oxford University Press, 1997). See also C. K. Prahalabad, "Rethinking the Primacy of Shareholder Value," in the same volume for a critique of the short-termism implicit in the stockholder maximization norm.

7. Gretchen Morgenson, "Investing's Longtime Best Bet is Being Trampled by the Bulls," *New York Times*, January 15, 2000, A1. For more information on high turnover rates, see Robert J. Shiller, *Irrational Exuberance* (Princeton: Princeton University Press, 2000), 39.

8. See Terrance Odean, "Do Investors Trade too Much?" *American Economic Review*, forthcoming; Brad Barber and Terrance Odean, "Trading Is Hazardous to Your Wealth: The Common Stock Performance of Individual Investors," http://www.gsm.ucdavis.edu/odean/papers/returns.html.

9. C. K. Prahalabad argues in favor of a model focusing on "corporate value

added" which balances stock price and stockholder value with the demands of a variety of other corporate constituents including suppliers, employees, creditors, and customers. Prahalabad, "Rethinking Shareholder Value."

10. Robert Levering and Milton Moskowitz, "The 100 Best Companies to Work For," *Fortune*, January 10, 2000, 82; Shelly Branch, "The 100 Best Companies to Work For," *Fortune*, January 11, 1999, 118.

11. Floyd Norris, "Visions: Power; Economic Thinking Finds a Free Market," *New York Times*, January 1, 2000, E4; Russell Reynolds Associates, "Toward A Common Standard: 1999 International Survey of Institutional Investors" (reporting worldwide trend toward adopting the stockholder value maximization norm and the increasing desire of German and Japanese institutional investors to instill American-style corporate governance in their countries); Laura M. Holson, "Can Europe Learn to Love Americans at the Gate?" *New York Times*, April 25, 1999, sec. 3, p. 1; Roger Coehn, "Big Business in Line to Get Large Tax Cut from Schroder," *New York Times*, February 10, 2000, A6 (describing use of German tax cut to develop American-style shareholder culture); Jeffrey N. Gordon, "Pathways to Corporate Convergence? Two Steps on the Road to Shareholder Capitalism in Germany: Deutsche Telekom and DaimlerChrysler," 5 *Colum. J. Eur. L.* 219 (1999) (noting likely pressure to shareholder-centric model in Germany as a result of the DaimlerChrysler merger). Some legal academics, apparently without much hard evidence, describe the battle as already over, the victory going to the forces of American-style corporate law. Henry Hansmann and Reinier Kraakman, "The End of History for Corporate Law," Yale Law School Law and Economics Working Paper no. 235, January 2000.

12. Leon Hadar, "America, America," *Business Times* (Singapore), December 31, 1999, 19.

13. Carolyn Kay Brancato, "Building on Sand," 35 *Asian Business* 8 (Aug. 1999); Conference Board, *Institutional Investment Report: International Patterns of Institutional Investment* (Conference Board, April 1999).

14. Norris, "Visions: Power"; Holson, "Can Europe Learn?"; Patrick J. Lyons, "A Global Vote for U.S. Style of Corporate Openness," *New York Times*, May 9, 1999, sec. 3, p. 4.

15. See, for example, the interesting argument made by former Monsanto CEO Richard Mahoney in "Shareholder Value: Sorting Out the Voices," 219 *Directorship* 1 (March 2000).

16. See, e.g., Schiller, *Irrational Exuberance*; Michael Useem, *Investor Capitalism: How Money Managers Are Changing the Face of Corporate America* (New York: Basic Books, 1996).

17. Michel Albert, a prominent French executive, has made this point quite well,

at least with respect to non-Anglo countries, in his book *Capitalism vs. Capitalism: How America's Obsession with Individual Achievement and Short-Term Profit Has Led It to the Brink of Collapse* (New York: Four Walls Eight Windows, 1993). I have also argued that Americans understand this, too, in *Stacked Deck: A Story of Selfishness in America* (Philadelphia: Temple University Press, 1998).

18. Seymour Martin Lipset and Gabriel Salman Lenz, "Corruption, Culture, and Markets," in *Culture Matters: How Values Shape Human Progress,* ed. Lawrence E. Harrison and Samuel P. Huntington (New York: Basic Books, 2000), 112.

19. On this point, see the following chapters in Harrison and Huntington, *Culture Matters:* Ronald Inglehart, "Culture and Democracy," 80; Mariano Grodona, "A Cultural Typology of Economic Development," 44; Michael E. Porter, "Attitudes, Values, Beliefs, and the Microeconomics of Prosperity," 14.

20. David Landes, "Culture Makes Almost All the Difference," in Harrison and Huntington, *Culture Matters,* 2.

CHAPTER 1. AMERICAN LIBERALISM AND THE FUNDAMENTAL FLAW

1. Aaron Bernstein, "Too Much Corporate Power? *BusinessWeek Online,* September 11, 2000.

2. I explored this cultural context in considerably more detail in *Stacked Deck: A Story of Selfishness in America* (Philadelphia: Temple University Press, 1998).

3. Constance L. Hays, "Coca-Cola to Cut 20% of Employees in a Big Pullback," *New York Times,* January 27, 2000, A1.

4. *John Doe v. Unocal Corp.,* 963 F. Supp. 880 (S. Dist. Calif. 1997).

5. Linda Wertheimer and Daniel Zwerdling, "Landmark Lawsuit Against U.S. Oil Firm Unocal Stemming from Its Operations in Myanmar," National Public Radio, *All Things Considered,* March 10, 2000.

6. There is evidence that some corporations, in their decision making about where to invest, are paying more attention to human rights abuses, but clearly there is a long way to go. Alison Matiland, "Human Rights Weigh Heavier with Investors," *Financial Times,* April 6, 2000, 15.

7. "Judge Slashes More than 3 Billion Dollars from GM Punitive Damages Award," Agence France Press, August 27, 1999.

8. For an expanded discussion of this point, see Elizabeth Wolgast, *Ethics of an Artificial Person* (Stanford: Stanford University Press, 1992).

9. *HB Korenvaes Investments, L.P. v. Marriott Corporation,* 1993 WL 257422 (Del. Ch.); *PPM America, Inc., v. Marriott Corporation,* 853 F. Supp. 860 (U.S. Dist. Md. 1994).

10. David Cay Johnston, "Corporations' Taxes are Falling Even as Individuals' Burden Rises," *New York Times,* February 20, 2000, 1.

11. Stating the formula is easy. Plugging in real numbers is difficult. I've made some suggestions as to how to go about this in *Stacked Deck*.

CHAPTER 2. THE PERFECT EXTERNALIZING MACHINE

1. Lawrence E. Mitchell, "Trust and Team Production in Post-Capitalist Society, 24 *J. Corp. Law* 869 (1999).
2. See also Robert Kuttner, *Everything for Sale: The Virtues and Limits of Markets* (New York: Alfred A. Knopf, 1997) (discussing norms of civility as a public good), 66–67.
3. Patricia McLagan and Christo Nel, *The Age of Participation: New Governance for the Workplace and the World* (San Francisco: Berrett-Koehler, 1997), xiii.
4. Levering and Moskowitz, "100 Best Companies," suggest that improvements in employee treatment by American corporations are unlikely to survive an increase in the unemployment rate, at least to the extent that they exist now. See also Kuttner, *Everything for Sale*, 74–77.
5. Albert, *Capitalism vs. Capitalism*, 75.
6. Contrast somewhat Michael Useem's argument, that to some extent the idea that stockholders want short-term price maximization is used as an excuse by underperforming managers (although question what "underperforming" means). Useem, *Investor Capitalism*, 78–79. While Useem has a point, his argument largely supports mine.
7. For more extended analysis of this assertion, see Lawrence E. Mitchell, "Close Corporations Reconsidered," 63 *Tulane L. Rev.* 1143 (1989).
8. Richard A. Posner, "The Ethical and Political Basis of the Efficiency Norm in Common Law Adjudication," 8 *Hofstra Law Review* 487 (1980).
9. Ronald H. Coase, "The Problem of Social Cost, 3 *J. Law and Econ.* 1 (1960).
10. *Ypsilanti v. General Motors Corporation*, 506 N.W. 2d 556 (Mich. Ct. App. 1993).
11. Theresa Gabaldon, "The Lemonade Stand: Feminist and Other Reflections on the Limited Liability of Corporate Shareholders," 45 *Vand. L. Rev.* 1 (1992).
12. Brian Reid and Kimberlee Millar, "Mutual Fund Assets and Flows in 1999," 61 *Investment Company Institute Perspective*, February 2000 (as to total mutual fund investments); Social Investment Forum, *1999 Report on Socially Responsible Investing Trends in the United States*, November 4, 1999 (as to dollars invested in all designated social responsibility funds, including those that employ only shareholder advocacy, those that employ only social screening, those that employ both, and community investment funds, all of which are discussed in more detail in chapter 5). Also, as to total dollars invested in mutual funds, see Margot Roosevelt, "How Green Is Your Money?" *Time*, October 16, 2000, and as to amounts invested in social responsibility funds, see Rob Wherry, "The Cleans and the Greens," *Forbes*, June 12, 2000.

CHAPTER 3. CORPORATE PSYCHOLOGY 101

1. The following argument is based in portion Lawrence E. Mitchell, "Cooperation and Constraint in the Modern Corporation: An Inquiry into the Causes of
Corporate Immorality," 73 *Texas L. Rev.* 477 (1995).

2. Kuttner, *Everything for Sale,* passim.

3. Perhaps the leading contemporary philosophical argument to this effect is
Michael J. Sandel, *Liberalism and the Limits of Justice* (Cambridge: Cambridge
University Press, 1982).

4. National Public Radio, *Fresh Air,* February 23, 2000.

5. Lon L. Fuller, "Two Principles of Human Association," in *Voluntary Associations,* ed. J. Roland Pinnoch and John W. Chapman (New York: Atherton Press,
1969), 1, 6.

CHAPTER 4. IS WEALTH A VALUE?

1. Ronald Dworkin, "Is Wealth a Value?" 9 *J. Leg. Stud.* 191 (1980).

2. See, for example, Lawrence E. Mitchell, "Understanding Norms," 49 *University
of Toronto Law Journal* 177 (1999).

3. Claude S. Fischer et al., *Inequality by Design: Cracking the Bell Curve Myth* (Princeton: Princeton University Press, 1996).

4. Robert A. Dahl, *A Preface to Economic Democracy* (Berkeley: University of California Press, 1985).

CHAPTER 5. CORPORATE MANAGERS

1. Kennedy, *The End of Shareholder Value,* 51.

2. *Blasius Industries, Inc. v. Atlas Corp.*, 564 A. 2d 651 (Del. Ch. 1988).

3. Prahalabad, "Rethinking Shareholder Value,"

4. 26 U.S.C. Sec. 162(m) (1994).

5. David M. Schizer, "Executives and Hedging; The Fragile Legal Foundation of
Incentive Compatibility," 100 *Colum. L. Rev.* 440 (2000).

6. Richard H. Wagner and Catherine G. Wagner, "Recent Developments in Executive, Director, and Employee Stock Compensation Plans: New Concerns for
Corporate Directors," 3 *Stan. J. L. Bus. and Fin.* 5 (1997).

7. Special Report, "The Package that Launched a Dozen Lawsuits, *BusinessWeek
Online,* April 17, 2000; National Public Radio, *Morning Edition,* April 13, 2000
(interview of Jennifer Reingold by Bob Edwards).

8. Donald E. Conlon and Daniel P. Sullivan, "Examining the Actions of Organizations in Conflict: Evidence from the Delaware Court of Chancery," 42 *Acad. of
Mngmnt. J.* 319 (1999).

9. See *Lewis v. Vogelstein,* 699 A. 2d 327 (Del. 1997). The *Vogelstein* case is particularly astonishing in that the court essentially held that the directors didn't

need to disclose their valuation of the options to be granted in seeking stock-holder approval because they were theoretically difficult to value. The court thus ignored the obvious practical fact that the directors had to have had some sense of the potential value of the options in deciding to grant them to themselves in the first place, and also the obvious legal fact that if they didn't, they were violating their duty of care to the corporation.

10. Although he recognizes some imperfections in capital markets, this is principally the basis upon which Nobel laureate Merton Miller defends the stockholder value maximization norm. Merton H. Miller, "Is American Corporate Governance Fatally Flawed?" in Chew, *Studies in Governance Systems.* Miller has good reason to be invested in the theory of efficient capital markets. See also Peter Bernstein, *Capital Ideas: The Improbable Origins of Modern Wall Street* (New York: Free Press, 1992), for a discussion of Miller's role in the development of modern finance theory.

11. Shiller, *Irrational Exuberance,* 186. Shiller canvases a variety of explanations for this phenomenon but finds none of them consistent with the conclusion that the stock market is efficient.

12. Kuttner, *Everything for Sale,* 197–201, shows how market short-termism results in underproduction of research and development.

13. Richard J. Mahoney, "Shareholder Value: Sorting Out the Voices," 26 *Directorship* 1 (March 2000).

14. National Science Foundation, *National Patterns of R and D Resources: 1999 Data Update,* http://www.nsf.gov/sbe/srs/nsf00306/start.html.

15. Kennedy, *The End of Shareholder Value,* 64–65, notes a number of leading American corporations which have increased their stock prices at the expense of their research and development expenditures.

16. Porter, "Capital Choices," 7. See also James M. Poterba and Lawrence H. Summers, "Time Horizons of American Firms: New Evidence from a Survey of CEOs," in Porter, *Capital Choices.*

17. Kuttner, *Everything for Sale,* 198, 199.

18. I'm not alone in this belief. Apparently many corporate CEOs agree. Porter, "Capital Choices."

19. For agreement on this point, see Carolyn Kay Brancato, *Institutional Investors and Corporate Governance: Best Practices for Increasing Corporate Value* (Chicago: Irwin Professional Publishing, 1997).

20. David M. Gordon, *Fat and Mean: The Corporate Squeeze of Working Americans and the Myth of Managerial "Downsizing"* (New York: Free Press, 1996).

21. Robert Putnam, *Making Democracy Work: Civic Traditions in Modern Italy* (Princeton: Princeton University Press, 1993).

22. *Lewis v. Vogelstein,* 699 A. 2d 327 (Del. Ch. 1997).

23. Martin Lipton and Steven Rosenblum, "A Proposal for a New System of Corporate Governance: The Quinquennial Election of Directors," 58 *U. Chi. L. Rev.* 187 (1991).

CHAPTER 6. TRADITIONAL STOCKHOLDERS

1. United States Department of Commerce, *Statistical Abstract of the United States 1999,* tables 839, 842, 843. The figure for new issues excludes, among other things, stock issued in employee stock plans and stock sold abroad. The aggregate number may be slightly overstated because the statistics break out stock from options and other derivatives for the exchanges but not for the NASDAQ.
2. Corresponding values were $123.11 billion, $522.85 billion, $1.99 trillion, and $21.37 trillion. Data for 1997 come from the *1999 Statistical Abstract of the United States.* All other data have been compiled from *2000 Securities Industry Fact Book* (New York: Securities Industry Association, 2000).
3. *1985 Statistical Abstract of the United States,* table 856.
4. Investment Company Institute and Securities Industry Association, "Equity Ownership in America" (Fall 1999), 13.
5. A fascinating, if somewhat uncritical, intellectual history of the development of modern finance theory is Peter L. Bernstein, *Capital Ideas: The Improbable Origins of Modern Wall Street* (New York: Free Press, 1992).
6. John Burr Williams, *The Theory of Investment Value* (Cambridge: Harvard University Press, 1938).
7. Eugene F. Fama, "Efficient Capital Markets: A Review of Theory and Empirical Work," 25 *J. Finance* 383 (1970)
8. Peter L. Bernstein, "A New Look at the Efficient Market Hypothesis," 25 *Journal of Portfolio Management* 1 (1999); Patrick J. Raines and Charles G. Leathers, "Veblenian Stock Markets and the Efficient Markets Hypothesis," 19 *J. of Post-Keynesian Economics* 137 (1996); David Dreman, "An Inefficient Market," *Forbes,* March 28, 1994, 146; Burton Malkiel, "The Influence of Conditions in Financial Markets on the Time Horizons of Business Managers: An International Comparison," in Porter, *Capital Choices;* cf. Merton H. Miller, "The History of Finance, 25 *J. Portfolio Management* 95 (1999) (supporting the theory in a very modest way but noting that substantial empirical evidence weighs against it. It might be noted that Miller, a 1990 Nobel Laureate, has a substantial personal and professional investment in the theory); see also Peter Coy, "This Alchemy May Yield Real Gold," *BusinessWeek Online,* April 17, 2000 (reporting on a study done at MIT suggesting there might be at least modest validity in the use of the widely mocked charting technique [or "technical analysis"] for predicting stock price movements).
9. *1999 Securities Industry Fact Book,* 47.

10. Data are based on an estimated U.S. population of 275 million individuals and 102,118,600 households. United States Bureau of the Census, *Current Population Reports*.

11. Investment Company Insitute and Securities Industry Association, "Equity Ownership in America" (Fall 1999), 5.

12. Laura Cohn, "Day Traders' Power Grows," *BusinessWeek*, May 1, 2000, 36.

13. Lawrence E. Mitchell, "The Human Corporation: Some Thoughts on Hume, Smith, and Buffett," 19 *Cardozo L. Rev.* 341 (1997).

14. Fred Block, *Postindustrial Possibilities: A Critique of Economic Discourse* (Berkeley: University of California Press, 1990). Brancato also identifies a number of ways in which corporations are trying to account for long-term investments in ways that are more evaluative than current accounting convention permits. Brancato, *Institutional Investors*.

15. Block, *Postindustrial Possibilities*, 189.

16. See Kuttner, *Everything for Sale*, 109, 162–63, for discussion of Tobin tax. See also James Tobin, "A Proposal for International Monetary Reform," 4 *Eastern Econ. J.* 153 (1978); James Tobin, "On Limiting the Domain of Inequality," 13 *J. Law and Econ.* 263 (1970) (proposing redistributive taxation for the purpose of providing relative equality of essential goods and services).

17. This last idea was suggested to me by the consultant and former business executive Harold Porosoff.

CHAPTER 7. THE NEW STOCKHOLDER

1. Conference Board, *Institutional Investment Report: Turnover, Investment Strategies, and Ownership Patterns* (2000) (noting that third-quarter dropoff in 1999 in percentage of institutional shareholdings indicates "a strong increase in equity ownership by individuals."), 5.

2. Ibid., table 20.

3. Ibid., 25.

4. Ibid., 7.

5. Porter, "Capital Choices," 9.

6. Social Investment Forum, *1999 Report on Socially Responsible Investing Trends in the United States*. The Social Investment Forum reports that almost ten times more socially invested assets were invested in privately managed separate accounts than in mutual funds.

7. Ibid. See also www.domini.com and www.calvertgroup.com.

8. Brancato makes careful, persuasive distinctions among them. Space limitations prohibit me from thoroughly evaluating her categories, but I believe that, even with her distinctions among long-term and short-term institutions, the textual points still hold. She also echoes Reichheld's interesting suggestion

that corporations work to cultivate the kind of stockholder they would like to attract, a point I think is valuable but beyond the scope of my analysis. See Brancato, *Institutional Investors.*

9. As to investment goals, the evidence is mixed. Richard A. Johnson and Daniel W. Greening, "The Effects of Corporate Governance and Institutional Ownership Types on Corporate Social Responsibility," 42 *Acad. of Mngmnt. J.* 564 (1999) (concluding that investment managers' behavior had no significant effect on certain dimensions of corporate social performance but that public pension fund behavior did); Keith C. Brown, W. V. Harlow, and Laura T. Starks, "Of Tournaments and Temptations: An Analysis of Mangerial Incentives in the Mutual Fund Industry," 51 *J. Fin.* 85 (1996) (concluding that investment managers change their behavior on the basis of short-term performance incentives and suggesting that this could be "effectively changing managerial objectives from a long-term to a short-term process"). As to legal regimes, see Tamar Frankel, *The Regulation of Money Managers* (Boston: Little, Brown, 1978, as supplemented) (with respect to investment advisors and mutual funds).

10. Conference Board, *Institutional Investment Report,* 6.

11. Conference Board, *Institutional Investment Report,* 5.

12. Useem, *Investor Capitalism,* provides evidence which largely supports this point.

13. Shiller, *Irrational Exuberance,* 39, reports it as high as 78 percent in 1999.

14. Conference Board, *Institutional Investment Report,* tables 1, 3; Brancato, *Institutional Investors,* 27.

15. Useem, *Investor Capitalism,* 31.

16. Investment Company Institute, *Mutual Fund Fact Book* (2000 edition), 70–71.

17. The age of thirty-six is given by Cindi Fukami of the University of Denver Business school, quoted in Jerd Smith, "People Power: Consulting Research Finds Companies that Invest in Workers See Higher Stock Prices," *Rocky Mountain News,* May 28, 2000, relying upon data in Jeffrey Pfeffer, *The Human Equation: Building Profits by Putting People First* (Boston: Harvard Business School Press, 1998); twenty-eight is the age given by money manager Charles Allmon, in Don Bauder, "Fear-Driven Money Is Fueling Market's Climb," *San Diego Union-Tribune,* June 7, 1998; forty-four is the age given in a survey performed by Morningstar, Inc. "Fund Experience," *Orlando Sentinel Tribune,* February 28, 1999.

18. Porter points out that "the performance of U.S. money managers is typically evaluated based on quarterly or annual appreciation relative to stock indices, and they thus seek near-term appreciation of their shares, holding stock for an average of only 1.9 years." Porter, "Capital Choices," 9. See also Kuttner, *Everything for Sale,* 160–61, quoting Robert Shiller: "The goal for a portfolio manager is to be right in the short run if he wants to be around for the long run."

19. Russell Reynolds Associates, *Toward a Common Standard: 1999 International Survey of Institutional Investors*, 3.

20. In addition to the material discussed in the text, see Kuttner, *Everything for Sale*, 187; Useem, *Investor Capitalism*, 55–56.

21. Reynolds 2000 Survey.

22. Russell Reynolds, 35.

23. Russell Reynolds Associates, *Corporate Governance in the New Economy: 2000 International Survey of Institutional Investors*, 21–22.

24. In 1975, 32 percent of workers with employer plans participated in a defined contribution plan and 87 percent participated in a defined benefit plan. By 1995, 81 percent of covered workers had defined contribution plans. http://www.urban.org/retirement/reports/4/retireþ4.html.

25. Samuel B. Graves and Sandra A. Waddock, "Institutional Owners and Corporate Social Performance," 37 *Acad. of Mngmnt. J.* 1034 (1994).

26. Richard A. Johnson and Daniel W. Greening, "The Effects of Corporate Governance and Institutional Ownership Types on Corporate Social Performance," 42 *Acad. of Mngmnt. J.* 564 (1999).

27. It has been highly successful in its informal letter writing to corporations. Willard T. Carleton, James M. Nelson, and Michael S. Weisbach, "The Influence of the Institutions on Corporate Governance Through Private Negotiations: Evidence from TIAA-CREF," 53 *J. Finance* 1335 (1998). None of the letters deal with social issues; they deal rather with issues of corporate governance.

28. Investor Responsibility Research Center (IRRC), *IRRC Corporate Governance Bulletin 8* (November 1999–January 2000); http://www.tiaa-cref.org/siteline/proxyefforts.html; John A. Byrne, "The Teddy Roosevelts of Corporate Governance," *Business Week*, May 31, 1999, 75.

29. Investor Responsibility Research Center, *Social Issues Reporter's Checklists of Shareholder Resolutions, 1995–2000*. To be fair, and as I will later note, TIAA-CREF usually makes its proposals more informally than through the shareholder proposal mechanism created by securities law, but *none* of these informal contacts involved social issues.

30. Betty Liu, "New York Pension Fund Calls for Coke Settlement," *Financial Times*, March 31, 2000, 29.

31. Available at its website, http://www.calpers-governance.org/alert/focus.

32. Audrey Y. Williams, "Pension Investor Takes Heat Off First Union," *Charlotte Observer*, February 26, 2000. ("CalPERS meets with the companies on its list and pushes for governance reform to improve stock prices.") There is some question whether these efforts succeed. Compare Carleton et al., "Influence of the Institutions on Corporate Governance" (finding some positive correlation

between TIAA-CREF's letter-writing campaign and stock price performance) with Barry Rehfeld, "Low-cal CalPERS," *Institutional Investor* (March 1997), 41 ("There is actually scant evidence that CalPERS—or, for that matter, any shareholder activist—has produced significant stock gains in targeted companies through standard corporate governance actions").

33. IRRC, *Corporate Governance Bulletin, Proponents Submit Innovative Proposals for 2000* (November 1999–January 2000), 1; IRRC, *Corporate Governance Bulletin, Binding Bylaw Amendments to Mark 1998 Shareholder Resolution Activity* (October–December 1997), 3.

34. IRRC, *Corporate Governance Bulletin, Proponents Submit Innovative Proposals for 2000* (November 1999–January 2000), 1.

35. Jinny St. Goar, "Labor Force," *Institutional Investor* (March 1996), 97.

36. Stewart J. Schwab and Randall S. Thomas, "Realigning Corporate Governance: Shareholder Activism by Labor Unions," 96 *Mich. L. Rev.* 1018, 1019–20 (1998).

37. www.domini.com. Most investment advisors and mutual funds do not disclose their voting records, although there is a current SEC proposal to require them to do so. Barry B. Burr, "One Form of Hidden Assets Could be Forced into View," *Investment News,* May 1, 2000, 36.

38. "Domini Social Investments Publishes Fifth Annual Proxy Voting Guidelines and Social Screening Criteria," *Business Wire,* March 30, 2000.

39. Investment Company Institute, *Mutual Fund Fact Book* (2000 edition), 69, 71.

40. Brancato, *Institutional Investors.*

41. Ilyana Polyak, "Packages Incentive-Heavy, Study Finds: Asset Managers Paid to Perform," *Investment News,* July 19, 1999, 3.

42. Beatrix Payne, "Penalty System: J. Sainsbury Plans to Charge Managers that Underperform," *Pensions and Investments,* January 24, 2000, 4. See also Floyd Norris, "When the Marketing Department Decides How to Invest," *New York Times,* May 5, 2000, C1.

43. AIMR and Russell Reynolds Associates *1999 Investment Management Compensation Survey.*

44. Linda Sakelaris, "Who Makes What: Compensation Story Is in the Incentives; The Little Extras—Like Stock Option Equity Ownership—Mean a Lot," *Pensions and Investments,* May 3, 1999.

CHAPTER 8. ABANDONING THE STOCKHOLDERS

1. See, generally, Lawrence E. Mitchell, "The Gentleman Scholar in Politics" (Honors thesis, Williams College, 1978); Henry Adams, *The Education of Henry Adams* (Boston: Houghton Mifflin, 1918); John G. Sproat, *The Best Men: Liberal Reformers in the Gilded Age* (New York: Oxford University Press, 1968).

2. *Bayer v. Beran*, 49 N.Y.S. 2d 2 (S. Ct. 1944).

3. *Aronson v. Lewis*, 473 A. 2d 805 (Del. 1984).

4. *In re Caremark International Inc. Derivative Litigation*, 698 A. 2d 959 (Del. Ch. 1996); *Kamin v. American Express Company*, 383 N.Y.S. 2d 807 (1976) (while this is a New York case, the standard of business judgment is pretty much the same as in Delaware).

5. See *Joy v. North*, 692 F. 2d 880 (2d Cir. 1982).

6. *Grobow v. Perot*, 539 A. 2d 180 (1988).

7. *Grimes v. Donald*, 673 A. 2d 1207 (Del. 1996).

8. For more, see Lawrence E. Mitchell, "Fairness and Trust in Corporate Law," 43 *Duke L.J.* 425 (1993).

CHAPTER 9. THE DILBERT SOCIETY?

1. Debora Vrana, "1998: Review and Outlook; Corporate Marriages: Not All Bliss," *Los Angeles Times*, January 2, 1999, C1 (BankAmerica and Challenger Gray and Christmas report of layoffs); Audrey Y. Williams, "Executive Pay Is Likely to be an Issue at Bank of America's Annual Meeting," *Charlotte Observer*, April 21, 2000 (BankAmerica merger); "Bell Atlantic Proxy Statement," April 14, 1999; *New York Times*, January 20, 1999 (BellAtlantic/GTE merger); Ross Kerber, "Fleet Boston Paid Executives Millions in Merger," *Boston Globe*, March 11, 2000 (FleetBoston/Bank Boston Merger); Timothy L. O'Brien, "Citigroup Says It Will Cut 10,400 Jobs," *New York Times*, December 16, 1998 (Citigroup layoffs); Robert D. Hershey, Jr., "Exxon Mobil Plans to Cut Payroll by 16,000 Jobs," *New York Times*, December 16, 1999, C1 (Exxon Mobil layoffs).

2. See Lawrence E. Mitchell, "Trust and Team Production in Post-Capitalist Society," 24 *J. Corp. L.* 869 (1999).

3. Jennifer Reingold, "Executive Pay," *Business Week*, April 17, 2000.

4. 198 U.S. 45, 25 S. Ct. 539, 49 L. Ed. 937 (1905).

5. For a general discussion, see Camille Guerin-Gonzales and Carl Strikwerd, eds., *The Politics of Immigrant Workers: Labor Activism and Migration in the World Economy Since 1830* (New York: Holmes and Meier, 1993).

6. Adam Smith, *An Inquiry into the Nature and Causes of the Wealth of Nations* (Indianapolis: Liberty Classics, 1981), bk. 1, chap. 8, pt. 1.

7. For earlier and similarly brilliant insights of the Supreme Court, see *Coppage v. Kansas*, 236 U.S. 1, 35 S. Ct. 240, 59 L. Ed. 441 (1915), and *Allgeyer v. Louisana*, 165 U.S. 578, 17 S. Ct. 427, 41 L. Ed 832 (1897).

8. United States Department of Labor Bureau of Labor Statistics, *Employment and Earnings*, March 2000, table A-7. The Household Data Survey is a survey of individuals and thus relies upon self-reporting.

9. United States Census Bureau, *Statistical Abstract of the United States,* table 878 (1999).

10. United States Department of Labor Bureau of Labor Statistics "Daily Labor Report," January 20, 2000.

11. Quoted in David I. Levine, *Reinventing the Workplace: How Business and Employees Can Both Win* (Washington, D.C.: Brookings Institution Press, 1995), 10.

12. I will discuss trust in more detail later in this chapter. For more general discussions of trust, see Francis Fukuyama, *Trust: The Social Virtues and the Creation of Prosperity* (New York: Free Press, 1995); Martin Hollis, *Trust Within Reason* (Cambridge: Cambridge University Press, 1998); Roderick Kramer and Tom R. Tyler, eds., *Trust in Organizations: Frontiers of Theory and Research* (Thousand Oaks, Calif.: Sage Publications, 1996); Christel Lane and Reinhard Bachman, *Trust Within and Between Organizations* (Oxford: Oxford University Press, 1998); Barbara A. Mistzal, *Trust in Modern Societies* (Cambridge: Polity Press, 1996); Matt Ridley, *The Origins of Virtue: Human Instinct and the Evolution of Cooperation* (New York: Viking Press, 1997); Adam B. Seligman, *The Problem of Trust* (Princeton: Princeton University Press, 1997).

13. Studs Terkel, *Working: People Talk About What They Do All Day and How They Feel About What They Do* (New York: Pantheon Books, 1974); Thomas Petzinger, Jr., *The New Pioneers: The Men and Women Who Are Transforming the Workplace and Marketplace* (New York: Simon and Schuster, 1999). Petzinger does not believe that the changes he describes have yet overtaken the American workplace, noting that "conformity and compliance remain the unwritten rule at many major American corporations, perhaps most" (24).

14. Patrick McGeehan, "At a Wall Street Firm, Juniors' Voices Roar," *New York Times,* April 8, 2000, A1.

15. Paul Sweeney, "Sharing in the Bounty: Dot-coms and HyperCompetition Have Raised Wall Street Compensation Levels to Unprecedented Heights, But Will It Last? *Investment Dealers Digest,* June 12, 2000.

16. Dean Foust, "Wooing the Worker," *Business Week,* May 22, 2000.

17. Denise Gellene, "Geekdom Is Awash in Perks," *Los Angeles Times,* May 23, 2000.

18. "Free Mercedes-Benz, Pets at Work, and Playrooms are the New Perks at High Tech Companies, According to Deloitte and Touche Survey," *Business Wire,* June 20, 2000.

19. Michael Skapinker, "Begging for Workers: The Unwritten Contract Binding Loyal Employee and Caring Employer—Shattered by Downsizing in the 1990s—Has Given Way to Fierce Competition for Footloose Staff," *Financial Times,* June 13, 2000.

20. Peter Drucker, *Post-Capitalist Society* (New York: Harperbusiness, 1993). Similar

ideas can be found in the somewhat breathless David Limerick and Bert Cunnington, *Managing the New Organization: A Blueprint for Networks and Strategic Alliances* (San Francisco: Jossey Bass, 1993).

21. Amy Zipkin, "The Wisdom of Thoughtfulness: In Tight Labor Market, Bosses Find Value in Being Nice," *New York Times,* May 31, 2000, C1.

22. *Statistical Abstract of the United States,* 1999, table 702 (number of service workers); table 705 (inflation-adjusted minimum wage).

23. Diane E. Lewis, "Working It Out," *Boston Globe,* November 29, 1998 (reporting Bureau of Labor Statistics).

24. United States Department of Labor, *Occupational Compensation Survey, Occupational Wages in the East North Central Division,* 1997, table 1, Summary, by Geographic Areas. As defined by the BLS, earnings include "the straight-time hourly wages or salaries paid to employees. They include incentive pay, cost-of-living adjustments, and hazard pay. Excluded are premium pay for overtime, vacations, and holidays; nonproduction bonuses; and tips."

25. *Statistical Abstract of the United States,* 1999, table 762.

26. Richard B. Freeman and Joel Rogers, *What Workers Want* (Ithaca: Cornell University Press, 1999), 13.

27. William Greider, *One World, Ready or Not* (New York: Simon and Schuster, 1997); Kuttner, *Everything for Sale,* 91.

28. Dahl, *A Preface to Economic Democracy.*

29. David M. Gordon, *Fat and Mean: The Corporate Squeeze of Working Americans and the Myth of Managerial "Downsizing"* (New York: Free Press, 1996).

30. Ibid., 33.

31. *Bureau of Labor Statistics Employment and Earnings Report,* March 2000, table A-7.

32. Erik Olin Wright, *Class Counts: Comparative Studies in Class Analysis* (Cambridge: Cambridge University Press, 1997).

33. Ibid.

34. Michael Useem, *Executive Defense: Shareholder Power and Corporate Reorganization* (Cambridge: Harvard University Press, 1993).

35. Ibid., 127.

36. Ibid., 118.

37. David Leonhart, "Report on Executive Pay: In the Options Age, Rising Pay (and Risk)," *New York Times,* April 2, 2000.

38. Greider, *One World,* 57.

39. Michael M. Weinstein, "Economic Scene: Cream in Labor Market's Churn; Why Job Losses Are Rising Amid Job Hunters' Nirvana," *New York Times,* July 22, 1999, C1.

40. Stephanie Armour, "Training Takes Front Seat at Offices: Workers Benefit from High-Tech Learning Boom," *USA Today,* January 19, 1999.

41. Jordan D. Lewis, "Trusting Companies Deliver More Shareholder Value," 26 *Directorship* 4 (March 2000).

42. Smith, *Wealth of Nations,* bk. 1, chap. 1, x.b.

43. "Retaining Your Valued Employees," *Strategic Finance,* October 1, 1999; Bruce Shutan, "They're Grrrreat! To Reviewer, Solid Benefits Link Best Places to Work," *Employee Benefit News,* April 1, 1999; Paul Osterman, "Work Reorganization in an Era of Restructuring: Trends in Diffusion and Effects on Employee Welfare," 53 *Ind. and Lab. Rel. Rev.* 179 (2000).

44. The stories of Morse and Sulik are reported in Zipkin, "The Wisdom of Thoughtfulness."

45. Robert Frank, "A Theory of Moral Sentiments," in *Beyond Self-Interest,* ed. Jane J. Mansbridge (Chicago: University of Chicago Press, 1990); Annette Baier, "Trust and Antitrust," in *Ethics and Personality: Essays in Moral Psychology,* ed. John Deight (Chicago: University of Chicago Press, 1992) See also Mitchell, "Trust and Team Production"; Lawrence E. Mitchell, "Trust.Contract.Process," in *Progressive Corporate Law,* ed. Lawrence E. Mitchell (Boulder: Westview Press, 1995).

46. Jack R. Gibb, "Climate for Trust Formation," in *T-Group Theory and Laboratory Method: Innovation in Reeducation,* ed. Leland P. Bradford et al. (New York: Wiley, 1964), 279.

47. Tom R. Tyler and Peter Degoey, "Trust in Organizational Authorities: The Influence of Motive Attributions on Willingness to Accept Decisions," in Kramer and Tyler, *Trust in Organizations,* 334.

48. But if you're interested see Mitchell, "Trust and Team Production."

49. Jennifer Laabe, "Employee Sabotage: Don't Be a Target," 78 *Workforce* 32 (July 1, 1999).

50. Kirsten Downey Grimsley, "Office Wrongdoing Common: Studies Find Ethics Often Take Back Seat to the Bottom Line," *Washington Post,* June 14, 2000, E2. At the same time, the National Business Ethics Survey found a sharp drop in pressure on workers to behave unethically and a substantial increase in corporate ethics training.

51. David Ignatius, "What's Wrong with Boeing? *Washington Post,* November 3, 1999, A35.

52. Levine, *Reinventing the Workplace.* Gregory Dow and Louis Putterman also find empirical evidence supporting high productivity in labor-managed firms, by which they mean corporations that go well beyond the more modest discussion of participation by workers that I am discussing in the text to corporations that are managed by the workers themselves. Gregory Dow and Louis Putterman, "Why Capital (Usually) Hires Labor: An Assessment and Proposed Explana-

tions," in *Employees and Corporate Governance,* ed. Margaret M. Blair and Mark J. Roe (Washington: Brookings Institution Press, 1999), 26.

53. A similar observation is made in Thomas A. Kochan, Harry C. Katz, and Robert B. McKersie, *The Transformation of American Industrial Relations* (New York: Basic Books, 1986), 175.

54. Levine, *Reinventing the Workplace,* 48.

55. Scott Hays, "Ownership Cultures Create Unity," *Workforce,* February 1, 1999.

56. Levine, *Reinventing the Workplace,* 56.

57. Lewis, "Trusting Companies Deliver More Shareholder Value," 4.

58. Jonathan P. Charkham, *Keeping Good Company: A Study of Corporate Governance in Five Countries* (Oxford: Clarendon Press: 1994).

59. Lewis, "Trusting Companies Deliver More Shareholder Value."

60. Joseph Schumpeter, *Capitalism, Socialism, and Democracy,* 3d ed. (New York: Harper Torchbooks, 1950), 123. Michel Albert picks up on this theme, noting the way that America's particular brand of capitalism winds up making a commodity of everything from wages and housing to education and even, to some extent, religion. Albert, *Capitalism vs. Capitalism,* 102.

61. Sheryl Gay Stolberg, "Report Says Profit-Making Health Plans Damage Care," *New York Times,* July 14, 1999, A18; David U. Himmelstein et al., "Quality of Care in Investor-Owned vs. Not-For-Profit HMOs," 282 *Journal of the American Medical Association* 159 (1999).

62. Linda Greenhouse, "H.M.O.'s Win Crucial Ruling on Liability for Doctors' Acts," *New York Times,* June 13, 2000, A1.

63. *Howard v. Sasson,* 1995 WL 581960 (E.D. Pa. 1995).

64. *Shea v. Eisensten,* 107 F. 3rd 625 (1997).

65. "Savings Due to Managed Care," *American Association of Health Plans Research Brief* (October 1999); see also "Quality of Care and Health Plans: Summaries of Individual Studies," *American Association of Health Plans Research Brief* (April 2000) (surveying literature and concluding that "the cumulative research shows a pattern of largely positive findings about quality of care in health maintenance organizations"). The research brief does not distinguish between for-profit and not-for-profit plans.

66. Dahl agrees but questions whether as a prior question stockholders are entitled to the money they invest in the first place, a question beyond the scope of this book. Dahl, *A Preface to Economic Democracy,* 80.

67. While Schumpeter saw democracy as an outgrowth of capitalism, he saw no reason why democracy couldn't exist in a socialist economy. Schumpeter, *Capitalism, Socialism, and Democracy.*

68. For an in-depth discussion of the differences among the various systems, see Albert, *Capitalism vs. Capitalism.*

69. John Rawls, *A Theory of Justice* (Cambridge: Belknap Press, 1971).

70. Michael Walzer, *Spheres of Justice: A Defense of Pluralism and Equality* (New York: Basic Books, 1983).

71. For a more extended discussion of this point, see Mitchell, *Stacked Deck*.

72. Smith, *Wealth of Nations,* bk. 1, chap. 1, pt. ii.

73. Jeffrey N. Gordon, "Employee Stock Ownership in Economic Transitions: The Case of United and the Airline Industry," in Blair and Roe, *Employees and Corporate Governance,* 317–18. See Henry Hansmann, *The Ownership of Enterprise* (Cambridge: Belknap Press, 1996), for a broad discussion of the different forms of firm ownership.

74. http://www.the-esop-emplowner.org/pubs/stats.html. Although the number of ESOPs is growing, the number of participants is declining because ESOPs are far more common in smaller, closely held corporations. wysiwig://279http://www.nceo.org/library/eopstat.html.

75. Hansmann, *Ownership of Enterprise,* 99–101. On Mondragón, see also Hans Wiener and Robert Oakeshott, *Worker-Owners: Mondragón Revisited* (London: Anglo-German Foundation, 1987).

76. William Foote Whyte and Kathleen King Whyte, *Making Mondragón: The Growth and Dynamics of the Worker Cooperative Complex* (Ithaca: ILR Press, 1988), 7.

77. Dahl, *A Preface to Economic Democracy,* 132.

78. Przeworski, *Democracy and the Market,* 126.

79. Dow and Putterman, "Why Capital (Usually) Hires Labor," 22–23.

80. *European Union Statistical Report on Cooperatives* (1994).

81. Just for starters, see Hansmann, *Ownership of Enterprise,* Blair and Roe, *Employees and Corporate Governance,* and the wide range of sources cited in each.

82. Among Smith's five components of wage determination is "the agreeableness or disagreeableness" of the occupation, a factor which is determined not only by the nature of the work but also by the way the worker is treated.

CHAPTER 10. CAPITALISM, SOCIALISM, AND DEMOCRACY

1. Smith particularly disliked corporations because of the fact that in his time the grant of a corporate charter almost invariably carried with it a right to a monopoly as well, an association which was clearly broken in the United States in the Charles River Bridge case: *Charles River Bridge v. Warren Bridge,* 36 U.S. (11 Pet.) 420 (1837). For a contemporary indictment of corporate capitalism, see David C. Korten, *When Corporations Rule the World* (West Hartford: Kumarian Press, and San Francisco: Berrett-Koehler Publications, 1995).

2. Przeworski, *Democracy and the Market,* 101.

3. Samuel Bowles and Herbert Gintis, *Democracy and Capitalism: Property, Commu-*

nity, and the Contradictions of Modern Social Thought (New York: Basic Books, 1986).

4. Schumpeter, *Capitalism, Socialism, and Democracy,* 296–99.

5. Dahl, *A Preface to Economic Democracy,* 46. See also Robert Frank, *Luxury Fever: Why Money Fails to Satisfy in an Era of Excess* (New York: Free Press, 1999); Schiller, *Irrational Exuberance.*

6. Quoted in Charkham, *Keeping Good Company,* 10.

7. Albert, *Capitalism vs. Capitalism,* 2.

8. *Merriam Webster's Collegiate Dictionary.*

9. Bowles and Gintis, *Democracy and Capitalism,* 16.

10. Giovanni Arrighi and Beverly Silver, *Chaos and Governance in the Modern World System* (Minneapolis: University of Minnesota Press, 1999).

CHAPTER 11. AMERICA RIGHT *AND* WRONG

1. Hilary Rosenberg, "The Shareholders are Restless in Europe," *New York Times,* December 12, 1999, sec. 3, p. 4.

2. Brancato, *Building on Sand,* 8.

3. Conference Board, *Institutional Investment Report: International Patterns of Institutional Investment* (April 2000).

4. Brancato, *Building on Sand.*

5. Conference Board, *Institutional Investment Report: International Patterns of Institutional Investment.*

6. Matthew Valencia, "European Business: Old Dogs, New Tricks," *The Economist,* April 29, 2000, 14.

7. Joseph Stiglitz, "For Economists, No Time To Party," *Newsweek, Special Supplement, Facing the Future Issues 2000,* December 1999–February 2000, 58.

8. For a report on the Czech Republic's problems with privatization, see Sabina Newman and Michelle Egan, "Between German and Anglo-Saxon Capitalism: The Czech Financial Markets in Transition, 4 *New Political Economy* 173, July 1999. For a suggestion that the Czech Republic is beginning to overcome its problems, see Oonagh Leighton, "A New Dawn," *Central European,* June 1998, 20.

9. On Poland, see Karen Lowry Miller, "An Eastern Star Looks Dimmer," *Business Week,* April 19, 1999, 50. Stiglitz mentions both Poland and Slovenia as exceptions.

10. Another commentator disagrees, tracing the success or failure of the adoption of market reforms to the willingness of particular countries to accept them: "Too many people who should know better are calling Russia's catastrophe a failure of capitalism — when in fact it is a failure of Russia to adopt capitalism." Kathryn Hanes, "The FDI Play in Central Europe," *Global Finance,* December

1998, 44. Comments like this suggest to me at best a failure to appreciate the variety of forms capitalism can take and the cultural sensitivity to those forms, and at worse a stunning arrogance that proclaims only one form of capitalism to be right, the very attitude Stiglitz criticizes.

11. For very thoughtful critiques of the hegemony of Enlightenment liberalism, see Alasdair MacIntyre, *After Virtue* (Notre Dame: University of Notre Dame Press, 1981); id., *Whose Justice? Which Rationality?* (Notre Dame: University of Notre Dame Press, 1988).

12. Seymour Martin Lipset, *American Exceptionalism: A Double-Edged Sword* (New York: W. W. Norton, 1996).

13. Jerry Mander and Edward Goldsmith, *The Case Against the Global Economy and For a Turn Toward the Local* (San Francisco: Sierra Club Books, 1996).

14. Lipset, *American Exceptionalism,* 268. Lipset does see much good in the American Creed and character, and in fact it is his thesis that the negative aspects of these are simply the flip side of the positive aspects.

15. Greider, *One World.*

16. Lipset, *American Exceptionalism,* 25, 234.

17. Jeff Faux and Larry Mishel, "Inequality and the Global Economy," in *On the Edge: Living with Global Capitalism,* ed. Will Hutton and Anthony Giddens (London: Jonathan Cape, 2000), 93.

18. Albert, *Capitalism vs. Capitalism,* 15–18.

19. Ibid; Charkham, *Keeping Good Company.*

20. Albert, *Capitalism vs. Capitalism,* 19.

21. See generally Charkham, *Keeping Good Company*; Klaus J. Hopt and Eddy Wymeersch, *Comparative Corporate Governance: Essays and Materials* (Berlin and New York: Walter de Gruyter, 1997). The principal exception is the German model, which under certain circumstances allows employees in corporations of at least five hundred workers to elect one-third of the supervisory board and employees in corporations of at least two thousand workers, half the members of the supervisory board in a system in which the supervisory board functions in a general oversight capacity and the managing board (which is appointed by the supervisory board) actually engages in the management of the company.

22. Charkham, *Keeping Good Company.*

23. Rafael La Porta, Florencio Lopez-De-Silanes, and Andrei Shleifer, "Corporate Ownership Around the World," 54 *J. Fin.* 471 (1999).

24. For other arguments that convergence is not likely to occur, see William W. Bratton and Joseph A. McCahery, "Comparative Corporate Governance and the Theory of the Firm: The Case Against Global Cross Reference," 38 *Col. J. Trans. Law* 213 (1999); Stefan Wagstyl, "Crumbs from the Table: The Fashionable Belief that Continental European Companies are Paying More Attention

to their Shareholders is Only Slowly Becoming a Reality," *Financial Times*, September 25, 1996 (quoting former consultant Ann Simpson: "It is arrogant to assume that American attitudes will prevail"). At the same time, it is hard to ignore legal changes in continental countries that are working toward an American-style model in increasing minority stockholder protections and easing takeover restrictions. Andrea Melis, "Corporate Governance In Italy," *Corporate Governance: An International Review* (Blackwell, 2000) However, as I make clear in the text, even if legal "reforms" do occur, corporate behavior is as much a matter of attitude as it is of law, and a culturally sensitive understanding of the issue does not lead to the prediction that the American model, even if it is adopted wholesale in the rest of the world, necessarily will lead in the long term to American-style capitalism. In fact, one reasonable fear is that to the extent the legal liberation permits foreign corporations to act like ours, they will cause significant social dislocations to which we may be accustomed but to which others are not; backlash is likely to arise in cultures that prize community over the pursuit of individual wealth.

INDEX

United States Supreme Court, 42, 211–2

Unocal, 22–25, 37, 40

Walzer, Michael, 92

Wealth: as value, 84–90, 256

Weber, Max, 35

Welch, Jack, 98

Workers: bargaining power of, 212; civic virtue and, 233–41; compensation ratios, 211, 218; effect of mergers on, 209–10; effect of stock price maximization on, 208–9, 223–4; effects of globalization on, 224–5; knowledge versus service, 216–7; minimum wage, 217; mistrust of, 210; ownership of enterprise, 241–5; participation in governance, 229–32; pension participation, 225–6 (*see also* Trust); revised accounting for, 245–50; wages, 217–8